JUSTIN CALABRESE, MSM

Mastering Momentum

Driving Success in Business Management

GREEN MOUNTAIN PUBLISHING
A CALABRESE COMPANY

First published by Green Mountain Publishing Company 2024

Copyright © 2024 by Justin Calabrese, MSM

All rights reserved. No part of this publication may be reproduced, stored or transmitted in any form or by any means, electronic, mechanical, photocopying, recording, scanning, or otherwise without written permission from the publisher. It is illegal to copy this book, post it to a website, or distribute it by any other means without permission.

Justin Calabrese, MSM has no responsibility for the persistence or accuracy of URLs for external or third-party Internet Websites referred to in this publication and does not guarantee that any content on such Websites is, or will remain, accurate or appropriate.

Designations used by companies to distinguish their products are often claimed as trademarks. All brand names and product names used in this book and on its cover are trade names, service marks, trademarks and registered trademarks of their respective owners. The publishers and the book are not associated with any product or vendor mentioned in this book. None of the companies referenced within the book have endorsed the book.

First edition

ISBN: 979-8-218-50035-1

This book was professionally typeset on Reedsy.
Find out more at reedsy.com

*There are so many people who will tell you that you can't.
What you've got to do is turn around and say "watch me."*

Contents

Preface		ii
1	The Root of Disengagement	1
2	From Chaos to Clarity	20
3	Building Your Dream Team	48
4	Matching Strengths With Opportunities	68
5	Creating a Culture of Care	87
6	Investing in Success	101
7	The Art of Retention	118
8	Creating a Shared Vision	140
9	Building a Community	158
10	Setting New Standards	185
11	Thriving in Transition	211
12	Firing With Compassion	252
13	From Theory to Practice	295
About the Author		298

Preface

Throughout my life, I've had the opportunity to participate in various unique experiences, and reflecting upon them has been a remarkable journey. By age 28, I had owned over seven businesses, mainly in eCommerce. I'd written several articles for the Huffington Post as a Contributing Journalist, published a few books on business startups, was invited to teach a summer business class at Clark University, and consulted over 150 small businesses, guiding them to different levels of success and self-sustainability. Oh, and let's not forget—somehow, I got a double-lifetime induction into the top three percent of global business students after earning my Masters of Management degree from the University of Hartford. It's been a wild ride, for sure—but I've loved every second of it!

Some of my colleagues would probably call me a risk-taker, a bit crazy, maybe even out of my league, and definitely out of touch with reality. But here's the thing: despite what anyone said about me, I continued my entrepreneurial journey in confidence. I was laser-focused, like a heat-seeking missile locked onto my goals, and there was no way I would let a little outside "noise" throw me off course. Sure, people were watching, and yeah, there were plenty of skeptics, but if they thought I was going to slow down or quit, they didn't know me very well. Stopping? Not a chance—I had too much to accomplish, and nothing would stand in my way.

I'll be honest—I wasn't exactly winning any "Student of the Year" awards in high school. Math, social studies, English, foreign language... let's say my brain wasn't exactly excited over those required subjects. In some of my classes, I barely scraped by. I just couldn't wrap my head around the history of the Straw Hat Riot. I mean, could you? No matter how much I tried, I had a different mindset, and, for some crazy reason, this different mindset worked for me.

After the final school bell rang, I got to hang up my "student" hat. I put on my entrepreneurial cape, and suddenly, everything clicked. It was like flipping a light switch. I'd dive into my after-school hustle and instantly find myself in this happy, content zone. While I understood the importance of learning social studies or mastering the trumpet in band class, nothing compared to the satisfaction I got from chasing my ventures.

But let's not sugarcoat it. The journey to mastering a winning business mindset wasn't always easy. For example, I had just one shot at pitching my business expertise and writing abilities to the Huffington Post when I begged them to be a Contributing Journalist. I didn't have time to pull out my eraser and ask for a do-over. It was downright stressful at times, and many sleepless nights when I questioned my sanity. As the sole owner of my businesses, I was responsible for everything: financial reporting, marketing, sales, technical support, troubleshooting, website maintenance, security, insurance, filing taxes, you name it. Let's not overlook customer service! Sure, customers can be a handful at times, but hey, without them, your return on investment would be as exciting as a snooze fest. Keep them happy, and watch those investments pay off in style! The true success of each business fell squarely on my shoulders. Sure, I'd met plenty of business partners along the way who were more than happy to lend a hand here and there, but at the end of the day, the buck stopped with me—I was the one legally on the hook for everything. There was no one else to blame if things went south. It was just me, my ideas, and my determination to make them work. Of course, I never passed up the chance to hear what my family had to say—they always had a fresh perspective (and sometimes a little too much honesty!).

I remember one particular moment as a turning point in my entrepreneurial career. National Public Radio (NPR) got wind of my business ventures in 2007, and I was approached by a local journalist who wanted to interview me about the importance of chasing after your dreams. I was 17 and launched my first eCommerce business, JC Surveillance, an online security retailer. I was young and a bit naive, but I was incredibly driven. I had never started a business before, but I figured, how hard could it be? With a ton of research and a little bit of determination, I was ready to educate myself. But then came the reality check— building a website. I suddenly was faced with learning HTML, CSS, PHP, and many other coding languages. Hiring a web developer wasn't in the budget, so everything was up to me. I still remember the night I bought my first website hosting service. It was just a blank web page waiting for my creative touch, but in my head, I knew it would be something fantastic—once I figured out what all those lines of code meant! I knew from the beginning that I wasn't going to fail. Sure, I might stumble along the way—that was unavoidable—but failure? No, that wasn't in my vocabulary.

During that NPR interview, I spoke about what drove me to start JC Surveillance and the early success I experienced. Thanks to my sister and her teenage relationship that went sideways, I was stepping into the role of family protector. Instead of suiting up with a superhero cape, the police had a more practical idea: installing a security camera. That's when it hit me—my family couldn't be the only one dealing with privacy and safety concerns. The security camera and home alarm industry was booming, and America entered a new era of crime awareness. Families nationwide were investing in safety and security, and the home security market showed no signs of slowing down. I saw my chance to grab a piece of the pie. So, after getting my hands on my first security camera and figuring out its features and how it works, I realized I'd stumbled onto something that captured my interest. Sure, it wasn't math class or social studies. This was the kind of hands-on interest that had me ready to roll up my sleeves and dive into a whole new way of learning. And just like that, my business journey began! It was surreal to be recognized at such a young age by a national news outlet, but it also came with immense pressure. I had set high expectations for myself, and I wasn't about to let anyone down, especially not myself. That mindset, that refusal to accept failure, became the foundation of my approach to business. It's what kept me going during the tough times, and believe me, there were plenty of tough times.

When I was 20, I got a call from my former middle school. Surprisingly, they wanted me to speak at their annual career day! Talk about a thrill! I mean, who wouldn't be excited to return to the place where it all started and share some wisdom? It felt surreal, stepping back into those familiar halls, but this time not as a student but as someone who had already carved out a little piece of the business world. There I was, a young entrepreneur, rubbing shoulders with seasoned professionals who had been at this game way longer than I had. Sure, some of them had years of experience under their belts, but I was asked to attend because my drive for success was genuine at such a young age. I began my presentation by reminding the students, parents, and teachers that not too long ago, I was the one sitting at those same desks. And now, I was—standing in front of them, hoping to spark some entrepreneurial excitement! The energy in the room was electric! The students were firing off questions left and right about my many business ventures, my failures, successes, and everything in between. To close, I left them with a quote that has always held a special place in my heart, one that guided me through my journey. It was the perfect ending to an unforgettable day, one that reminded me just how far I'd come and how much further I wanted to go.

> *"If your actions inspire others to dream more, learn more, do more, and become more, then you are a leader."*
> - John Quincy Adams

One of the wildest rides in my entrepreneurial journey kicked off in 2013 when I decided to buy the intellectual property rights of a defunct national retailer. After researching and building seven companies, selling them, and reinvesting the profits, I still hadn't had my fill. So naturally, I jumped headfirst into this massive endeavor. What can I say? I was crazy enough to take on the challenge. The work was grueling, and the financial pressure was intense. I managed a global team of eCommerce professionals while also dealing with the whirlwind of media attention. I mean, it's one thing to hear about someone's success on the radio, but it's a whole different experience when your own story is being broadcast. I'd be driving home, listening to my news, and then getting calls from friends saying, "Hey, I just heard you on the radio!" Suddenly, reputation management became an almost full-time job. Here I was, trying to build a business, forge partnerships with national vendors, manage customer service inquiries, and create meaningful business relationships while the media shaped my public image. It wasn't easy. By the end of the day, I felt like I was juggling twenty balls in the air, knowing that if I dropped even one, everything could come crashing down, and most likely, the media would build a story out of it.

In 2015, I sold the business and the intellectual property, closing that chapter of my life to focus on consulting. Looking back, I feel incredibly blessed for every opportunity I had, and I knew that despite the challenges, I had so much more to offer. The adventure was far from over!

Even though I've embarked on many business ventures, you won't catch me chatting about them over coffee. I spend quite a bit of time making sure my entrepreneurial achievements stay under the radar. Each adventure brought unique thrills, but I'm a forward thinker, looking ahead to the next big thing. These days, I'm more focused on developing my skill set—finding that sweet balance and channeling my energy into helping others through consulting and research. It's all about keeping the momentum going, one client at a time!

Trading the entrepreneurial roller coaster for a nine-to-five gig with a better work-life balance sounded like a breeze—until I realized it came with a new set of challenges! I inherited a team of workers who were… let's say, less than motivated. They were resistant to change, unwilling to go the extra mile, and seemingly indifferent to the company's mission. It was a tough situation, and I quickly realized that this wasn't just about business strategy or analyzing financial charts. This was about people. I knew that without a "dream team," success would be out of reach.

Building trust with that team was no small feat. They were skeptical of me from the start—an outsider who had entered their workplace made the change and instilled new guidelines on office procedures. However, I knew that to turn things around, I needed to get them on board to align their efforts with the company's mission. And that meant putting their needs above mine, creating an environment where they felt valued, heard, and part of something bigger than themselves.

I started by listening—really listening—to their concerns and frustrations. I didn't come in with all the answers. Instead, I made it clear that I was there to work with them, not against them. Slowly but surely, I began to see a shift in their attitudes. I encouraged creativity, rewarded teamwork, and showed that I was just as invested in their success as they were. It wasn't easy, and there were plenty of bumps along the way, but eventually, we started to see real progress.

The experience taught me so much about leadership and the importance of a winning mindset—not just for myself but for the entire team. Success isn't just about having the best ideas or the most money. It's about the people you surround yourself with, the culture you create, and the mindset you bring to the table daily.

Many leaders struggle when they inherit a new team, especially one that isn't eager to follow their lead. It's a common challenge, and it can feel incredibly daunting. But I'm here to tell you that it's not impossible. With the right approach, you can turn things around. You can build trust, inspire creativity, and foster an environment where everyone feels part of something meaningful. Once you do that, you'll see just how powerful a winning mindset can be—not just for you, but for your entire team.

This book is a compilation of my winning business approach—a blend of strategies, experiences, and lessons learned from years of navigating the highs and lows of team building and entrepreneurship. It's about mastering a mindset that refuses to accept failure, embraces challenges as opportunities, and sees every setback as a stepping stone to something greater.

We're about to embark on a journey together. Whether you're a seasoned entrepreneur or just starting, I hope this book will inspire you to adopt a winning mindset of your own and that it will equip you with the tools you need to achieve the success you've always dreamed of. In every adventure you embark on, keep your head held high. Aim for the moon because if you miss, you'll still find yourself among the stars.

1

The Root of Disengagement

On paper, Logan looked like a dream come true for the web designer role I desperately needed to fill for my eCommerce venture. As I flipped through his resume, it was like checking off every box on my wish list. Smart? Check. Well-educated? Check. A track record that made me do a double-take? Absolutely. His technical skills were impressive—he was up to speed on the latest hardware, knew his way around web security, and could navigate servers and web coding like a pro. With years of experience at a high-powered firm, Logan seemed like the exact person who could catapult my startup to the next level.

I couldn't help but feel excitement at the thought of bringing Logan on board. His background practically screamed "technical wizardry," and his hands-on experience was what my business needed to thrive. Sure, great ideas are important, but I've always believed that the real magic happens when you've got a rock-solid team to bring those ideas to life. And in Logan, I saw someone who could be a real MVP in building that dream team. His knowledge and experience made me think he just might hold the golden ticket to our success.

When I finally got the chance to interview Logan, my good vibes about him only got stronger. He spoke with thought, showing he was committed to a collaborative work environment. It was a breath of fresh air, especially in a field where I've seen plenty of people ready to hog all the credit for a team's hard work. Logan's take on teamwork clicked with my belief that success is a team sport, not a one-man show.

One thing that made Logan stand out was his knack for all things cybersecurity—a field where my startup was lacking. Cybersecurity isn't the most exciting topic, and many small businesses, especially in eCommerce, tend to brush it off. But in today's digital world, ignoring cybersecurity is like leaving your front door wide open. The fact that Logan was up-to-speed on the latest practices was a huge win in my book. I was confident that he could help protect the business from digital dangers. This wasn't just a nice-to-have; it was an absolute must-have that many entrepreneurs don't think about until it's too late.

After a lot of hemming and hawing, I realized there was only one option: I had to hire Logan. But this wasn't just about filling a spot on the team; it was about bringing someone on board who'd be as invested in the business's success as I was. So, after some serious thinking, I decided to sweeten the deal with a partnership opportunity in the startup. Sure, the compensation wasn't anything to write about, but it came with a 5% ownership stake in the company. The idea was simple: the harder Logan worked, the more he'd benefit as the company grew.

I've always believed that when someone has a piece of the pie—whether through stock or voting rights—they're way more invested in making sure the pie gets bigger. Logan was thrilled with the offer, and that kind of enthusiasm was exactly what I was looking for. From the get-go, Logan showed up with a winning attitude. His mindset was about, "What can I do for you?" instead of, "What can you do for me?"—and let me tell you, that was a major score!

As Logan started getting his feet wet with the startup I had dreamed up, I was already knee-deep in building the website for this new venture. I had taken the lead on most of it, but there was a catch—I was working with an international web development team, and that brought its own set of challenges. Picture this: communication happening through business chat boards and instant messengers, with most of the work being done remotely across different time zones. The kicker? Most of the development happened while I was catching some Z's, making real-time collaboration feel like chasing a moving target.

Logan would have to bring his A-game in communication and use his expertise to sync up with the international team. They were already well-versed in my vision, but getting everyone on the same page would take some serious coordination. Luckily, Logan was up for the challenge, and I was excited to see how he'd bridge the gap between time zones and turn our ideas into reality.

In just a few months, Logan had taken the reins and was holding weekly phone calls with me and our international website development team. But those weekly chats quickly morphed into daily meetings—and, before I knew it, we were sometimes hopping on multiple calls a day. It was like we were all in a fast-paced startup groove. With every call, my confidence in Logan grew. It was clear he was fully invested in the mission, and I couldn't have been more thrilled to have him on board.

Plot twist—I was also juggling a regular nine-to-five job on top of everything else. Since my startup wasn't exactly rolling in cash yet, managing an international team quickly drained my wallet. My daily routine turned into a circus act of delegating projects to Logan, website development, and a never-ending list of startup tasks. I had to become a prioritizing ninja, juggling all these responsibilities with the finesse of a plate spinner. But let's be real—I was running on fumes. The constant demand for my time and energy was wearing me down, and after a full day of business consulting, the last thing I wanted to do was come home and dive into my business venture.

Logan, meanwhile, had his own juggling act going on. He had a family to care for, was quite a bit older than me, and lived eight states away. But despite all that, Logan somehow managed to carve out time for the business. At the least, he was a solid hire—his commitment never wavered. He wanted the startup to succeed just as much as I did, and his dedication was like a shot of espresso, keeping me going even when I felt like I was running on empty. Logan's determination was the spark that kept the fire burning, no matter how hectic things got.

Most nights, I was burning the midnight oil until 2:00 a.m., only to grab a few hours of shut-eye before my alarm went off at 8:00 a.m., signaling the start of my regular job all over again. It was like living in a never-ending loop, and I can't tell you how many times I wished I had a clone—someone who could go full throttle on the business while I hustled to keep it financially afloat with my second job.

But I had this one motto that kept me going: "The more you put into the business, the more you'll get out of it." It became my mantra; the little voice kept pushing me forward, convincing me that all this craziness would eventually pay off.

Despite my constant exhaustion and those moments when my motivation was running on fumes, I knew it was time to take a leap of faith and trust Logan with more responsibility. It was time to pass the torch—or, in this case, the login information and all those personal details—so he could take the reins. This was his moment to shine, to show me that he could steer the ship without me hovering over his shoulder. It was sink or swim time for Logan, and I was ready to see him dive in and take charge of the website development team and cybersecurity like the rockstar I knew he could be.

I knew I was jumping the gun a bit, but the truth was, I just didn't have the time to give Logan a proper crash course. My philosophy? Sometimes, the best way to learn is by diving in headfirst, and in this case, Logan was going to have to figure things out on the fly. Sure, I knew there might be a few bumps along the way—mistakes were pretty much a given. However, I also knew that failure can be the best teacher, and I decided to roll with that mindset. After all, what's a little trial and error between friends, right?

As Logan dove into the tasks at hand, he started asking way more questions than I had anticipated—and that's when the little voice in my head began to question his true qualifications. Was it because I hadn't given him the proper training? Maybe. Was it because I hadn't coached him to be the leader he claimed to be? Possibly. Or was Logan simply losing interest? My mind was spinning with doubts.

Questions like, "How do I log into the vendor portal to add a new vendor to the storefront?" started popping up. Then there were the more basic ones, like "What level of security do we want on our website?" I mean, as an IT and cybersecurity professional, shouldn't he already know the answers to these? My patience started to wear thin, and I found myself doubting the very person I once thought I couldn't live without. Suddenly, Logan wasn't looking like the superhero I had envisioned, and I wondered if I had made a mistake.

The turning point came when Logan called me with an urgent issue: we needed to implement a firewall to protect our customers' data on the server. As he cautiously started with, "I believe we should...," I cut him off mid-sentence. Without missing a beat, I said, "Logan, just go ahead and use your expertise to set up a strong firewall that fits our business needs."

A week later, the phone rang late at night—around 11:00 pm, when I was already half-asleep and not in the mood for another one of Logan's "brilliant" questions. But to my surprise, instead of asking something trivial, Logan was confronting me about the possibility of getting more compensation for his expertise. I was caught off guard. I mean, how could I even think about paying him more when he was still asking me basic questions he should've already known the answers to?

It hit me like a ton of bricks that the 5% ownership stake I'd offered him wasn't cutting it. If the company tanked, Logan would essentially have been working for free. I couldn't shake the feeling of being a bit selfish—I was relying on his skills and experience to keep the business afloat, but I just didn't have the resources to compensate him properly.

I found myself in a tough spot with Logan—he had become crucial to the business, and I realized I needed to do more to show my appreciation for his knowledge and time. Moving forward without him seemed impossible, and the thought of any conflict that might push him to quit was terrifying. The harsh reality was that while I couldn't afford to lose Logan, he held the power to walk away, leaving me in a quandary. After all, he knew more about the website development than I did. This imbalance of power was uncomfortable, to say the least, and it was something I had to confront head-on.

The thought of letting Logan go did cross my mind, but the reality hit me—

finding someone as skilled as Logan, who'd be willing to work for next to nothing, was like searching for a needle in a haystack. I even thought about bringing on an intern desperate for college credit, but I quickly realized that was a pipe dream. My brain went into overdrive, spiraling with unhelpful thoughts as I tried to figure out how to keep Logan on board without pushing him away.

It was like I'd stumbled into some weird employment paradox: the guy I was considering replacing was the same guy I needed to figure out how to pay more. Talk about a frustrating and ironic predicament! So, I started brainstorming ways to trim the fat in other business areas, hoping to free up some cash to keep Logan from feeling undervalued—and from walking out the door.

Then, a month later, Logan called me. I'd kind of hoped he'd forgotten about that whole compensation conversation, but instead, he hit me with some heavy news. He needed to take a month off for a family emergency. Of course, I couldn't deny him the time—family comes first, after all. I offered my condolences, hung up the phone, and realized that with Logan out of the picture for the next month, it was time for me to step up and carry the torch alone. There was no way I would let the business falter while he was dealing with personal issues.

But, I must admit, my curiosity got the best of me. I wanted to know more about Logan's situation, so I became a bit of a Facebook detective. I found myself trolling his profile like never before, trying to dig up any clues about what was going on with his family. It was a strange mix of concern and a desperate need to stay in the loop—because, let's face it, with Logan temporarily out of the game, the pressure was all on me.

Finally, after days of playing amateur detective, I stumbled upon a photo of Logan lounging on a beach in Mexico, beer in hand, looking as relaxed as ever. I leaned back in my chair and thought, "Family emergency, huh?" I double-checked the date on the Facebook post, and that's when it hit me—Logan had completely let me down. He hadn't been dealing with a family emergency; his only emergency was figuring out how to bail on his commitment at the last minute so he could kick back with his friends in

Mexico.

To make matters worse, I'd sent a flower bouquet to Logan's family, offering my condolences. That's when things got awkward. Logan's family called me, confused about the unexpected floral arrangement. When I explained what Logan had told me, they were as baffled as I was—there was no "family emergency." Logan was officially busted.

Letting Logan go was tough, not just because of the betrayal but because I had to explain the whole mess to my international website development team, who had developed a relationship with him. Now, I had to pick up the pieces Logan had left behind before his impromptu vacation. Inside, I was fuming. My emotions were all over the place, but I knew I had to stay focused and learn everything I'd trusted Logan to handle.

According to CareerBuilder, the cost of a bad hire can be nearly 30% of their salary. That's a hefty price for any business, but it's not just about the money. There's the cost of wasted time, disrupted partnerships, and the general chaos that follows when an employee doesn't fit. And let's not forget the sleepless nights thrown in as a bonus for the boss.

After Logan left my startup venture, I'll admit, I took every opportunity to vent about him. I was angry, and I wanted to get even. I'm not the person who just wakes up the next day and moves on. But as I kept chugging along with the startup's development, I reminded myself that terminating people is just part of the entrepreneurial journey. Not everything in business is sunshine and rainbows.

It wasn't until I agreed to participate in an interview with an old college professor that things clicked. The last question he asked was, "What's one thing you've learned recently that could change the direction of your business?" That's when it all came together, and I responded, "No more bad hires."

* * *

The Engagement Target

Over time, I got better at spotting the warning signs of bad employees. I started combing through resumes like a detective on a mission, hunting for those red flags. Sure, you won't catch every single one—some bad hires are bound to sneak through no matter how sharp you are. But even with all that effort, I still found myself struggling to keep everyone engaged and to build that dream team where everyone was just as invested as I was. It's like trying to herd cats—sometimes it feels impossible, but you keep trying anyway!

After selling my most recent business and transitioning into a nine-to-five role, I made it a priority to engage my team effectively. I understood that the foundation of any successful company lies in a team that not only supports your ideas but also challenges you to think outside the box. While I was eager for everything to fall into place quickly, I knew that wasn't realistic. Assembling my "dream team" proved more challenging than anticipated, and it became clear that I had significant work ahead of me.

I often felt like I was playing a game of darts, aiming for that elusive bullseye. And when I didn't hit the center of the dartboard as closely as I wanted, I simply picked up my darts and tried again. First, I communicated clearly—I laid out my vision and goals as plainly as possible. I ensured everyone knew exactly what I expected and what the outcome should look like. I connected the dots for each team member, showing how their work fits the bigger picture. I kept them updated regularly, making sure they knew how their efforts were moving the needle. But let's just say it didn't quite hit the mark as I'd hoped.

So, I switched tactics. I tried empowering my team and delegating authority, encouraging them to take the initiative and bring new ideas. I stood by their decisions, offering guidance when needed. This approach worked better than my first attempt, but it still wasn't the magic formula I was looking for.

The real game-changer turned out to be building strong relationships. I took the time to get to know my team on both a professional and personal level. I learned each person's strengths, weaknesses, successes, and areas for improvement. I also worked to create a sense of belonging in the workplace, encouraging bonding through team-building activities, social events, and open communication. That's when things started to click.

So, why did I zero in on this "engagement target" thing? Well, employee engagement is basically how much your team is "committed" when it comes to helping the organization hit its goals. It's not just about what they do—how they think, feel, and connect with their work, colleagues, and the company. If you don't understand your team, if you don't know their strengths and weaknesses, how are you supposed to prioritize or train effectively?

When employee engagement is high, everyone's happier and more productive, and they feel like they're making a difference. My team started to feel connected to the company, which led to better morale, greater satisfaction, and a noticeable boost in productivity.

The secret sauce? I had to learn who my team members were, get into real conversations with them, and ditch the "untouchable boss" attitude. I stepped down from the pedestal, got on the same level as them, and started thinking like one of them. And that's when things started to change for the better.

* * *

Giving it Your All

I knew I had to "give it my all." What does that mean? It means I had to fully commit—no half ass efforts allowed. If I wanted my team to be just as committed to their work, I had to show the same level of commitment to them. My team was already putting in the effort, so it was time for me to step up and commit to leadership.

Leading by example isn't just about barking orders from behind a desk; it's about rolling up your sleeves, diving into the work, and showing exactly how it's done. I had to be in the trenches with my team, demonstrating the work ethic and attitude I expected from them. And it didn't stop there—I also needed to be fully dedicated to the team's success.

I had already invested in my team through company resources, salaries, and training, so giving up wasn't an option. I needed to keep that investment going. The turning point came when one of my team members pulled me aside to discuss a weakness she had—her typing speed. She asked if there was any additional training available to help her improve. That's when it hit me: investing in my team means committing to their growth. It was my responsibility to find the resources she needed to improve, and that's exactly what I did.

When she asked me for help, I didn't hesitate. I gave her a clear answer and committed to a timeline for her success. I told her that within a week, I'd have a typing training program installed on her computer so she could practice during her downtime. But I didn't stop there—I held her accountable for making progress. I even added a bit of fun by challenging her to a "type-off" within a month to see if she could outpace me.

But "giving it your all" wasn't just about investing in my team's skills—I wanted to take it further by encouraging innovation. I pushed my team to think creatively and come up with new ideas. Sure, not every suggestion was a winner, but I clarified that I'd listen to every idea they had. Some of them made us laugh out loud, while others had me putting my head down, muttering, "God help me." But that's the beauty of it—fostering a culture where creativity is welcomed, even if it sometimes leads to a few facepalm moments!

As you can see, there's a difference between running a team and being an entrepreneur. The office environment brings its own unique set of challenges. But at the heart of it all is teamwork. Teamwork is the secret sauce for success in the workplace.

Communication hiccups, conflicts between team members, uneven contributions, and poor coordination can easily derail your day. But here's the thing—when you "give it your all," you start to truly understand your team. And when you understand your team, you build stronger relationships and get better results. In the end, the work gets done better, faster, and with a team that's more invested and motivated.

***

Are You Really "Giving it Your All"?

You might wonder, "Justin, do you *really* care about your employees? Are you genuinely invested in their success, or is it just about you winning?" The truth is, as leaders, we often have a different perspective on the workplace than our employees. And until we grasp this difference, no amount of caring will build the dream team we aim for.

Check this out: according to HRDConnect, 85% of employees worldwide aren't fully engaged. What? That's a massive chunk of the workforce! On the flip side, Deel.com reports that 94% of employees stick around longer when their company invests in their professional development. Say what? Do you see the gap here? Over eighty percent of employees globally say they're not engaged in their jobs. But when a company lays down the foundation for its future, and leaders "give it their all," ninety-four percent of those employees are likelier to stay.

It's time for leaders to pick up this book and start building a winning mindset. All is not lost, though. According to Randstad Enterprises, research shows that more than three-quarters (76%) of companies are now putting a greater emphasis on employee skill development and career engagement. The tides are turning—let's make sure we're riding that wave!

I've discovered that committing to your team's success means fully investing in their growth, development, and achievements. When one of my staff members came to me concerned about her skillset, I listened closely. She felt comfortable sharing her weaknesses, trusting I'd help her. And that's what it's all about—prioritizing their needs, supporting their goals, and creating an environment where they can thrive.

Let's be real for a second—it's all too easy for some leaders to park themselves behind their desks, fire off orders like they're launching missiles, and bask in the glory when things go right. And when things go south? Well, they're the first ones to hurl the team under the bus, sometimes even shifting into reverse to ensure everyone's thoroughly flattened. I've seen it happen, and let me tell you, that's not how I roll.

For me, being "all in" as a leader means you rise with the team, and, yes, if it comes to it, you sink with the team, too. There's no playing the blame game or pretending you're above the fray. When we're in it together, we're in it together—through thick, thin, and everything in between. After all, there's no "I" in "team," but there is a whole lot of "we."

I'm the kind of leader who's not just standing on the sidelines with a clipboard. Nope, I'm in the trenches, sleeves rolled up, getting my hands dirty with the rest of the crew. When we win, we all get to share the spotlight. And if we stumble? We figure it out together and come back stronger. Because that's what a real team does—we've got each other's backs, no matter what.

After years of education and riding the rollercoaster of my ups and downs, I've finally cracked the code of what it means to be committed to your team's success. Spoiler alert: it's not about chasing personal glory or racking up individual wins. Nope, it's all about putting the team's goals front and center, making sure the collective achievements take the spotlight.

And let's be real—you've got to celebrate those wins, too! Now, don't get me wrong, I didn't go all out with candles and cake every time we hit a milestone (though come to think of it, that might've been fun). Instead, I made it a point to sprinkle some praise into our weekly team meetings. Just a little shoutout here, a "great job" there—it's amazing how those small moments of recognition can keep everyone pumped up and appreciated.

Honestly, those little celebrations do wonders for morale. It's like fueling the engine that keeps the team running strong. So, while I may not have been throwing office parties every Friday, I made sure my team knew I saw their hard work and was cheering them on every step of the way. Because when the team wins, we all win—and that's worth celebrating every time.

Let's pause for a second and think about your leadership style. Maybe you've never officially led a team before—and that's cool. But hey, chances are you've taken the reins on a group project or even a study group at some point. So, how'd that go? Did you just guide them to the edge, stand back, and watch as they tumbled over the waterfall? Or did you give it your all, diving headfirst with them, taking charge like a fearless leader, and steering the ship with all the leadership skills you could muster?

* * *

The Commitment Formula

Let me tell you, there's no magic wand when it comes to the recruiting process. I wish there were! It'd make life a whole lot easier, wouldn't it? But, alas, we've got to do it the old-fashioned way—trial and error, a sprinkle of intuition, and patience.

Now, don't get me wrong, there are plenty of interview questions out there that sound clever but end up being as useful as a chocolate teapot. Take something like, "Do you always shop for bargains in the store or use coupons to save on full-priced items?" Sure, it might give you a little insight into their shopping habits, but it tells you absolutely nothing about whether this person will be the next star player on your team.

And asking your top performers to refer their "excellent friends" to the job? It sounds promising on paper, but let me tell you, it rarely leads to the golden results you're hoping for. The truth is, not everyone's circle of friends is filled with people who are just as amazing at work as they are. You might end up with a great pal but not necessarily a great employee.

Then there's the classic: the resume. A resume packed with relevant experiences might seem like a recruiter's dream. It's easy to get your hopes up when you see all those check boxes ticked off. But here's the thing—resumes can be some of the most dangerous misleaders in the recruiting game. They're like those fancy, glossy brochures that make every vacation destination look like paradise. You get there, and suddenly, the beach is full of seaweed, the hotel's under construction, and the "ocean view" is more like a "parking lot view."

The point is that the recruiting process is full of traps if you're not careful. It's not about finding someone who looks perfect on paper or answers quirky questions just right. It's about digging deeper, getting to know the person behind the resume, and determining if they're the right fit for your team. That takes time, effort, and a willingness to see beyond the surface. No magic wand is required—just a commitment to doing it right.

Sometimes, we think we can solve staffing issues with a quick fix, like making a "one-time exemption" and hoping it'll work magic. But let's be real—humans don't function that way, and they certainly don't get motivated by a one-and-done approach. No interview question will magically attract the best candidates while filtering out the worst. And I'm sorry to break it to you, but your existing team, whether a bit broken or running like a well-oiled machine, isn't going to transform overnight with the flick of a switch. They won't suddenly become the dream team you envisioned during your perfect night's sleep.

If we want our teams to grow, develop, and truly thrive, we've got to create the right conditions. And those conditions aren't born out of wishful thinking or quick fixes—they're crafted by great leadership. Over time, I've built winning teams by fostering a sense of belonging, promoting open communication, ensuring a safe environment, and showing real commitment.

What's worked for me—and for the countless teammates I've talked to over the years—wasn't about one particular strategy being better than another. There's no secret sauce that outperforms everything else. Instead, it's been about creating a formula that ensures my team cares about the company as much as I do. And let me tell you, it's not about discipline or micromanaging (ugh, I can't stand micromanaging).

When I started my career, let me tell you, it was a wild ride of trial and error. Picture a young, eager me, thinking leadership was about handing out tasks like candy on Halloween and barking orders like a drill sergeant. I was convinced that if I kept micromanaging everyone and ensured they did everything properly and on time, I'd have this whole leadership thing down pat. Spoiler alert: I was so wrong.

Fast forward a bit, and after a few bumps, bruises, and many lessons learned, I finally cracked the code. I realized that leadership isn't about being the loudest voice in the room or micromanaging every little detail. Nope, the real magic, the winning formula, boils down to three key steps that transformed not only how I lead but also how my team responded and thrived. This winning formula is simple:

Define + foster + empowerment = *winning team*

***

The Winning Formula Explained

Every leader out there has their take on what makes a team win. It's kind of like cooking—everyone's got their recipe. Some leaders have perfected their approach over years of experience, like a well-seasoned chef who knows the right amount of spice to add. Others, like me when I first started, have learned through a whole lot of trial and error—think of it as experimenting in the kitchen and sometimes ending up with a few burnt dishes along the way. And then, well, some just tossed in the towel entirely, deciding that maybe the heat of the kitchen isn't for them after all.

Now, here's the thing: no one-size-fits-all answer to what makes a team truly click. What works for me might not be the secret sauce for you, and that's perfectly okay. Leadership is as much about finding your style as it is about guiding others. But because I love sharing what's worked for me (and because I've had my fair share of "aha!" moments), I'm going to let you in on my recipe for success—a three-step winning formula that's helped me turn my teams into high-performing powerhouses:

- **Define:** First, you've got to define what success looks like for your team. First things first, let's talk about defining success for your team. And no, I don't mean some vague idea of "doing a good job." I'm talking crystal-clear, can't-miss-it goals that everyone on the team can rally around. Without that clarity, your team might as well be trying to hit a bullseye blindfolded—trust me, it's not pretty. So, here's how I roll. I kick things off by laying out a vision everyone can get behind. I'm not just throwing out some fancy words and hoping they stick. I make sure our team's purpose is spelled out in big, bold letters and that it fits like a puzzle piece into the organization's bigger picture. And guess what? Everyone on the team must know exactly how their role fits that puzzle. When they get that "aha" moment and realize their work is moving the needle for the whole company—well, that's when the magic happens. But we're not stopping there. Oh no. Next, I'm all about setting goals as *SMART* as they come. That means we're not just shooting for the moon and hoping to land somewhere in the stars. Nope, we're setting goals that are Specific, Measurable, Achievable, Relevant, and Time-bound—*SMART*, for short. These are the kinds of goals that make you wake up in the morning knowing exactly what you need to do and why it matters. So, there you have it. Define success, clarify it, and set some *SMART* goals to get your team fired up and ready to crush it. That's how to build a winning team, one step at a time.

- **Foster:** Alright, let's get into the good stuff—fostering the right environment for your team. And no, I'm not just discussing ensuring everyone's on good terms (though that's a big plus). I'm talking about creating a space where people feel safe to throw out their wildest ideas, make a few mistakes, and, most importantly, grow from those experiences. It's about making your team feel like they belong, and what they bring to the table matters. So here's how I tackle it. First, I'm all about building trust and respect—think of it as the foundation of a killer office culture. Without it, you're just spinning your wheels. I make it a point to cultivate an atmosphere where trust isn't just a buzzword but a way of life. Respect for one another isn't optional; it's baked into everything we do. Next up, I'm a huge fan of open communication. I want my team to feel like they can share their ideas, give feedback, and even disagree—without worrying about getting side-eye or judgment. The goal is to create a vibe where everyone feels heard and valued. And let's talk about collaboration. I support creating chances for my team to work together, swap knowledge, and play into each other's strengths. I'm constantly promoting teamwork because, let's face it, no one achieves greatness alone. Sure, individual accomplishments are wonderful, but it's the collective wins that take things to the next level. Remember, there's no "I" in "team." And when your team feels like a tight-knit crew, that's when the real magic happens.

- **Empowerment:** Alright, let's talk about the final piece of the puzzle—empowering your team. You hired these folks because they're talented, so now it's time to trust them to do what they do best. Give them the tools, resources, and space they need, and then—here's the tricky part—step back and let them shine. Now, this doesn't mean you vanish into thin air. Oh no, you're still around, ready to guide, support, and be their biggest cheerleader. But you're not hovering over their shoulders or questioning their every move.

I'm all about delegation. I hand over responsibilities and let my team take the reins. I empower them to make decisions, own their tasks, and feel that sense of responsibility and accountability. And guess what? It works wonders. When people feel trusted, they step up in ways you might never have expected.

Now, let's not forget about recognizing and rewarding achievements. I'm all for celebrating wins—big, small, and everything in between. But here's the kicker: I also celebrate the failures. Why? Because every stumble is just a stepping stone to the next success. We learn we grow, and we come back even stronger.

My secret sauce is keeping morale high. I constantly encourage continuous improvement and development because a team that's always learning is a team that's always winning. So, empower your team, trust them, and watch them soar. You'll be amazed at what they can accomplish when you give them the freedom to fly.

When you combine these three steps—**define, foster, & empowerment**—you create a team that's not just working for you but with you. A team that's invested in the company's success because they feel valued, understood, and empowered to do their best work. And that, my friends, is how you turn a group of individuals into a dream team.

Each part of my winning formula works well on its own, but when you put them together, the effect is downright magical. It's like combining the perfect ingredients in a recipe—the result is more than just the sum of its parts. And who doesn't love a good acronym to keep things easy to remember? I sure do!

Let me take you back to my middle school days. I tried my hand at Spanish, and, well, let's just say it wasn't exactly a success story. I could barely remember anything, especially when we had tests, and I had to translate a paragraph. By eighth grade, I thought I'd be clever and switch to Latin—because, you know, Latin is supposed to be easier, right? Spoiler alert: it wasn't. I constantly used acronyms to remember all those Latin-to-English translations (and vice versa). Honestly, I don't miss those days at all, and to this day, I can't remember one bit of a foreign language!

But out of that struggle came my love of acronyms. One of my most memorable acronyms, "*B.U.I.L.D.*," stands for Bonding, Understanding, Investment, Leadership, and Dedication—key qualities to *B.U.I.L.D.-ing* a winning team. Let's break it down:

- **Bonding:** Building strong relationships and camaraderie.
- **Understanding:** Appreciating team members' diverse skills and perspectives.
- **Investment:** Investing time and resources into team development.
- **Leadership:** Providing strong, supportive leadership to guide the team.
- **Dedication:** Committing fully to the team's success.

THE ROOT OF DISENGAGEMENT

So there you have it—*B.U.I.L.D.* a winning team focusing on bonding, understanding, investment, leadership, and dedication. This acronym might not be as tricky as Latin, but it is much more rewarding and easier to remember!

2

From Chaos to Clarity

So, you've poured your heart and soul into building a winning team. You've sacrificed sleep, spent countless nights tossing and turning, wondering why the plan fell apart and then basked in the sweet glory of high-fives and team celebrations when everything clicked. It's like you've finally cracked the code on leadership, and you're rolling with your dream team. And then—bam!—just when you think you've figured it all out, life throws you a curveball out of left field. Classic, right?

Here's the thing: teams are kind of like a perfect summer vacation—amazing while they last, but eventually, everyone's got to pack up and head home. Sure, positions are more permanent, but no one stays in the same job forever—not even your star employee. Spoiler alert: not even you. People evolve, interests shift, and life's weird little detours can lead us to unexpected places (like that time I accidentally got really into cross-stitching—don't ask).

Maybe you start as a business leader, laser-focused on hitting targets and leading your team to victory. But who knows? A few years later, you could trade that suit and tie for a hard hat and steel-toed boots, living your best life as a construction worker. It's all about following your passions, setting new goals, and rolling with the punches that life throws your way—kind of like bobbing and weaving through a never-ending obstacle course.

And hey, let's not forget the old saying: "It's not *what* you know, but *who* you know." It's cheesy but oh-so-true. Along your journey, the people you meet can open doors you never knew existed. They can also shut doors (but hey, maybe you didn't want to go through that door anyway). Whether you're leading a team, starting a new career, or just figuring out what's next, those relationships are pure gold. They can make all the difference when you're trying to navigate the next big move.

Now, here's the kicker: people come and go. That's just how life works. Sometimes, your star player moves on to chase their dreams, and sometimes, you find yourself shaking hands with someone new who's about to make their mark on your team. If you want to be a truly effective leader, you've got to embrace this reality. It's not just about the *person* doing the job but about understanding the *job* itself and why it's so essential to the company's success.

So, things will change, people will move on, and you might even end up in a career you never saw coming (hello, future llama farmer?). But if you can focus on what makes the role important and stay open to the twists and turns life throws, you'll be fine. Plus, if all else fails, there's always cross-stitching.

Take an accountant at an accounting firm, for example. You might be thinking, "They handle the books, right?" Well, sure—but that's like saying the Chief Financial Officer just "makes deposits." There's a *lot* more going on behind the scenes. Your accountant might be a rock star, balancing the books with one hand while sipping coffee with the other, all while keeping the financial gears turning. But guess what? They're not going to be there forever. People move on, careers change, and that's just the way the cookie crumbles (or, in this case, the ledger balances).

What matters is that *you*, as the leader, understand the role itself. An accountant isn't just the person who files your taxes and ensures the IRS doesn't come knocking. No, they're the unsung hero of your business—the financial backbone, the vendor-payer, the customer-payment-depositor, and the reason your staff gets paid on time (which, fun fact, people appreciate). They're like the oil that keeps the engine running smoothly, and if they're not there, well, that engine's going to sputter.

Now, recruiting perfection isn't about finding someone with a resume that looks like a "Greatest Hits" album. It's about understanding exactly what the role needs before starting the search. Think of it like building a puzzle—you've got to know what the final picture looks like before you can even start looking for the right pieces. Otherwise, you'll end up with a puzzle that's half-sea turtles, half-city skyline, and no one wants that mess.

Most of us get stuck on resumes, focusing on all the shiny things someone's done in the past. "Oh, they worked at a Fortune 500 company? They must be amazing!" But here's the deal: experience is great, but what's even more important is knowing the core functions of the role you're filling. You need to know exactly what you want from this role and then find someone who can nail those tasks.

Take hiring an accountant, for instance. You think, "I need someone to crunch numbers," and boom—you've got a list of twenty candidates who can turn a balance sheet into a work of art. You probably even have a list of ten job duties lined up, ready to slap on that job posting. But here's the catch: are *all* those duties necessary for this role?

It's easy to get caught up in the checklist, but have you stopped to ask yourself which tasks are mission-critical? Which ones could maybe be shuffled off to another department or automated? What if one of those candidates is a rock star at five tasks but isn't so hot at the other five? Would they still be a good fit?

The truth is, hiring isn't about finding someone who checks every single box—it's about finding someone who can do what matters most and do it well. So maybe your accountant can't recite the tax code backward in their sleep, but if they can keep the business running smoothly, pay your staff on time, and help you make sense of the finances, I'd say that's a win. Because let's face it: no one's perfect. And at the end of the day, you're not looking for perfection—you're looking for the right fit.

Sometimes, the perfect candidate isn't the one who checks every single box but the one who nails the most important ones. And if we're being honest, *nobody* ticks every box anyway—unless they're some kind of superhero with a cape and an endless supply of coffee.

When I was growing my eCommerce ventures, I prided myself on being super organized. My desk? Oh, it was a masterpiece of order. Everything had its place and purpose, and if something didn't get used daily, it was exiled from my line of sight like it was caught committing a crime. I was like a neat freak ninja, swooping in to keep everything tidy.

But, as time went on, things started to get a little...chaotic. Between juggling homework assignments from school, invoices piling up in my accounting software, and keeping track of phone messages scribbled on sticky notes, my once-pristine desk slowly morphed into what I affectionately call the *paper jungle*. Piles grew taller, and the dust settled like it was moving in for good. Business cards started mingling with contracts like they were at some sort of paperwork mixer. Sure, messages got buried—but hey, they weren't lost, just, you know...temporarily misplaced. (That's my story, and I'm sticking to it!)

This gradual descent into chaos? Inevitable. It's just one of those facts of life. You can start as organized as you want, but sooner or later, things are going to get messy. And as a leader, you've got to learn to roll with it. Embrace the chaos—because whether you like it or not, it's coming for you. The trick is not to let it stress you out. Know that it's part of the ride, and if you're managing a business, that ride has twists, turns, and a few surprise loop-the-loops.

Here's a little analogy for you: life and business are a lot like water and ice. When things are more structured—like ice—you've got a solid, predictable shape. But as soon as things heat up and start moving—boom, you've got water. Fluid, unpredictable, and slipping through your fingers no matter how hard you try to contain it. Chaos is higher in a state of flow, just like water, and that randomness can bring more freedom for things to shift and change. So, yes, more chaos—but more room for creativity and innovation, too. A little chaos isn't always bad; it keeps things interesting. Plus, ice melts eventually, right?

The same goes for teams. As your business grows, so does the complexity. Suddenly, there are more tasks to juggle, bigger goals to hit, more funding to manage, and a hundred other moving parts. Early on, everyone's wearing all the hats—sometimes literally. You've got people stepping out of their usual roles, diving into new responsibilities, and tackling things that probably weren't in their job description (but hey, they're game). That's the beauty of a growing business—it's messy, it's unpredictable, but it's also full of potential.

So, yes, understand that chaos will happen, especially as your team evolves and the business expands. But instead of trying to fight it, learn to embrace it. When you can thrive in chaos, real magic happens. And if your desk looks a little like mine, welcome to the club.

As teams grow and evolve, especially in today's fast-paced, "blink-and-suddenly-everything-changed" environment, we promote top performers, shuffle people around, and bring in fresh faces. Amidst all this glorious chaos, it's pretty easy for people to lose sight of what their actual job is. You know, that thing they were hired to do in the first place. And before you know it, their role looks like a patchwork quilt of tasks and projects they didn't exactly sign up for. I've seen it happen more times than I care to admit.

Let's be real for a second—teams morph. People take on "just for now" tasks that stick around longer than leftovers in the office fridge. One minute you're covering for a colleague on vacation, the next minute you're managing a whole new department! (Okay, maybe not that extreme, but close enough.) And those unofficial duties? They have a way of hanging around like that one friend who says goodbye at a party but never actually leaves. This phenomenon? I call it "departmental chaos."

Once you accept that "departmental chaos" is just part of the workplace ecosystem, like coffee spills and Monday morning sighs, you can start taking steps to handle it. Think of it like taming a wild beast—you're not trying to eliminate it, just get it to behave better. Just like you'd clean up a messy desk (or at least shove everything into a drawer and call it "organized"), you can refocus your team to reduce the chaos. The trick? Fewer, but more meaningful, rules. Focus on the big picture. It's like setting your GPS—you've got to know where you're going, or you'll drive in circles.

Managing and reducing chaos? That takes time and skill. And patience.

Oh boy, the patience. Some people will get frustrated and question why they signed up for this circus in the first place. I can't tell you how often I've heard someone say, "This is *not* what I originally signed up to do!" My response is usually, "Welcome to the club!" But seriously, I always remind them: "Departmental chaos happens everywhere, but we can do something about it."

Without clear goals and great communication, chaos will run the show, complete with juggling and disappearing acts. If you're clear on where to go, you can pave a straight path and clear out as many obstacles as possible. As a leader, you're handing out the maps and shouting directions from the front of the pack. It's up to you to clear up the confusion, eliminate the unnecessary distractions, and give everyone a sense of direction—otherwise, it's like herding cats. And trust me, I've tried that. Cats don't like to be herded.

Ultimately, your job as a leader is to combat departmental chaos like a superhero with a clipboard and a plan. Bring focus, organization, and a sense of calm to the storm. And when things get crazy, remember: it's not about stopping the chaos—it's about learning to dance in it, preferably without stepping on anyone's toes.

* * *

The Chaos of Circuit City

Circuit City was a major retail chain founded in 1949 by Sam Wurtzel, who rapidly expanded the business into a national presence. His son, Alan Wurtzel, took the reins and transformed Circuit City into a household name. By 2000, Circuit City had grown to employ over 60,000 people across more than 616 locations throughout the United States. At its peak, it felt like Circuit City was everywhere you turned.

Circuit City's origins date back to 1949, when founder Sam Wurtzel was getting a haircut in Richmond, Virginia, on his way to a family vacation in

North Carolina. During the conversation, the barber mentioned that the first television station in the South had opened in Richmond less than a year earlier. Fresh off a failed import-export business, Sam saw this new entertainment device as his next big opportunity.

Sam initially considered naming his store "Wards," figuring it would be easier for people to pronounce than his last name. Instead of competing directly with large retailers like Walmart, he targeted lower-income Americans by offering purchase installment plans. But that wasn't his only innovative strategy. He also introduced a unique sales technique: free in-home demonstrations. A salesman would drop off a television at a customer's home for the night, free of charge, and offer to pick it up the next day. Once the set was in the family's living room, it almost always stayed there—customers couldn't resist buying it. I'd say that was a pretty smart move.

With his sales strategy firmly in place, Sam Wurtzel decided to join the ranks of national retailers and began expanding his business. After opening his first big-box discount retail space in New England in 1952, he took the company public to secure the additional capital needed for further expansion. Energized by early successes, the company embarked on an aggressive expansion strategy—one that nearly led to bankruptcy by 1975.

To navigate this crisis, Sam's son, Alan Wurtzel, stepped in as CEO in 1973. Under his leadership, the company underwent a significant restructuring, which included closing many underperforming stores. By the late 1970s, the company was ready to grow again, but this time with a crucial change—a new name: "Circuit City."

The re-branded stores featured larger showroom floors with attached warehouses in the back. Customers could browse the items on display, select what they wanted from the shelves, and purchase at one of the many checkout kiosks throughout the store. This new approach set the stage for Circuit City's rapid growth and solidified its place as a major player in the retail industry.

Circuit City's rapid rise to fame is a story of incredible success and one of America's most notable retail failures. In November 2008, after nearly

60 years in business, the company filed for bankruptcy. Within months, Circuit City closed its doors, liquidated over $1 billion in merchandise, and turned off the lights at the last remaining store on March 8, 2009.

So, how does a company go from startup success to national growth, only to end in national failure? The answer lies in chaos and poor management.

The company's 700,000-square-foot headquarters in Richmond, Virginia, which once buzzed with activity, has since been taken over by other successful retailers who have continued to expand. This begs the question: why did other retailers survive and thrive during the early 2000s while Circuit City did not?

The key difference lies in how management approaches their employees and business decisions. While other retailers prioritized well-trained and well-invested staff, Circuit City's management made a series of questionable choices. These included the ill-fated acquisition of a Canadian-based electronics retail chain and an aggressive round of store expansions that overstretched the company. To cut costs, management also laid off more than 3,400 of the company's most experienced and dedicated employees—decisions that ultimately contributed to the company's downfall. Experienced staff were replaced with less knowledgeable employees who received minimal, if any, company training.

Circuit City's story is a powerful reminder that even the most successful businesses can falter without strong leadership, sound decision-making, and a genuine commitment to valuing their employees. Chaos is inevitable in any organization, but how you, as a leader, choose to address it will ultimately determine your success.

Great leaders don't start by simply recruiting the best people they can find. Instead, they identify the most critical functions and responsibilities within their team or organization and then focus on finding—and retaining—the best employees to perform those functions. Achieving organizational clarity begins with setting clear objectives and expectations. Once these objectives are established, the right match can be made with existing or new team members (remember, you can always recruit from within your current staff), ensuring everyone is aligned and working toward the same goals.

Essential Leadership Qualities

As leaders, one of the biggest traps we can fall into is thinking everything is equally important. You know that supervisor who says, "Everything is urgent, and it all needs to be done perfectly"? Yeah, we've all been there. It's like they're handing you a to-do list that stretches longer than a CVS receipt and then expecting you to sprint through it like a superhero. But let's face it—only a few things have a *huge* impact, while a lot of the other stuff? Not so much.

Being truly committed to your team means getting real about what matters most. It's not about throwing everything at the wall and hoping it sticks. It's about sitting down, sorting through the clutter, and making sure your employees know their main priorities. You've got to help them focus on the core functions of their role, not the random side quests they've picked up along the way. Because let's be honest—who's got time for all those side quests when you've got dragons (or deadlines) to slay?

Take our friend the accountant, for example. Sure, their job description might read like a novel—paying bills, balancing the books, handling banking, processing payroll, and probably making sure the office plant doesn't die (just kidding, I hope). But at the end of the day, their number one job is maintaining accurate financial records and interpreting those records effectively. You're not hiring them to be the next great customer service hero or the office's official copy machine whisperer. You're hiring them to keep the company's finances in check.

Now, let's switch gears and think about a Barista at Starbucks. Their job description? Well, it's probably longer than your coffee order (and if you're ordering a triple venti, half-sweet, non-fat, caramel macchiato, that's saying something). They're responsible for taking orders, operating the cash register, cleaning, ensuring safety, making drinks—and running a mini-empire. But their *real* job, their essential job duty, is much simpler: giving the customer an unforgettable experience and serving the perfect cup of whatever keeps them going. It's not about having the cleanest blender in the city (though, points if they do), but about making sure that when the customer walks out, they're smiling—and, more importantly, coming back for more.

Here's the kicker: when we, as leaders, focus on the core functions of a job and make those the priority, everything else falls into place. Your employees aren't running around like headless chickens, trying to balance a thousand different tasks. Instead, they're laser-focused on what matters, and they feel more accomplished when they're nailing those key tasks. It's a win-win: better performance, happier employees, and a better environment.

Start by writing down every task the employee will be responsible for. It's important to include not only the major responsibilities but also the smaller, seasonal, and one-off tasks they may need to handle.

Next, identify the primary job function for which the employee will be accountable. Make this as clear and specific as possible to avoid any ambiguity.

Then, organize your list of responsibilities in order of importance, with the primary job function at the top. This ensures that the most crucial responsibility is highlighted from the outset.

Once the list is ordered from most important to least important, highlight the critical functions of the organization's success. These highlighted tasks should be ones that the new employee can perform with ease and proficiency.

For example, if you're hiring an accountant, the list might look like this (with the primary function listed at the top):

1. Preparing and analyzing financial statements (Primary function)
2. Filing and follow-through on tax returns
3. Budgets and forecasting
4. Managing accounts payable (ensuring bills are paid)
5. Handling cash flow and bank deposits
6. Updating the business plan

This structured approach ensures that you hire someone who understands their primary responsibilities and can effectively contribute to the organization's overall success.

Over the years, working at various companies, I've seen it all—colleagues getting promoted, demoted, transferred, and some just packing up and moving on. It's like a never-ending game of musical chairs but with job titles. And if there's one thing I've learned from all this shuffling, it's that when hiring for a role, you need to be crystal clear about the type of person you're looking for.

Take hiring an accountant, for example. The primary job function is "preparing and analyzing financial statements," but what does that mean regarding the qualities you need? You'll want someone who's a stickler for accuracy, with laser-sharp attention to detail, and can spot a loophole in a financial report from a mile away. Patience is key here, too—after all, this isn't a job for someone who likes to rush through things. Do they have financial and auditing experience from a previous firm? Even better!

Once you've got a list of the qualities you're after, it's time to bring out the ranking system again—just like you did when you listed the job functions. Write down all the qualities you've identified and rank them in order of importance for the role. But here's the catch: the more "must-have" qualities you insist on, the fewer candidates you'll have to choose from. It's all about balance, so keep your "must-haves" to a few essentials for the job.

This approach works particularly well for employees who are transferring into a new role within your company or who are already familiar with your company culture. But let's not forget that there are some qualities you just can't teach—things like energy, passion, morale, and attitude. I've always believed that if you can't bring a positive attitude and strong work ethic to your role, you won't be able to inspire and motivate others.

At the end of the day, it's all about knowing what you need, prioritizing those needs, and finding the right person who can not only do the job but thrive in it. And if they can bring a little extra spark to the team, all the better!

*　*　*

Unlocking the Mindset of Amazing Employees

Over the years, I've had the incredible fortune of working with some truly high-performing teams. These teams weren't just good at their jobs—they were filled with colleagues who brought an infectious energy, a great sense of humor, and a level of competence that meant they needed minimal supervision. Honestly, it's like finding a treasure trove of talent that makes coming to work something you look forward to.

Now, there are plenty of stars in the universe, but when I come across a true superstar, I can't help but feel this overwhelming urge to lock them into their position forever. The thought of losing them is almost too painful to consider. I mean, how do you even start to imagine replacing someone who's not just good but irreplaceable?

But here's the flip side—it would be completely wrong to hold back an employee eager to grow, develop, and possibly even be promoted within the company. As much as I'd love to keep them in their current role, doing so would be selfish. The very qualities that make these high performers so special are exactly what drive them to seek new challenges and opportunities.

The thing is, what makes these ultra-high performers so exceptional is unique to them. You can try to find a replacement, but let me tell you, good luck with that. It just doesn't work that way. Each of these superstars brings something to the one-of-a-kind table, and finding someone exactly like them? That is not going to happen.

So, while it's tough to think about letting go of these incredible talents, it's also a reminder of why they're so special in the first place. And if we're lucky, we get to watch them soar to even greater heights, knowing that we played a part in their journey.

Let's be honest—leaders often fall into the same trap when they've got a high-performing employee on their hands. Suddenly, job duties start to form around that person. Think about it—if you've got someone who's not only capable but hungry for more work, why wouldn't you give them the chance to tackle new projects? Of course, you would! It's almost a no-brainer.

So, what happens? Job responsibilities start to morph into something that the employee never initially signed up for. It's like, "Oh, you can do this too? Great, let's add that to your list!" You've heard leaders say, "I didn't know you could handle that! Let's make it part of your role." Before you know it, this high performer's job description is bursting at the seams with tasks and projects that weren't there originally.

But here's the kicker—what happens when that superstar employee decides to leave the company or move to a different position? Chaos. Absolute, unfiltered chaos. Suddenly, there's this gaping hole where your rock star used to be, and everyone's scrambling to figure out who will pick up the slack.

It's like watching a well-oiled machine suddenly lose a key gear. Now, the company is stuck trying to throw darts at the wall, hoping something sticks, or worse—pressuring other employees, who might not be nearly as capable, to take on tasks they aren't fluent in. This is just to keep the business running smoothly and avoid major disruptions.

This is where the danger lies—relying too heavily on a single high performer can leave you vulnerable when they're no longer there. Suddenly, the workload that was once managed so effortlessly by your superstar is now causing stress and confusion across the board. And let's face it, trying to replace that kind of talent isn't as simple as just finding someone new. So, while it's great to tap into your employees' hidden talents, it's just as important to have a plan for when the inevitable happens and they move on. Otherwise, you're left with chaos—and nobody wants that.

When you find yourself in this leadership situation, it's time to hit the pause button and have a little heart-to-heart with yourself. Grab a cup of coffee, sit down, and get real. What exactly made that rock star employee so incredible? Was it their magnetic personality? Their infectious positive outlook? Maybe it was their insatiable hunger for growth or the fact that they were laser-focused on climbing the company ladder.

Let's be honest: it's not every day you stumble across someone who can juggle a million tasks with a smile and still ask for more. So, why were they able to do it? What were those magical qualities that made them stand out from the crowd? It's time to dig deep and compile a list of everything that made them a superstar. Was it their ability to think on their feet? Their knack for solving problems before they even became problems? Or maybe it was their commitment to always going above and beyond?

Once you've got that list of rock star qualities in hand, you can start the search for someone who might be able to fill those very big shoes. Now, let's be clear—you're probably not going to find an exact clone of your former superstar (because, let's face it, they were one of a kind), but you can find someone who has the potential to take on some of those rock star tasks.

This is where the fun begins! It's like a treasure hunt, where you're looking for the next hidden gem who might just surprise you with their brand of awesomeness. Sure, it might take some time, and you might need to shift around responsibilities, but that's all part of the adventure. And who knows? Maybe you'll find someone who brings something entirely new and exciting—something you didn't even know you needed.

Jake Thompson was hands down one of the best employees I've ever had the pleasure of working with. I used to call him "The Innovator" because he always thought up new ways to make our business processes faster and more efficient. See, I grew up hearing the phrase, "Work smarter, not harder," but I can't say I always followed that advice. I'm the kind of person who would dive headfirst into a task, only to realize later that there were a million shortcuts I could've taken to get the same results. Sigh!

But Jake? Jake was different. He was smart, positive, creative, and knew exactly what he was doing. Plus, he had a great sense of humor, which is always a bonus in the workplace. I could bring him to team meetings with full confidence, knowing he'd not only deliver solid strategies but also make me look like a superstar leader in the process.

Over the years, Jake's role evolved significantly. He started as a data processor, where he was responsible for analyzing reports, customer satisfaction levels, and internal business software reports, you name it. If it involved data and analytics, Jake was all over it, and he handled it with both speed and accuracy. He was the go-to guy, the one you could always count on to get the job done right.

But then came the day I knew would eventually arrive—Jake was promoted. Our CEO recognized his talents and made him the Director of Quality Control. Suddenly, Jake's job shifted from analyzing reports to writing proposals on improving our business functions. It was a huge step up for him, and while I was incredibly proud, I couldn't help but think, "What am I going to do without Jake?"

Replacing someone like Jake? That's like trying to find Waldo in the middle of New York City—nearly impossible! The original position Jake signed up for had transformed so much over the years as he grew with the company. Every time he mastered a task, we added more to his plate, and of course, Jake could handle it all without breaking a sweat.

But now, my department was in chaos. Some gaps needed filling, and they needed to be filled fast. I knew I had to figure out what made Jake tick and replicate that in his replacement. So, I reviewed his responsibilities over time, especially those he handled right before his promotion. It became clear that I needed to identify his primary job function and find someone to step into those shoes sooner rather than later.

***

Leadership vs. Managing

Throughout my career as a business consultant, I've seen firsthand the impact that managers and leaders can have on an organization. "Manager" and "leader" are often used interchangeably, but the roles are distinct. Understanding the difference between the two is essential for anyone who wants to build a successful, engaged, and high-performing team. More importantly, understanding why it's better to be a leader than just a manager can make all the difference in your career and the growth of your organization. Throughout this book, you'll see a common trend - I will refer to "managers" as "leaders."

A manager is typically responsible for maintaining the systems and processes that keep an organization running smoothly. Their role is operational, ensuring that tasks are completed on time, budgets are adhered to, and policies and procedures are followed. Managers set goals, assign tasks, and measure performance. Their focus tends to be on efficiency, productivity, and achieving short-term objectives.

In many organizations, managers ensure that day-to-day operations run smoothly. They track metrics, supervise work, and maintain order. Their success is measured by their ability to deliver results within the company's established framework. Managers are often seen as the individuals who "keep the trains running on time," and while this is an important function, it has limitations.

A leader, on the other hand, inspires, motivates, and influences others to achieve a vision that goes beyond the immediate tasks at hand. Leadership is less about process and more about people. While leaders also have goals, their primary focus is cultivating an environment where employees feel empowered, valued, and inspired to perform at their best.

A leader looks beyond today's goals to consider the long-term success of the organization and its people. Instead of managing tasks, they build relationships, foster trust, and encourage creativity and innovation. Leaders are visionaries who guide their teams through change, help them overcome obstacles, and inspire them to see possibilities beyond their limitations.

There are several key differences between a manager and a leader that shape the way they interact with their teams and the broader organization:

1. **Focus**: Managers focus on tasks and processes, while leaders focus on people and vision. Managers are concerned with the "what" and "how," whereas leaders are more concerned with the "why" and "who."

2. **Approach to change**: Managers maintain the status quo, working

within established systems to ensure consistency. Leaders, on the other hand, embrace change, pushing their teams to innovate, grow, and adapt to new challenges.

3. **Decision-making**: Managers often decide based on data, metrics, and established policies. Leaders, while also using data, are more likely to make decisions based on values, vision, and a broader perspective of the organization's future.

4. **Motivation**: Managers motivate through control and structure—clear roles, expectations, and rewards for meeting performance standards. Leaders motivate through inspiration, creating a sense of purpose and ownership that drives employees to exceed expectations.

5. **Authority vs. influence**: Managers derive their authority from their organizational position. Their power comes from the title and the responsibility it carries. Leaders, on the other hand, derive their influence from the trust and respect they earn from their teams. Leadership is not about a title but how well you inspire and guide others.

In today's business environment, being a manager is no longer enough. While management skills are essential, they don't fully address the needs of a workforce that craves engagement, purpose, and connection. Organizations that succeed in the long term are led by people who understand the value of leadership over mere management.

Here's why it's better to be a leader than a manager:

1. **Leaders create engagement and commitment**: Leaders foster a sense of purpose and ownership among their teams. When employees feel that their work is meaningful and part of something larger than themselves, they are far more engaged and committed. This level of engagement leads to higher performance, increased job satisfaction,

and lower turnover rates. Managers may be able to get their teams to meet deadlines, but leaders inspire their teams to take ownership and strive for excellence.

2. **Leaders build trust and loyalty**: Leadership is about building relationships based on trust and respect. Employees are far more likely to stay loyal to a leader they trust than a manager they simply follow out of obligation. In my experience, organizations that cultivate leaders see lower turnover rates and stronger, more cohesive teams. When employees feel their leader cares about their growth and well-being, they are likelier to invest their best efforts in the organization's success.

3. **Leaders drive innovation**: Managers often focus on maintaining existing systems and achieving immediate results, which can stifle innovation. Leaders, however, encourage risk-taking and creativity, allowing their teams to experiment and explore new ideas. This forward-thinking approach fosters innovation and helps organizations stay ahead in a constantly evolving market. A team led by a strong leader will be more agile, adaptable, and better equipped to face new challenges.

4. **Leaders cultivate future leaders**: One of the most valuable contributions a leader can make is developing the next generation of leaders within the organization. While managers may focus on managing the current team, leaders are invested in helping their team members grow and develop their leadership potential. This investment in people leads to a culture of continuous growth and development, ensuring the long-term success of the organization.

5. **Leaders inspire resilience:** In times of difficulty or change, teams look to their leaders for guidance and strength. While managers may rely on rules and procedures to overcome challenges, leaders inspire their teams to push forward with resilience and confidence. A true

leader can turn a crisis into an opportunity for growth, motivating their team to not only overcome obstacles but to emerge stronger on the other side.

To be clear, management skills are necessary. Processes, organization, and structure are all important elements of a successful business. However, when we combine strong management with effective leadership, the result is far more powerful.

In my work with organizations, I've found that the most successful companies are those where managers also see themselves as leaders. They understand the need to balance efficiency and productivity with vision, inspiration, and personal connection. These organizations have teams that are not only effective in the short term but are also motivated and prepared to meet the challenges of the future.

***

Aligning Skills With Responsibilities

I've encountered plenty of colleagues who, for lack of a better term, seemed allergic to learning. I'd run training sessions, walk them through policies like a patient kindergarten teacher, and offer more guidance than a self-help book, but somehow, the knowledge never seemed to stick. It was like trying to teach a cat to fetch—they'd look at me, blink, and then wander off to do something completely unrelated.

I even went as far as developing customized training programs tailored to fill the specific gaps in their knowledge, but despite my best efforts, some employees just weren't hitting the mark. Naturally, when someone's not meeting performance expectations, the knee-jerk reaction is to think, "Well, maybe they're just not cut out for this." But here's the twist: I've realized it's not always about them not being the right fit for the company. Sometimes, it's about us putting them in the wrong job. It's like hiring a chef and then wondering why they're not crushing it as the front desk receptionist.

Here's the deal: everyone's got their thing. Some people are great at numbers; some can charm customers and others? Well, they might be really, *really* good at organizing the office supply closet (and hey, that's a skill too). The point is, if an employee is struggling, it's worth asking: did we stick them in a role that aligns with their actual strengths, or did we just need someone to fill the vacancy? Because if it's the latter, you might have a diamond in the rough just waiting for the right opportunity to shine.

Now, trying to change someone's entire personality or work style? That's like trying to convince a dog to become a vegetarian—it's not happening, and it's a waste of perfectly good bacon. Instead, we should focus on channeling what they *are* good at and finding a way to make it work for them and the company. When you help people play to their strengths, magic happens—suddenly, they're more engaged, more productive, and less likely to leave passive-aggressive Post-Its on the office fridge.

I firmly believe in treating my team like an actual team, not just a bunch of people who work in the same building. Everyone brings something unique to the table, and if we're not making room for that, we're missing out on some serious potential. Without each person's contributions, we'd all be fumbling through our workday like toddlers trying to use chopsticks.

As a leader, it's our job to give people the freedom, tools, and encouragement they need to *grow* into their roles. Think of it like raising plants—you don't expect an oak tree to sprout overnight, but with a little sunlight, water, and time, it'll grow into something pretty impressive. And trust me, when your team feels valued and supported, they'll contribute their best work, and that's what pushes the whole organization forward. Plus, it's way more fun to work with a happy, engaged team than a bunch of people counting down the minutes to 5 PM.

Now, when you're using what I like to call the "commitment formula," you might notice something: some of your employees aren't quite in the right roles. And that's okay! It's all part of the process, especially as your business grows and the demands on your team shift. When this happens, it's not just about creating new positions—it's also about trimming the fat, so to speak. I call this process "weeding the garden."

Think about it: in any business, tasks tend to pile up like weeds. Some of these tasks were essential at one point, but now? They're just clutter, weighing everything down. By "weeding the garden," we're freeing up space for the important work to thrive. Less busy work means more time for your team to focus on what moves the needle for your business—honestly, who wouldn't want that?

Now, when it comes to leveling up your team, here's something to keep in mind: lots of people can handle entry-level tasks, but only a few are ready for the big, complex jobs. But guess what? Your existing employees—yes, the ones who already know the quirks of the company and where we hide the extra coffee filters—have way more potential to grow into those bigger roles than someone you just brought in off the street. Sure, a new hire might look great on paper, but they will need time to learn the ropes before making a real impact.

Before you rush to hire externally, look at your current team. Can you align their skills with your needs in those more advanced roles? If you can, do it. Let them step up. Then, bring in new hires to tackle the entry-level stuff. That way, you're fostering internal growth, keeping the team cohesive, and ensuring all that knowledge stays in-house. Plus, it saves you from explaining how the coffee machine works for the millionth time.

* * *

Creating Synergy to Eliminate Chaos

Throughout our lives, we've witnessed countless examples of teamwork being the key to success. But building a truly effective team goes far beyond just holding meetings and checking off tasks on a list. It requires making difficult decisions and working selflessly for the benefit of others, even when the final outcome is uncertain. One of the hallmarks of a great team is its ability to foster a sense of psychological safety across the entire organization—from senior executives to entry-level employees. This environment encourages everyone to contribute their best ideas and efforts without fear of failure.

One of the most profound examples of a high-performing team in action is NASA's 1969 Apollo 11 mission. This mission was a monumental milestone for science and humanity, capturing the world's attention as three astronauts embarked on a historic journey to the moon. While Neil Armstrong, Buzz Aldrin, and Michael Collins are the names we remember, their success was built on the hard work and dedication of a vast support team.

Years of research, planning, and expertise laid the foundation for this achievement. For two years before the mission, planners meticulously studied the moon's surface, analyzing satellite images and data from the Surveyor spacecraft. They had to account for every detail—craters, boulders, cliffs, and the sun's position—to determine the safest landing site. NASA estimates that more than 400,000 people played a role in making the moon landing possible. This included not only scientists, engineers, and technicians but also individuals who had never worked in aerospace before and were tasked with designing the technology to safely transport humans to the moon and back.

What made this mission successful was the unwavering commitment of all 400,000 people involved - working together in synergy. Their collective dedication ensured that every detail was executed flawlessly. In our rapidly changing world, we face our own "Apollo 11" challenges regularly, especially as new technologies and ambitious goals are introduced in the workplace. These "reach goals" often require assembling teams from various departments and sometimes even bringing in external experts to achieve a successful outcome.

In these situations, team members often have to step outside their usual roles, much like those who contributed to the Apollo 11 mission without prior aerospace experience. What sets apart these great achievements, whether in space exploration or the business world, is the shared commitment to the project's success. It's this collective effort and dedication that turn ambitious dreams into reality. As leaders, it's our responsibility to cultivate this level of commitment within our teams, ensuring that everyone is aligned with the mission and motivated to contribute to its success.

In the wild and ever-changing business world, where things move at lightning speed and the pressure is always on, success is rarely about just one person's talent or effort. It's all about the magic that happens when a team clicks—*synergy*. Now, I know "synergy" might sound like one of those corporate buzzwords, but trust me, it's the real deal. It's that special sauce that takes a bunch of individuals and turns them into a powerhouse team capable of achieving things that would be impossible on their own.

Why is synergy such a big deal? Well, in a world where challenges are getting more complex by the day, no single person, no matter how much of a rock star they are, can handle everything alone. Synergy is like the ultimate team superpower—it lets everyone pool their unique talents, skills, and perspectives to devise solutions that no person could dream up solo.

Imagine a company facing a huge challenge, like breaking into a new market. If everyone on the team is working in their little bubble, focused only on their specific task, they might miss out on some key insights or overlook potential pitfalls. But when that team works synergistically, they're not just playing their instruments—they're making beautiful music together. They draw on each other's strengths, challenge each other's ideas, and come up with a strategy that's not only solid but also adaptable.

Synergy is like a creativity booster shot. When team members build on each other's ideas, the real magic happens—innovative solutions start popping up left and right. And it's not just about solving problems; synergy also gives everyone a serious morale boost. When you know you're part of something bigger, when you're contributing to a shared goal, it's hard not to feel motivated and proud of what you're achieving together.

Creating synergy within a team doesn't just magically happen—it takes some serious effort and thoughtful leadership. But don't worry, it's doable, and honestly, it's pretty fun when you see it all come together. Here's how I like to stir up some synergy on my team:

1. **Establish clear communication:** Let's start with the basics—

communication is the bedrock of any team clicking. I make sure everyone on the team feels comfortable sharing their ideas, concerns, and feedback without fearing being shut down. We hold regular meetings and keep updates transparent, and I always make time for some good old-fashioned active listening. When everyone's on the same page and ideas are flowing freely, the magic happens.

2. **Define roles and responsibilities:** Synergy loves collaboration, but it's crucial that everyone knows their role in the team. I make sure roles and responsibilities are crystal clear to avoid confusion or overlap. Of course, these roles aren't set in stone—there's always room for flexibility so team members can jump in and support each other when needed.

3. **Learn to trust and respect:** Trust is the secret sauce of any synergistic team. We must trust each other's abilities and believe everyone is as committed to the team's success as we are. I work hard to build that trust by recognizing everyone's contributions, nipping conflicts in the bud, and ensuring every voice is heard. Mutual respect and reliability are the name of the game here.

4. **Leverage diversity:** Diversity isn't just a buzzword—it's a powerhouse for synergy. When people from different backgrounds and with varied experiences come together, they bring unique perspectives that can lead to some pretty innovative solutions. I actively seek out and embrace diversity, not just in terms of demographics but also in how people think and approach problems.

5. **Share visions and goals:** Synergy hits its stride when the team is united by a common vision and shared goals. I make it a point to articulate a clear vision that resonates with everyone and aligns with our values. By setting specific, measurable, and achievable goals, we can all work together toward a common purpose, keeping our efforts

aligned and focused.

6. **Encourage collaboration:** Collaboration is the beating heart of synergy. I create plenty of opportunities for the team to collaborate on projects, share ideas, and solve problems as a unit. Whether it's through collaborative tools, cross-functional teams, or fun team-building activities, I make sure there's always space for cooperation and camaraderie.

* * *

Effective vs. Exceptional Leadership

Change is a gradual process. It's rare for someone to instantly replace one behavior with another. For most of us, change is a journey of experimentation, discovering what works and what doesn't. Those who dive in headfirst and attempt drastic changes shouldn't be surprised if the results don't align with their expectations. But the key is not to give up—quitters don't become leaders! There isn't a "one-size-fits-all" approach to business leadership because every company is unique.

It's important to play devil's advocate and challenge your assumptions about what will work and what won't. However, it's crucial to do this in measured steps. If you don't achieve the desired outcome on your first attempt, don't abandon the effort; instead, adjust your approach. Small tweaks might lead to success where the original plan did not.

Great leaders understand the importance of adapting their beliefs to align with the company's policies and principles. They are open to showing themselves that thinking outside the box can lead to different, and often better, outcomes. This willingness to evolve and refine one's approach distinguishes effective leaders from exceptional ones.

Here are some of the qualities that set us apart as leaders:

Effective Leaders

1. **Clear communication**: An effective leader ensures the team is well-informed about objectives, expectations, and tasks. They maintain regular communication to provide updates and resolve any confusion.

2. **Sound decision-making**: Effective leaders make thoughtful, fair decisions considering the team's well-being. They gather input when needed and choose actions that benefit the organization.

3. **Supportive behavior**: An effective leader offers support by providing resources, guidance, and encouragement. They help the team navigate challenges and ensure everyone has the tools to succeed.

4. **Accountability**: Effective leaders hold themselves and their team accountable. They set clear expectations and follow up to ensure commitments are fulfilled.

5. **Recognition of efforts**: They actively recognize and celebrate the achievements of team members, which boosts morale and motivation.

Exceptional Leaders

1. **Visionary leadership**: An exceptional leader has a compelling vision for the future and can inspire their team to work towards it with enthusiasm. They focus not only on current tasks but also on long-term goals and innovation.

2. **Empowering team members**: Exceptional leaders empower their team by delegating responsibility, encouraging autonomy, and fostering a sense of ownership. They trust their team to take initiative and make decisions.

3. **Emotional intelligence**: Exceptional leaders have a keen understanding of their team members' emotions and needs. They connect personally, building strong relationships and creating a supportive, inclusive environment.

4. **Mentorship and development**: An exceptional leader actively mentors team members, helping them grow in their careers. They invest in the development of others by providing opportunities for learning and advancement.

5. **Resilience in challenges**: When faced with adversity, exceptional leaders remain composed and optimistic. They guide their team through difficulties with confidence and adaptability, turning challenges into opportunities.

6. **Building a legacy**: Exceptional leaders create a lasting impact on their organization and the people they lead. They establish a culture of excellence, innovation, and integrity that continues to thrive even after they move on.

7. **Ethical leadership**: Exceptional leaders consistently uphold high ethical standards, lead by example, and make decisions that reflect their core values. They inspire others to act with integrity.

Incorporating these qualities into your leadership approach is best done incrementally. Rather than trying to adopt too many at once, it's more effective to introduce them gradually. This allows you to fully evaluate how each strategy is working for you and to make any necessary adjustments along the way.

I don't expect everything to fall into place perfectly from the start—change is a process that requires time and persistence. It's important to give yourself the space to experiment and refine your approach as you go. By doing so, you can assess what resonates most with your leadership style and what areas may need further development.

The journey from being an effective leader to an exceptional one doesn't happen overnight. It's a continuous process of learning, adapting, and growing. With patience and determination, you can gradually integrate these qualities into your leadership practice, enhancing your impact and elevating your leadership to the next level.

3

Building Your Dream Team

Y ou can find me just about anywhere—whether I'm in a business meeting or making my way through an airport. Trust me, I'm pretty hard to miss. I'm usually the one who kicks off the conversation, maybe talks too much, or throws in a quirky comment for good measure. But do I care? Not one bit! I love putting myself out there and connecting with people. I'm not the type to lurk in the back of the room and sneak out five minutes early to beat the parking lot rush. Nope, I'm grinning and nudging my way into a conversation. And if the other person isn't into it? Well, that's their loss—I'm off to find my next chat buddy.

Luckily, my knack for striking up conversations has worked in my favor. While working at my first retail job, a customer walked in, interested in buying a mattress. Now, I wasn't about to let this be just any sale. I brought my A-game, using my energetic customer service skills and product knowledge, to not sell just one mattress but two— and these weren't your run-of-the-mill mattresses, either.

When it came time to ring up the sale, I headed to the register, and that's when things got interesting. The customer pulled out a Black Card. If you're unfamiliar, a Black Card is like the holy grail of credit cards—it's made of heavy metal, has high credit limits, and is typically reserved for the ultra-wealthy. So there I was, holding this card, trying to decide if I was more in awe of selling $12,000 worth of mattresses or that I was holding a

Black Card. It was a toss-up!

After wrapping up the sale, I handed over my business card and ensured the customers knew they could reach out anytime with questions or concerns. For me, the after-sale experience is just as important—if not more so—than the in-store experience. I mean, how many times have you bought something expensive and never heard from the salesperson again? Not on my watch. I'm all about making sure that the experience continues to be top-notch long after the sale is completed.

Naturally curious, once the customer walked out the door, I couldn't resist—I dove straight into the paperwork to find out her name. My curiosity was through the roof. Who exactly had I just crossed paths with? A quick Google search later, and boom—there it was, her Wikipedia page. That's right, not only did this customer hold a Black Card, but she also had her own Wikipedia page. Now, I was intrigued. Who was this mystery celebrity?

Her name was Rachna, and as it turns out, she's no ordinary shopper. Rachna is an American marketing executive and a politician, serving as a member of the Connecticut House of Representatives. And not just any district—she represents parts of Greenwich and Stamford, some of the wealthiest areas in the entire country. Talk about impressive! Rachna's success was fueled by her drive and passion for excellence, and now I could see why.

Fast forward almost ten years later, and I'm at a Beta Gamma Sigma Honors Society meeting at the University of Hartford, celebrating my double lifetime induction for my entrepreneurial endeavors. I'm mingling, enjoying the event when someone familiar strolls into the room. I knew I recognized her, but I couldn't quite remember from where. Then she spoke, and it all clicked—I was the one who told her those mattresses! Talk about a small world, right?

There she was, the same Rachna I had Googled, now standing in front of me at an honors society meeting. It was one of those surreal moments where the world suddenly felt like a much smaller place. From selling mattresses to rubbing elbows at a prestigious event—it just goes to show you never know who you're going to meet or how your paths might cross again.

Among many inspiring topics, Rachna got the room buzzing when she opened up about the challenges she's faced in her business career. And let me tell you, the biggest hurdle she mentioned was one we can all relate to building your dream team. See, Rachna gets it—she knows that without the right people in her corner, her business would never reach its full potential. She didn't shy away from admitting that this was one of her toughest battles, but she also acknowledged that her current team is nothing short of exceptional.

Listening to Rachna break down her "dream team" woes, I couldn't help but think about her revolving success. It's all about connecting with people, understanding what drives them, and creating an environment where they can thrive. And if Rachna's story is anything to go by, when you get the right team together, there's no limit to what you can achieve.

After her inspiring speech, the evening was just getting started. I had the chance to mix and mingle with the other guests, but I knew exactly who I wanted to chat with first. I went over to Rachna and, with a big grin, asked if she remembered me. She turned and, without missing a beat, said, "Yes, of course, you sold me the mattresses!" We both smiled and before I knew it, we shared a handshake. I told her how much her success story had inspired me, and I gave her a quick rundown of my adventures in the business world. The connection was instant, and it felt like we were on the same wavelength.

But the real magic happened a little later when I was outside in the atrium, grabbing a quick bite. As I was enjoying some hors d'oeuvres, Rachna wandered over, and we started another conversation. She asked me what I liked most about her presentation, and I didn't hesitate. I told her that her approach to building her team was rather interesting.

Rachna nodded, a mischievous smile spreading across her face, and then she shared some wisdom that stuck with me. She laughed and said, "You'll never hear this from an HR professional, but it's been my secret weapon: I hire people with zero experience!"

"Zero experience?" I shot back, genuinely surprised. "How can you possibly have hope for someone without any idea what they're doing?"

Rachna just grinned and explained her strategy, which, to my surprise, has worked repeatedly. "I hire for potential, not based on experience," she confidently said. And you know what? She's right. Let's think about this.

At first glance, it might seem like a no-brainer to hire an experienced and highly qualified candidate. I mean, they've already got the skills and know the ropes, and everything should be smooth sailing, right? So, why take a chance on someone who's inexperienced and doesn't have a clue?

But here's the twist—hiring for potential isn't just some wild gamble; it's a brilliant strategy. Rachna's approach is all about seeing beyond the resume and spotting the raw talent, drive, and passion that can't be taught. These are the people who, with the right guidance, can grow and adapt, bringing fresh ideas and energy to the team.

I thought about this concept a bit more. I was quite intrigued. When you hire with an eye on potential rather than just ticking off a checklist of competencies and experience, you're not just filling a position—you're opening up a whole world of opportunities several times over! People with high potential often bring fresh perspectives to business, which can lead to possible new directions and smarter approaches. Inexperienced employees with high potential can sometimes be the ones to come up with the best ideas.

When a leader is looking to make a good hire, I know that a candidate's experience and fit for the position are just the starting points. What matters the most is whether the person has the desire and ability to keep learning, the flexibility to adapt to new situations, and the drive to be genuinely involved in the work. These qualities are just as important, if not more so, for someone to grow and thrive in their role.

In my experience, people with less experience often bring more flexibility. They tend to learn quicker, they're more eager to dive in and contribute, and they usually have a higher potential for growth. That combination of hunger and adaptability can make all the difference in a professional's journey.

**

Curiosity Reveals Winners

Have you ever gone with friends to an art studio for a painting workshop? I'm not the biggest fan of painting, so I've never done it myself, but I know plenty of you probably have. So, picture this: you're sitting in front of a blank canvas with a palette full of beautiful, vibrant paints. Now what? Where do you even start? Are you the type to quickly whip out your phone and search Google for inspiration, or do you dive right in and let your creativity take the wheel?

Some people will start painting immediately like they've been secretly planning this masterpiece for months. Others, though, might stare at that brush like a foreign object, totally stumped on what to do next. Every workshop has a mix of people—those eager to learn something new and those who just dive in headfirst, letting their curiosity lead the way. And some take curiosity to a whole new level, approaching the canvas with a sense of wonder that's almost contagious.

The potential always reveals itself in three stages—like leveling up in a game. First, you've got the curious ones. These are the people who start to show a spark of interest, poking around to see what's out there. Then, you move to those who want more—they've tasted a little bit of success or interest, and now they're hungry for seconds. Finally, there are the ones with an unquenchable desire. These are the folks who can't stop themselves from diving deeper and deeper, always looking to improve and become a professional in whatever they set their minds to.

Curiosity is like the gateway to potential. Even if someone has all the raw talent in the world, if they don't have that initial curiosity to learn, they're probably not going to explore things in much detail. But when someone desires to do something, you can almost see the gears turning—they automatically start seeking ways to improve, quickly picking up the skills they need to get better at whatever they're doing.

And at the highest level, you've got those unstoppable learners. These are the people who are always pushing themselves, always striving to be better. They're the ones who, given enough time, are most likely to become true masters of their craft. It's like they've got this internal drive that just won't quit, and it's amazing to watch.

Always keep an eye out for the curious ones—they're the ones who reveal the most potential. When narrowing down your candidates, focus on those who show genuine desire. That's where you'll find the real gems and the best talent for the job. Hire for desire because that's where potential turns into action. Those who want to learn and grow will apply their potential and make things happen.

Instead of just posting a job offer in the local newspaper, why not shake things up a bit? Consider hosting a round table, workshop, or even a class. You can set it up at the local public library, a nearby university, or your office. It's a fun and creative way to scout for talent while getting a firsthand look at who's got the right stuff for the job.

Here's the best part—you get to create the guidelines for what attendees will do during the session. Tailor these activities to fit the specific requirements of the role you're hiring for. Let's say you're hunting for the next receptionist to hold down the front desk. You need someone who's engaged, can collaborate across departments, shows great teamwork, multitasks, and has sharp critical thinking skills.

Once your group is all gathered for the workshop, kick things off with a motivational game. Why a motivational game, you ask? Those who shine in these games will naturally demonstrate their engagement, ability to collaborate, teamwork, and critical thinking. It's a fun, low-pressure way to see who's got what it takes. So, who's ready to play?

At my current company, staff enjoy a good scavenger hunt game, and over the years, it's become a tradition! Here's how we roll: I break everyone into groups of five, and once the teams are set, I let them huddle up and pick a team captain. This lucky person gets the job of recording answers to clues and leading the charge to the next hint. If they crack the riddle, they move forward. But if they get stumped... well, no cheers for that round!

While the teams are buzzing around, solving riddles, and having a blast, I keep a close eye on who's stepping up. Did someone immediately volunteer to be the team leader? Is there a teammate who's super encouraging or showing a level of engagement off the charts? These are the little things that reveal so much about who's got what it takes.

And let's not forget—this game is on the clock! The time pressure adds a fun twist and naturally brings out those with top-notch time management skills. As a leader, I'm all about spotting those employees who push themselves to finish first. They have the most potential, and this game is the perfect way to see it in action.

***

The Five C's to Team Success

Teamwork is crucial in today's fast-paced world. Without it, you'd have everyone doing the same task a little differently, which is not just unproductive—it's downright silly. The success of your organization hinges on collaboration, cooperation, and communication. We've chatted about communication before, but now it's time to implement it. Effective teamwork doesn't just boost productivity (yep, there's that "P" word again); it also ramps up employee engagement (and there's the "E" word) and makes for a much happier workplace all around. As a leader, the strength of your team depends on your skills and how well you connect with your crew. Whenever I'm leading a business seminar, I always talk about the five C's. So, you've hosted your workshop, you've run a scavenger hunt, and now it's time to roll up your sleeves and start building that dream team.

Let's jump into the five C's and get this party started:

1. Communication
2. Camaraderie
3. Commitment
4. Confidence
5. Coachability

Communication

Communication is the secret sauce of any successful team. Without it, you're setting up a game of telephone where everyone's left guessing what's going on—not ideal! It's vital to keep those communication channels open so everyone knows exactly what they're supposed to do and how it fits into the bigger picture.

Effective communication isn't just about talking; it's about listening, clarifying your ideas, and giving constructive feedback. I'm all about encouraging my team to ask questions, seek out clarifications, and throw in their own two cents. When everyone's on the same page, you can dodge misunderstandings, keep conflicts to a minimum, and make way better decisions as a group. Plus, it just makes everything run a whole lot smoother!

Camaraderie

Camaraderie is that awesome sense of community and friendship that just clicks when you're part of a great team. I'm sure we've all been on those high-performing teams where camaraderie was the secret ingredient that made everything gel. When a team has strong camaraderie, it's not just more productive—it's also more cohesive and can bounce back from challenges like champs.

To build that camaraderie, I'm all about throwing in team-building activities, organizing fun social events, and creating shared experiences that bring everyone closer. When a team has a positive vibe, collaboration becomes second nature, everyone's got each other's backs, and work becomes something they look forward to. It's like the magic glue that holds everything together and makes the ride much more enjoyable!

Commitment

Commitment is all about how much dedication and energy your team brings to smashing those common goals. It's the drive to put in the time, effort, and resources to hit those big objectives. When a team is truly committed, they're all in—working together toward a shared vision and tackling any obstacles that come their way like a bunch of pros.

I'm all for encouraging my team to take ownership of their tasks, hold themselves accountable, and support each other. We're all on the same boat, rowing in sync toward the finish line. And, of course, it's my job to ensure everyone has the right tools to crush their roles effectively. When everyone's committed, it's amazing what you can accomplish together!

Confidence

Confidence is all about believing in yourself and knowing that your team has what it takes to crush those goals. A team that is brimming with confidence is not afraid to take risks, get creative, and roll with the punches when things change.

Building confidence starts with setting achievable goals, celebrating every win, and learning lessons from the bumps. I love encouraging my team to take calculated risks, think outside the box, and let their creativity run wild. When a team is confident, it's laser-focused on tackling challenges and not shy about raising its hand when it needs a little backup. It's like having a superpower that helps us push the limits and keep moving forward!

Coachability

Coachability is all about being eager to learn, adapt, and level up. No matter how experienced we are, there's always something new we can pick up from each other and outside perspectives. The key is to stay open to feedback, be willing to try out new approaches, and actively look for ways to sharpen our skills.

I'm all about encouraging my team to seek feedback, learn from any slip-ups, and share their best tricks with the rest of the crew. When you have the ability to coach your team, they become more adaptable, innovative, and high-performing. It's like having a built-in upgrade button for the whole team!

* * *

Teamwork Makes The Dream Work

The phrase "teamwork makes the dream work," originally coined by John C. Maxwell in his 2002 book of the same name, has become a staple in discussions about effective collaboration. While the quote might seem a bit dated, it's just as relevant in today's work environment as when Maxwell first wrote it. In full, Maxwell's quote reads, "Teamwork makes the dream work, but a vision becomes a nightmare when the leader has a big dream and a bad team."

Now, don't get hung up on the term "bad team." We all know there's no "I" in the word team, and every member is in it together. When a team struggles, it's often due to negative behaviors, lack of trust, low productivity, misalignment, or a lack of vision and purpose. But the beauty of a team lies in its potential to overcome these obstacles.

Picture a soccer game where one team isn't working together. Each player tries to cover every position—goalkeeper, defense, midfield, and attack—independently. This disjointed approach will likely lead to defeat against a team that understands and embraces the power of collaboration.

Now, imagine that the same team realizes that some players excel at scoring goals while others are stronger in defense. By leveraging each player's strengths in specialized roles, the team becomes more cohesive, effective, and likely to win—their common goal.

The essence of "teamwork makes the dream work" is about the power of shared responsibilities. When a team divides tasks based on individual strengths, they can achieve greater outcomes than anyone else. This collaborative approach not only enhances productivity but also ensures that the team's vision is realized effectively.

***

The 17 Laws of John C. Maxwell

Maxwell outlined 17 laws of effective teamwork in his book, each designed to enhance a team's ability to work together and achieve success. By integrating these principles, your team stands a greater chance of turning the dream into reality through their collective efforts:

1. **Law of significance:** According to the law of significance, individuals acting alone may not achieve significant success. Maxwell notes, "Behind an able man, there are other able men."

2. **The law of the big picture**: Emphasizes that everyone must be willing to sacrifice their own personal best interest when it impedes the potential for the group to reach its common goal.

3. **Law of the niche:** The team's leader can utilize the law of niche by recognizing everyone's unique strengths and assigning roles accordingly. Within this law, Maxwell identifies that each team member can be pushed outside their comfort zone but stay within the zone of their strengths.

4. **The Law of Mt. Everest:** Individuals working alone may struggle to achieve big dreams. As the goal becomes more challenging, unified teamwork can become more crucial for the project's end goal.

5. **Law of the chain:** According to Maxwell's book, a chain is only as

strong as its weakest link, and the same goes for team performance. Maxwell explains that anyone not serving the group can be trained or leave to serve a team that's a better match. When asking someone to leave the group, Maxwell emphasizes the importance of honesty, brevity, and discretion.

6. **Law of the catalyst:** For the team to continue reaching out of their comfort zone, there must be a member who makes the team perform better and try harder. This may be someone whose own enthusiasm or energy inspires others to be more enthusiastic and energetic in return.

7. **Law of the compass:** An effective team must have a vision that provides clear direction and inspiration.

8. **The law of the bad apple:** When one team member has a negative attitude or poor communication skills, they may interfere with the entire team's effectiveness. The team leader can address bad attitudes, but they may ultimately impact the energy of the whole team.

9. **Law of accountability:** According to this law, an effective team can benefit from trusting each other and being able to count on one another. The most effective teams may be honored to work alongside their teammates and hold a deep respect for each other.

10. **Law of the price tag:** According to the law of the price tag, each group member may pay a price for the team to succeed, such as making a time commitment, striving toward personal development, or putting the group's goals ahead of one's own.

11. **Law of the scoreboard:** Without accounting for their current position, teams may struggle to see how far they are from their goals. To keep their goals on track, teams can implement measurable milestones and accountability.

12. **Law of the bench:** According to this law, great leaders are those who have people on the bench who are training to become the starting players of the team. These team members are often compared to the army reserves, who are ready for action whenever needed.

13. **Law of identity:** For a team to succeed, it may be beneficial to have a unified set of values. These values provide a foundation and can act as the glue that holds the group together. Individuals with similar values may join and strengthen the team by establishing a clear, unified identity.

14. **Law of communication:** Communication can require active listening, courtesy, and connection. When teams have strong communication, they uplift each other. When they don't, they may cause unhealthy patterns to develop.

15. **Law of the edge:** When two teams are equally talented, the leadership may give them an edge. A team may struggle to reach its full potential without effective leadership, guidance, shared responsibility, and encouragement.

16. **Law of high morale:** Teams with high morale may overcome obstacles and achieve their goals. Morale can encourage greater performance, make wins seem more significant, and give team members the confidence to tackle obstacles and take risks.

17. **Law of dividends:** Investing in your team can compound over time. Although investment can require time and energy to build and develop an effective team, it may be the key that makes the dream work.

**

The Hidden Cost of a Bad Hire

According to Influx.com, the hidden costs of hiring in 2023 are mind-blowing. When you factor in things like advertising, the time investment, training, or turnover, the costs can pile up and become way more than you initially expected. And let's not forget the potential moral damage—a bad hire can lead to negative online reviews, damage to your company's reputation, and other headaches.

A recent poll found that 57% of HR leaders struggle to recruit and keep valued employees. In addition, 36% say they don't even have the resources to attract top talent. It's no wonder hiring has become such a challenge!

Here's the kicker: for companies with fewer than 500 employees, it costs an average of $7,645 to bring on a new hire, and it takes about 42 days to fill a position. Plus, it usually takes around six months just to break even on that new employee. So, yeah, the investment in onboarding a new team member is no small thing.

But here's the real jaw-dropper: according to the US Department of Labor, a bad hire can cost up to 30% of that employee's wages in the first year alone. And it's not just about the money. A whopping 34% of CFOs said that bad hires hurt productivity, and leaders end up spending 17% of their time babysitting these under-performers.

Bad hiring decisions aren't just costly in dollars—they can cause a ripple effect across the entire organization. A bad hire can be like a tiny wrecking ball, smashing company culture, shaking up team dynamics, crushing morale, and creating a toxic environment where good employees start heading for the exit. It's like watching a snowball of disaster roll downhill, and trust me, it gets bigger and bigger.

There are plenty of warning signs when you've made a bad hire. Some people might talk up their abilities, only to under-deliver once they're on the job, constantly needing oversight and "hand-holding" like they're still on training wheels. Others crack under pressure or struggle to adapt when things don't go according to plan. And let's not forget those who find it nearly impossible to learn new skills or roll with the changes—especially when flexibility is key to thriving in today's fast-paced work environment.

Now, what's the worst-case scenario? A bad hire doesn't just impact themselves—it can drag down the performance of the whole team or even derail the entire company. It's like putting one wrong piece in a machine; suddenly, everything else starts misfiring.

You can usually spot a bad hire by these tell-tale personality traits:

1. **A change in expected personality and work ethic:** Let's be real—interviews alone don't always cut it when figuring out if a candidate is truly a good fit. Sure, during the interview, it might feel like you're vibing with the person across the table, but once they're in the role? Well, that's when the differences start to show up. It's like thinking you've found the perfect puzzle piece, only to realize it doesn't quite fit once you try to put it in place. The good news is that you can minimize the risk of this disconnect by beefing up your interview process with more targeted, meaningful questions. Trust me, asking the right questions can make all the difference, and we'll dive into exactly how to do that in this article. A person's resume might tell you where they've been and what they've done, but it doesn't always give you the full picture—especially regarding personality and work ethic. And let's face it, those are the things that can make or break a hire. That's why a more thorough, well-rounded interview process is key to evaluating whether someone fits your team.

2. **Employee skills do not match candidate claims:** Most interviews will revolve around the candidate's skill set. If they have the skills the company needs? Boom! You've hit the jackpot, and the job's practically done. But let's be honest, some candidates might stretch the truth a little (or a lot) to land the gig. So, how do you know if they can walk the talk? One solid way is to follow up with their previous employers and do a reference check. But why stop there? You can get creative and build assessments or hands-on activities into the interview process that let them show off their skills in real time. Whether it's a quick

task or a full-on project, these activities give you an early peek at how they'll perform in the role. No more guessing, just results!

3. **Unwilling or unable to adapt to the working environment:** Let's discuss culture—the secret sauce to a company's success. When employees are fully engaged, they don't just clock in and out— they buy into the company's vision, mission, and culture as if it's part of their job description. It's not just about doing the work; it's about how they do it. Of course, there are also some non-negotiables, like showing up during standard working hours, using company assets responsibly, and treating everyone with respect. You know, basic things. But when someone decides to ignore those expectations, that's when things can get messy. It's like trying to fit a square peg into a round hole. If an employee constantly pushes back against the company's values and rules, it's probably a sign they're not a great fit, and you'll start to feel the friction with the rest of the team. The bottom line is that if someone's not onboard with the company's culture, the role is likely not theirs.

* * *

Interviewing For A Great Fit

I've had the pleasure (and, let's be honest, sometimes the daunting task) of conducting more interviews than I can count. I've done them all—face-to-face, over Zoom, and even remotely from across the globe. Throughout all of that, I've learned a thing or two about "interviewing for a great fit."

When I bought the intellectual property rights for my last eCommerce venture, I knew one thing: I wasn't building the website myself. The website *was* the business. It was my storefront, my product, my everything. And if the website were mediocre, customers would take one look and head straight for the competition. I needed a dream team behind me, and so the hunt began.

Now, I didn't just dive into interviews with random questions, hoping to stumble upon the right team. Oh no, there was strategy involved—lots of it. First, I must remember that my potential web development team was international. Their work culture, holidays, and even working hours weren't going to match up with what I was used to in the U.S. I had to adapt, and more importantly, I had to ask the right questions to get the answers I needed. After all, if I wanted a tailored answer, I had to ask a tailored question.

So, before starting any interview, I spent a solid amount of time prepping. I didn't just wing it. I started by reviewing the job description, dissecting it, and then creating questions specifically aimed at the role. Take HTML, for example—it was a must-have skill for the position, so I'd ask, "At what speed can you write HTML to create an interactive search feature on a website?" It was specific, and I'd be able to gauge their ability from their response.

I call this process my "interview checklist." I created a two-column spreadsheet, where the left column was filled with all the questions I wanted to ask. The right column? That was where I listed the "dream characteristics" I hoped the candidate would embody. It was like building my dream team on paper before meeting them. This system kept me organized and focused, ensuring I didn't overlook any key details during the interview.

To dodge bad hires, companies can (and should) use a handy checklist of questions for each candidate—covering both behavioral and skills-based inquiries. Why? Because it gives you the full picture, not just a highlight reel of their skills and qualifications. You'll get to see if they're a true fit, not only for the role but for the company culture as well.

Let's face it—interviewing can be awkward, but it doesn't have to be a stressful ordeal. Companies can improve their game by creating a smooth and positive candidate experience. One way to do this is by setting clear expectations from the get-go. For example, you can provide materials ahead of time to guide them through the interview process and even have a live chat function for any quick questions about the role or the company. The goal? Both sides walk away feeling good. The candidate should feel more confident in their career direction, and you end up with top-notch talent excited to join your team.

When it comes to interviews, why not kick things off with a little icebreaker? Drop your guard, crack a joke, or start with an informal conversation. It's a great way to put the candidate at ease, and hey, you might learn something unexpected about them that could benefit the company down the line.

Conversely, a bad interview experience can leave a lasting mark. If things go south, candidates may not only hesitate to apply again but could also spread the word to others. So, keep an open mind. If someone isn't the perfect fit for the role, don't write them off completely—it could just be a "not right now" situation. Or, if you're unsure but see potential, why not offer a trial period for freelance or part-time work? This way, the candidate and the company get a feel for the working relationship before diving into full-time commitments. Plus, you'll have a chance to see how they gel with the rest of the team, something that's hard to gauge until they're in the thick of it.

In the end, it's all about creating a hiring process that benefits everyone involved—both the candidate and the company.

* * *

Asking The Right Questions

We've all been there. You're in the middle of an interview, and it's not going well. The conversation is awkward; you feel like you're asking the same questions repeatedly, and it's pretty clear the person just isn't a good fit. Cue the internal sigh.

But let's rewind a bit. The key to avoiding these situations is to ask the *right* questions—ones that let the candidate open up and give you a real sense of who they are. Open-ended questions are your best friend here.

Think like: "Tell me about a time when..." and let them run with it. From there, dig a little deeper. Ask about the result of their actions and how those results impacted their organization. This will help you gauge their value and how they approach challenges.

Now, don't stop there. You also want to get a peek into their character and ability to reflect on their experiences. For example:

"We all have to make tough decisions. Can you tell me about a time you had to make a difficult choice? What led up to it, what decision did you make, and what was the outcome?"

This one's a gem because it reveals how they think, how they approach critical decisions, and how aware they are of the ripple effects of their actions. You're looking for how coherent their story is, their ability to think critically, and whether they grasp the cause and effect of their decisions. Another favorite of mine:

"How would you describe your work ethic?"

This one is golden. You'll quickly determine if the person is driven and motivated and how they view work. Are they the go-getter you need or just someone looking to punch the clock? And last, if you want to know if they've been investing in their growth?

"What kind of training have you received in your field?"

This shows whether they're committed to developing their skills and staying sharp beyond just what's on their resume. And, of course, there are some other classic questions to help you weed out those candidates who might just be going through the motions:

- *"What do you think is your greatest strength?"*
- *"What do you think is your greatest weakness?"*
- *"When was the last time you failed at something?"*
- *"What made your previous boss or coworkers happiest/unhappy with you?"*

BUILDING YOUR DREAM TEAM

Asking these behavioral-based questions can help determine if the candidate is serious about the role or just looking for a paycheck. And trust me, they'll help you spot potential bad hires before they become your problem!

4

Matching Strengths With Opportunities

Kara is one of the best hires I've ever made. When I first interviewed her, my receptionist team was a revolving door. Turnover was through the roof, and it felt like every other week, someone was either quitting or planning to leave. I needed someone solid, someone who could bring the department back from the edge of chaos. That's when Kara was hired as a Lead Receptionist.

During her interview, she outlined her strengths in customer service, communication, multitasking, and staying calm under pressure—everything I needed for a dream receptionist team. I knew almost immediately that Kara was special. But here's the thing—it wasn't just her skills that caught my attention. It was her can-do attitude. It was contagious, and I could already picture her bringing that positive energy to my team.

Fast forward a few months, and Kara was an absolute game-changer. She transformed the receptionist department, stabilizing everything with her dependability and knack for keeping things running smoothly. The constant turnover stopped. The entire team seemed happier and more cohesive, and I had Kara to thank for that. But it didn't stop there. Kara's leadership abilities became more and more apparent. I knew she wasn't just a star in her current role—she was destined for bigger things.

Sure enough, about a year later, a new opportunity opened up for both Kara and the company. We were looking to break into the property

MATCHING STRENGTHS WITH OPPORTUNITIES

management game, and Kara, with her dedication to superior customer service, stepped up. She offered her skills to help launch the new venture and was soon promoted to a newly created role: "Head Customer Service Training Support Specialist." In this position, she trained new employees, taught them the ins and outs of excellent customer service, and showed them what it meant to embody the company's culture.

This wasn't just a win for Kara—it was a huge win for the company. Why did I recommend Kara for the promotion? My answer is simple. She was dependable, flexible, team-oriented, and goal-driven. Kara didn't just do her job—she took ownership of it. She was trustworthy and showed incredible leadership, making her an obvious choice for the role.

Kara was more than an asset—she was a key player in driving the company forward. Her work onboarding and training rock-star employees was moving the needle in a big way. Kara wasn't just changing her career—she was shaping the company's future, and we were all better because of her desire to excel.

Organizations are all about people. Your business is only as strong as the team behind it. So, if you're aiming for growth and chasing those long-term goals, it's crucial to know your employees' key strengths.

Why does this matter so much? First, if you understand where your team members might be struggling, you can help them improve. Think of it as leveling up their professional skills. On the flip side, knowing their strengths means you can play to them, putting their unique talents to work where they'll shine the brightest.

The result? You've got an organization running like a well-oiled machine where everyone grooves. You boost productivity, increase employee satisfaction, and position your business more competitive. Plus, who doesn't want a happier, more efficient team? It's a total win-win!

You've probably heard the buzz around soft skills—things like being organized or having killer communication—and hard skills, like speaking a second language or mastering a specific technology. We all know the difference, right?

But when discussing employee strengths, it's a mix of both. It's not just about those technical skills or how well someone manages their email inbox. It's about those unique character traits, talents, and quirks that make an employee thrive in their role. It's the stuff that sets them apart and helps them crush it on the job.

Recognizing, nurturing, and leveraging those strengths is like finding the secret sauce for your team. Whether in sales, customer service, or any other department, knowing how to tap into what makes your employees awesome will take your organization to the next level. So yeah, figuring out what makes your people tick is vital!

Employee strengths can manifest in so many different ways, and trust me when you start to spot them, it's like finding little gems in your team. Some employees are crazy organized and detail-oriented (you know, the ones who color-code their to-do lists), while others have the magic touch when it comes to leading or negotiating—basically, they are the glue that brings everyone together.

***

Top Traits of All-Star Employees

Let me tell you, there are a few key employee strengths that can level up your organization, and when I say they're game-changers, I mean it. So, let's break it down—these are the all-star traits every team needs (and maybe toss in a dad joke or two, because why not?):

1. **Dependability:** Imagine if your Wi-Fi was dependable as your best employee—no buffering, no dropping out! That's what you want in your team. Someone who meets deadlines, owns up to mistakes (because who doesn't spill coffee on the keyboard once in a while?), and is reliable through and through. Dependability isn't just a nice-to-have; it's the glue that keeps the business machine running smoothly.

2. **Goal-oriented:** Who doesn't love an employee who sets goals and crushes them? I mean, it's like watching someone finish a marathon while you're still tying your shoelaces. When people focus on their growth, it lifts the entire team. They're motivated, they tackle challenges head-on, and their energy? It's contagious!

3. **Team-oriented:** We all know teamwork is like the oil that keeps the engine running—without it, the whole machine grinds to a halt. A team player keeps everyone on track, communicates like a pro, and makes sure all those pesky silos disappear faster than donuts at a Monday meeting.

4. **Flexibility:** Let's be real. Life (and business) is one giant game of Whac-A-Mole. Plans change, things go sideways, and you need employees who can roll with the punches. Flexibility keeps everything from derailing when things don't go as planned. It's the secret sauce to keeping the ship smoothly—even through choppy waters.

5. **Optimism:** You know that one person who's always in a good mood, even if it's pouring rain? That's the optimistic employee. Not only do they lift everyone's spirits, but they're also the ones who make feedback sessions feel less like a roast and more like a pep talk. Let's face it, work is more fun when there's a little sunshine in the room.

6. **Emotional awareness:** We all need a bit of emotional intelligence to get through the day (especially after that second cup of coffee). Employees with emotional awareness are like the Jedi Masters of communication. They reflect, grow, and make those around them feel heard. Whether in leadership or just chatting by the water cooler, they keep the team vibe smooth and connected.

7. **Trustworthiness:** Trust is like pizza—everyone needs it, and when it's missing, things get awkward fast. A trustworthy employee can be

counted on to handle sensitive information, take accountability, and represent the company professionally. When you've got a trustworthy team, you're building confidence from the top down. No pineapple on this pizza!

8. **Leadership:** Wondering about the company's future? It's in the hands of your leaders. You need people who can rally the troops, inspire creativity, and bring out the best in everyone. The earlier you develop these leaders, the faster your organization will hit those big-picture goals.

9. **Resilience:** The resilient employee is the one who gets knocked down, dusts off their shoulders, and says, "Is that all you've got?" They learn from mistakes, adapt to challenges, and turn problems into opportunities. With resilience, nothing can hold your team back.

10. **Ambition:** Nothing revs up a team like ambition. When you've got people who constantly set the bar higher and higher, it creates a ripple effect of success. They're always learning, growing, and driving the team forward. It's like having a turbo button for your organization!

11. **Teachability:** No matter how awesome someone is, there's always room to grow. Teachability is what separates the good from the great. Employees open to feedback and eager to learn will evolve alongside the company, making them irreplaceable in the long run. Plus, they're the first to dive into coaching or mentoring programs—a total bonus!

12. **Focus on improvement:** Here's the thing—if you're not evolving, you're falling behind. That's why you need employees constantly pushing for growth, both for themselves and the company. A team focused on improvement keeps your business sharp, competitive, and ready for the future. You're future-proofing your company—who doesn't love that?

13. **Accountability:** Everybody messes up now and then, but it's how you handle it that counts. Accountability means owning your mistakes, learning from them, and figuring out how to improve next time. Lindsey Scrase from Checkr says, "Whether you're an Account Exec or a Sales Manager, it's about owning your number, knowing the issues, and figuring out the plan to fix them." No excuses, just solutions.

14. **Managing up:** Ah, "managing up"—it's the secret weapon of every superstar employee. It's all about adapting to your leader's style to improve communication, problem-solving, and workplace harmony. When employees "manage up," it leads to smoother projects, better relationships, and everyone's happy.

***

Beyond the Muscles

When we think about strength, the image that probably pops into your head is a bodybuilder lifting weights. Me? I think of something slightly different—mainly because I struggle to lift a 5-pound bag of flour. But when it comes to employee strengths, it's a whole other ballgame. Employee strengths are the skills, traits, and magic each person brings to the table that contribute to the overall effectiveness, productivity, and success of the organization. Sure, some employees are stronger in certain areas than others, but that makes a diverse team! We need to embrace that.

Now, what exactly is employee strength, you ask? Great question! I'm glad you're here for the answer. Employees' strengths are those unique abilities, skills, attributes, and qualities that individuals possess. These aren't just your run-of-the-mill job descriptions either. We're talking about everything from technical expertise (let's be real, the younger generation has the upper hand with tech) to problem-solving skills, leadership, creativity, communication, adaptability, resilience—you name it, it's in there.

Identifying and leveraging these strengths is like unlocking your team's hidden superpowers. It leads to better productivity, higher job satisfaction, and a truly engaged team. And let's not forget the overall success that comes with all that greatness!

Now, when talking about employee strength, it's more than their ability to lead meetings or hit deadlines (although those are pretty important). One thing I've taught myself while managing multiple teams is a five-factor checklist, which I will describe in detail. No, I didn't pick this up during my Master's degree (though that would've been useful), but after conducting a ton of annual reviews, I realized I needed a solid standard for assessing what makes an employee truly shine.

1. **Time management:** The employee should be able to manage, prioritize tasks, and work organizationally. Their ability to meet deadlines and handle multiple responsibilities greatly affects their productivity.

2. **Communication skills:** Good communication is the key to articulating thoughts and ideas effectively, indulging in active listening, and responding mindfully to resolve conflicts and build better relationships.

3. **Adaptability and flexibility:** In a fast-changing work environment, employees must be flexible, adapt to situations, and work through changes.

4. **Effective teamwork:** Employees who are adaptive and collaborative can contribute easily and positively to the team and appreciate various perspectives, which allows them to achieve collaborative goals and overall organizational success.

5. **Emotional intelligence:** Workers with emotional intelligence have strong self-awareness and pay attention to their colleagues' motivation levels. This allows them to be empathetic and supportive, which helps to avoid conflict within the team.

I had the pleasure of working with some incredible Sales Associates during my time at a retail job I started back in high school. I was with that company for 13 years—my entire adult life—until they went under due to bankruptcy. It was a tough pill to swallow, especially since retail was all I knew, but hey, all good things must come to an end, right?

During those years, I climbed the ladder from Sales Associate to Store Manager, and let me tell you, it was a wild ride. One of my Assistant Managers, bless her heart, needed extra guidance—okay, maybe a lot of hand-holding. She had her strengths but some glaring weaknesses, too. She'd miss deadlines, get overwhelmed by small tasks, and have no clue how to prioritize. Honestly, watching her try to juggle was like watching me trying to juggle actual bowling pins—chaos everywhere. The thing was, she had so much potential, but her lack of self-confidence held her back.

Now, on the flip side, I had other employees who were absolute rock stars. They knew the ins and outs of the retail world, understood the company goals, and could give thoughtful, spot-on advice to customers. These were the employees who went the extra mile—constantly. They didn't just do the job; they looked for opportunities and proactively solved problems before I even had a chance to point them out. Because of them, our little retail corner of the world was able to reach new potential customers and grow in ways we hadn't thought possible.

* * *

Delegating Tasks Based on Strengths

Delegating tasks based on strengths is like finding the secret sauce for a happy, thriving team. Not only does it make *your* life easier, but it also makes your employees feel like superheroes. When you hand out tasks that match their skills, interests, and talents, you're essentially giving them a confidence boost, a reason to be more engaged, and the motivation to knock it out of the park. Plus, you lower the chance of them burning out or getting frustrated. Trust me, nobody wants to juggle many tasks that feel like pulling teeth. By playing to their strengths, you're telling your team, "Hey, I see you, I value you, and I trust you to crush it." And who doesn't love a little trust?

Now, to get the delegation ball rolling, you have to first *know* your employees' strengths. It's not just about guessing or throwing tasks at them to see what sticks (that's a little chaotic, even for me). You've got tools! Use surveys, interviews, or feedback sessions to ask your team what they love, what they're good at, and what gets them fired up. You could also get fancy with assessments like StrengthsFinder, DISC, or Myers-Briggs if you want to dive deeper into their personality traits and potential. Oh, and don't forget the golden opinions of customers and peers—they can offer some pretty valuable insights too!

Once you've got the strengths pinned down, it's time to match them with the right tasks. Think of it like a puzzle but with fewer frustrating corner pieces. Prioritize what needs to be done into four categories:

- Urgent
- Strategic
- Routine
- Repetitive

Then, line up those tasks with the people who are practically *built* for them based on their strengths. Clear communication is key here! Lay out the expectations, objectives, deadlines, and resources they'll need to succeed.

After all, you're not throwing them into the deep end; you're handing them the reins.

Of course, it doesn't stop there. To unleash your team's potential, give them the freedom to own their tasks. Let them make decisions, solve problems, and take a few risks without you breathing down their necks like a helicopter leader (I've mentioned how much I dislike micromanagers). Seriously, nobody likes that. And give them room to grow! New challenges and projects help them develop their strengths even further. Oh, and don't forget the *high*-fives—whether it's literal or metaphorical. Recognizing their contributions and celebrating their wins is like fuel for their motivation.

But hey, delegating based on strengths doesn't mean you get to sweep their weaknesses under the rug. We all have areas that could improve (like my baking skills... but we won't talk about that). If someone's weakness is affecting their performance, you've got to address it. But here's the trick— find out *why* they're struggling. Is it a lack of knowledge? A motivation issue? Or maybe their environment is working against them? Once you figure that out, you can offer constructive feedback and give them the resources to tackle those weak spots head-on.

Finally, don't forget to build a culture of teamwork while you're at it! Encourage your employees to lean on each other's strengths and help fill in the gaps where weaknesses arise. That way, everyone's lifting each other, and the whole team is stronger. It's like assembling the Avengers without the fancy costumes (unless that's your thing).

***

Personal S.W.O.T. Analysis

There's a little gem in the business world called the SWOT analysis—aka the tool that saves businesses from flying blind. It determines a company's Strengths, Weaknesses, Opportunities, and Threats. You'll usually find it tucked into the marketing section of a business plan, right next to buzzwords like "synergy" and "disruption" (you know the drill).

But hang on a second! If businesses can do a SWOT analysis to boost their game, why can't *you* do one to showcase the superpowers that lie within your team? Was this even a thing? Naturally, I hit up my trusty friend Google, half-expecting to be the genius behind a new self-improvement trend. Nope. Google quickly humbled me—turns out that a personal SWOT analysis is *very much* a thing.

So, why not use this awesome tool to assess your teams' strengths (and weaknesses)? Let's dive into the details of a personal SWOT analysis and figure out how to market your team like the leaders you were born to be (no buzzwords required, I promise!) Additionally, a personal SWOT analysis can also help you figure out if your goals are realistic for where you are in your career right now for both leaders and employees. Spoiler alert: it's like putting your teams' characteristics through a reality check—but in a good way!

Once you've mastered the art of self-SWOT, you can apply it to all kinds of situations: planning for that promotion you've always dreamed of, managing a tricky work project, designing a service, leading your team, or even launching your side hustle. It's like your secret weapon for leveling up—no capes required, but highly recommended.

- **Strengths:** Alright, let's dive into the fun part of your personal SWOT analysis—your strengths! Think of it as your highlight reel, where you show off all the awesome traits you bring to the table. Start by looking at the internal factors that work in your favor. Do you have some fancy qualifications? Special skills? That degree you worked your butt off for? Yup, throw all that in. Don't forget any cool certifications, work experience, or even the gold star your boss gave you for crushing it at work. Now, if you're job hunting, this is where it gets juicy. Your strengths can also include testimonials from previous bosses, professional connections, or even the fact that you're open to relocating or working remotely (extra points for flexibility!). Once you've got your list of strengths, you can use it to boost your resume or write a killer cover letter. Highlight the best of the best, and leave the fluff behind—because who's got time for fluff? And if you're getting ready for an interview, think of a few times when you flexed those strengths like a pro. Having real-life examples up your sleeve can make you stand out. Just try not to dazzle them *too* much... okay, maybe a little.

- **Weaknesses:** When listing weaknesses, it's important to be honest and objective. This ensures that your analysis is effective and helps generate meaningful insights. By thoroughly assessing your weaknesses, you can identify key areas for improvement and create a plan to address them. In a recruitment scenario, employers appreciate candidates who are self-aware and have logical, actionable strategies for growth. Weaknesses might also include factors that could impact your productivity, such as health conditions or limited availability at certain times. Being upfront about these challenges shows you're realistic and proactive in managing them. This self-reflection is essential for personal and professional development and helps you take control of your growth path.

- **Opportunities:** Any external factors that benefit your situation should be listed as opportunities. These can include available resources, industry trends, or broader market developments that can support your professional growth.

- **Threats:** Any factor that arises from a situation and puts you at a disadvantage is a potential threat you should address and prepare for. Threats can include challenges like a limited job market, low earning potential, heightened competition, or specific constraints within an industry. Once you've identified these threats, it's crucial to develop strategies to minimize their risk or mitigate their impact. Proper assessment and thoughtful planning can often turn threats into opportunities. For instance, imagine you own a retail store specializing in stationery, and a new eCommerce site enters your market, consistently undercutting your prices by offering bulk orders and leveraging effective marketing. In response, you could explore listing your products on that eCommerce platform to boost sales while maintaining competitive prices. Alternatively, you might consider securing a bank loan to purchase stationery items in bulk, allowing you to lower your prices and remain competitive. By proactively addressing these challenges and turning them into actionable plans, you not only reduce their negative impact but also position yourself to seize new opportunities that may arise.

***

Building a Personal S.W.O.T. Analysis

I've known Jacob for several years, and throughout that time, he has struggled with recognizing his strengths. When he first joined our company as a consultant, around the same time I started my role at my nine-to-five nonprofit job, it was clear that he had a great deal of potential. However, he needed to recognize his abilities to build the self-confidence necessary for further growth.

  I suggested that he conduct a personal SWOT analysis to help him gain a clearer perspective. The goal was to outline his strengths and accomplishments, as well as identify areas where he could focus on personal development. By seeing his abilities and opportunities for improvement laid out in front of him, I hoped it would give him both the confidence and direction he needed to move forward in his career as a computer engineer. Jacob's SWOT analysis looked like this:

Strengths:

- **Technical background**: Strong analytical and problem-solving skills from years of experience in software engineering. Earned the trust

MATCHING STRENGTHS WITH OPPORTUNITIES

of top management by completing several online training programs relating to confidentiality.

- **Adaptability**: Proven ability to learn new skills quickly and adapt to different challenges.

- **Detail-oriented**: Keen attention to detail, which can benefit marketing analytics and campaign strategies.

- **Project management**: Experience leading software projects, which translates well to managing marketing campaigns and initiatives.

Weaknesses:

- **Limited marketing experience**: Lack of formal training and hands-on experience in the marketing field.

- **Industry knowledge**: Less familiarity with marketing trends, consumer behavior, and best practices.

- **Networking**: Fewer professional connections in the marketing industry compared to established networks in software engineering.

Opportunities:

- **Growing demand**: Marketing is evolving rapidly, especially with the increasing focus on digital channels and data-driven strategies.

- **Transferable skills**: Strong analytical and technical skills can be a great asset in digital marketing, SEO, and marketing automation.

- **Learning resources**: Numerous online courses, certifications, and workshops are available to quickly build marketing knowledge.

Threats:

- **Competition:** The marketing field may have more experienced candidates with traditional backgrounds in marketing or business.

- **Initial learning curve:** Transitioning to a new field could require additional time and effort to reach the level of proficiency needed to compete effectively.

- **Uncertainty in Career Shift:** There's a potential risk in leaving an established career path in software engineering for a new, less familiar industry.

***

S.O.A.R.

In the fast-paced world of business, one of the most important roles I've taken on as a leader is coaching and developing my team. Building a cohesive, high-performing team requires ongoing support, constructive feedback, and, most importantly, a strategic framework to guide their growth. Over the years, I've utilized several tools for personal and professional development within my companies, and one that stands out for its effectiveness is the S.O.A.R. analysis.

S.O.A.R. stands for:

- Strengths
- Opportunities
- Aspirations
- Results

Unlike the traditional SWOT (Strengths, Weaknesses, Opportunities, Threats) analysis, which often focuses on identifying and mitigating weaknesses and threats, S.O.A.R. takes a strengths-based approach. The idea is to leverage what's already working well within an individual or a team and build from that foundation.

The focus is more forward-looking, emphasizing aspirations and desired results rather than focusing on the problems that might hold us back. This makes S.O.A.R. an incredibly powerful tool for developing a team because it fosters an environment of positivity and possibility rather than fear or caution.

In my experience, applying S.O.A.R. as a framework has been a game-changer in creating stronger, more resilient teams. It encourages people to align their personal growth with the broader goals of the organization. The shift in focus from addressing "weaknesses" to identifying and amplifying "strengths" results in increased engagement, ownership, and morale.

* * *

Effective Team Development

SWOT analysis, though useful in many contexts, can sometimes have a limiting effect on people. Focusing on weaknesses and threats can inadvertently cause individuals to dwell on their shortcomings, leading to decreased confidence. While it's essential to recognize areas for improvement, coaching teams to fixate on their weaknesses can stunt growth and limit their potential.

S.O.A.R., on the other hand, begins with a strength-based approach, which not only empowers individuals but also creates a culture of continuous improvement without the burden of self-doubt. When team members focus on their strengths and envision aspirational goals, they are more motivated to take the necessary steps to reach their desired outcomes. S.O.A.R. helps people take a broader view of their role and how their aspirations align with the company's vision for success.

One of the best parts of S.O.A.R. is that it's inherently team-centric. It naturally fosters collaboration and open dialogue between employees and leadership. This emphasis on working together to explore opportunities and aspirations often results in a heightened sense of ownership and commitment, which is key to building long-term team morale and cohesion.

* * *

S.O.A.R. in Action

A few years ago, one of my receptionists, Lucy, began to feel stagnant in her role. Although she was efficient, punctual, and performed well, she didn't see much room for growth or any clear way to take on additional responsibility. Recognizing this as an opportunity to coach her through the S.O.A.R. framework, I sat down with Lucy to help her understand how to leverage her strengths and think about her role from a broader perspective.

Together, we conducted a *S.O.A.R.* analysis:

- **Strengths**: Lucy was excellent at customer service, had great attention to detail, and was a natural communicator. She was well-liked by the entire team and had a strong ability to multitask.

- **Opportunities**: We identified areas where Lucy could contribute beyond her immediate responsibilities, such as training new hires and helping to streamline office processes. We also recognized that with her people skills, she could take on more client-facing responsibilities.

- **Aspirations**: Lucy wanted to grow her role but wasn't sure how to do so. Through our discussions, she expressed a desire to be more involved in administrative tasks and potentially lead a team in the future. This was an aspiration she had never voiced before but felt confident about after seeing her strengths laid out.

- **Results**: We outlined a set of goals—both short-term and long-term—for Lucy to achieve. In the short term, she would start by creating a manual for new hires and helping with administrative projects. In the long term, she wanted to advance into an office management role.

This process completely transformed Lucy's outlook on her job. Instead of feeling stuck in her role, she saw growth opportunities. The results were immediate: Lucy took on updating our office protocols, making them more efficient and organized. Over time, she began mentoring new team members, eventually leading to her stepping into a supervisory role. This not only boosted Lucy's confidence but also elevated team morale as others saw the possibilities for growth within the company.

Lucy's experience was a great example of how applying S.O.A.R. can unlock potential not just in individuals but within the entire team. When employees are coached to recognize their strengths and align their aspirations with the company's goals, they feel more connected to the overall success of the business. This connection is what fosters long-term engagement and loyalty.

When I apply S.O.A.R. with other team members, we collectively focus on building a culture where individual strengths are celebrated and growth opportunities are always on the table. S.O.A.R. encourages forward-thinking and opens up conversations about what's possible rather than what's limiting.

Over time, I've found that when my team feels empowered and aligned with the company's aspirations, overall morale improves. There's a palpable sense of excitement in the air—a contagious optimism. Everyone knows they can shape not only their future but also the future of the company.

By coaching my team using the S.O.A.R. framework, I've turned challenging situations into opportunities for growth and development. Lucy's story is one of many where a simple shift in perspective—focusing on strengths rather than weaknesses—led to transformative results. As a leader, I've found that the key to cultivating a thriving team lies in showing them their potential and aligning their goals with the larger vision of the company. S.O.A.R. is the tool that helps make that happen.

5

Creating a Culture of Care

Many years ago, when Microsoft was skyrocketing above all its competition, I heard an interesting story from a colleague who used to work for the software giant. As the legend goes, Microsoft, the company famously founded by Bill Gates in his garage, had a system that trimmed the bottom 10% of every team during layoffs. The idea was simple—create a fiercely competitive environment where everyone constantly fought to be the best. In theory, this sounds like a solid plan, but in practice? Chaos ensued, and panic set in.

Soon, the cut-throat competition meant that no one enjoyed coming to work. People weren't striving to grow or collaborate; they were trying to survive the next round of cuts.

Here's the main issue: when your job security is based on the performance of your peers, things get messy fast. Instead of working together, people avoid those they think are "mediocre." While that might seem like a natural response, it leaves the so-called weaker team members out in the cold. No one's coaching or helping them improve because, let's be honest, why would they? Everyone's too busy protecting their position.

Worse still, this environment breeds unnecessary rivalries between projects that should work harmoniously. Teams that need each other to succeed start withholding information, not out of malice but out of self-preservation. Why collaborate when someone's going to be cut no matter what? It's a lose-lose situation. Communication breaks down; teamwork suffers, and productivity—well, that takes a nosedive, too.

It's like playing musical chairs, but instead of fun, it's a constant sense of dread because you know someone's losing their seat, and it might just be you. Needless to say, it wasn't exactly a recipe for job satisfaction or innovation. At the end of the day, no one's winning in a system designed for constant elimination, and that's the opposite of what a healthy workplace should feel like. I can assure you that Microsoft was not creating a culture of care.

Microsoft eventually abandoned this unproductive incentive program, but the story doesn't end there. In 2024, Microsoft laid off its Diversity, Equity, and Inclusion (DEI) team as part of broader cost-cutting measures in response to economic uncertainty. This decision has raised many eyebrows, prompting serious questions about Microsoft's commitment to diversity and inclusion.

And Microsoft isn't alone. Google also reduced its workforce, with cuts impacting its own DEI team as part of a strategic shift to streamline operations and refocus on core business areas. Even Zoom, which experienced rapid growth during the pandemic, found itself in a position where downsizing was necessary.

This recent trend points to a larger concern about corporate priorities. While these companies justify the layoffs as part of broader operational efficiency efforts, cutting teams responsible for fostering diversity and inclusion sends a conflicting message. It raises doubts about how committed these organizations are to creating inclusive cultures where all employees feel welcomed and valued. Microsoft's decision, in particular, extends a troubling pattern of missing the mark when it comes to building a true culture of care, especially now that they've scaled back departments designed to uphold those very values.

When great leaders create policies, they are focused on the intended outcomes and avoiding any unintended negative consequences. They strive to implement policies that support their team rather than hinder them. Moreover, effective leaders closely monitor the success of these newly implemented policies, ensuring they work as intended and making necessary adjustments along the way.

When a team feels unsafe or perceives a policy as harmful, it can impact every aspect of their work experience, ultimately limiting their potential. On the other hand, when employees feel safe, welcomed, and confident that policies are designed with their best interests in mind, they are more likely to build momentum and strive for greater achievements. Creating a work environment where staff know they are protected allows them to focus on growth and performance, ultimately driving success for the entire organization.

When employees don't feel safe being themselves at work, it's impossible for them to take on new tasks or, let's be honest, even *care* about what they're doing. And it's not just about DEI—your team might be hesitant to share their ideas, concerns, or even conflicts because they're afraid of retaliation, getting shut down, or being labeled as "that outspoken person."

The thing is, when people feel psychologically unsafe, all that potential you saw when you hired them fizzles out. They're too busy worrying about stepping on toes to shine. So, instead of reaching their full potential, they play it safe, which means you're missing out on all the great things they could bring to the table. And let's face it, as a leader, that's not what you want in a workplace!

* * *

Creating a Culture of CARE

As leaders, we have to admit something: no one's perfect! Our days get busy, deadlines pile up, and sometimes, we don't communicate as clearly as we'd like. We might miss the mark on listening to ideas, seeing things from different perspectives, or making sure everyone's equipped with the tools and energy they need to succeed. It happens—life gets chaotic.

This breakdown in team dynamics often stems from one thing: leaders not fully *CARE*-ing for their teams. And no, I'm not just talking about saying "good morning" (although that helps).

A culture of CARE means showing compassion, which is baked into the company's DNA. It's amazing how much empathy, support, and genuine connection can transform the daily 9-to-5 grind. When your team feels cared for, they'll return the favor by giving their all. It's like the workplace version of "you get what you give"—except, in this case, you're giving out genuine support, not free donuts (although both are nice!).

Culture is a direct reflection of leadership, and as the saying goes, "the fish rots from the head." So, if we want our teams to truly care, it starts with us as leaders caring first.

It's time to stop the culture conning—where we preach values, hang motivational posters on the walls, and behave in ways that contradict those messages. This kind of inauthentic leadership not only fails but backfires. Employees can spot when there's a disconnect between what's being said and what's happening, and when they do, it breeds resentment.

For CARE to be meaningful, it must be woven into the organization's values and aligned with the business strategy. It's not just about words on a wall; it's about demonstrating genuine care in every interaction, every decision, and every day. CARE stands for clarity, autonomy, relationships, and equity:

- **Clarity**: In a culture of CARE, clarity is everything. Everyone understands their roles and goals with precision, which not only closes gaps in understanding but also empowers individuals to contribute meaningfully. Clear communication fosters an environment where people know exactly what's expected of them, and as the saying goes, "To be clear is to be kind."

- **Autonomy**: Caring leadership fosters an environment where teams are encouraged to take initiative, no matter their position. When people are empowered to lead from wherever they are, it sparks innovation, collaboration, and self-sufficiency. The potential unleashed in such a space is truly transformative—like fireworks lighting the sky.

- **Relationships**: Building authentic, genuine relationships is at the heart of a caring culture. It's about ensuring everyone feels seen, heard, and valued. In this kind of culture, no one is left on the sidelines—you've got a whole team of star players, and everyone feels like a vital part of the game.

- **Equity**: Caring cultures ensure everyone is valued, respected, and inspired. It's about a personalized approach to recognizing people's unique needs and contributions. The impact? It's like that moment in *The Wizard of Oz* when everything turns from black-and-white to Technicolor—suddenly, the possibilities are endless.

* * *

The Benefits of a CARE-ing Culture

Nearly 69% of the global workforce says their boss has a bigger impact on their mental health than their therapist, doctor, or even their spouse. Yep, you read that right! Leadership carries some serious weight. When leaders create a culture of CARE—where employees don't feel like just another cog in the machine—the daily grind starts feeling much more like daily satisfaction. And guess who else wins? The company, with happier employees sticking around longer and slashing those onboarding costs.

In a culture of CARE, engagement isn't forced—it just happens. Employees feel like they're part of a work family that supports their growth and cheers for their wins. As a leader, your job is to cultivate that vibe of clarity—starting with the "why" and the "what." Let's be real: would *you* give 100% if you had no clue why you were doing something? Clarity isn't about shouting orders from your corner office. It's about inspiring your team and turning their scattered efforts into a well-oiled machine.

Think of clarity as the fuel that keeps everything running: clear communication, open dialogue, well-defined goals, and constant feedback. That's what turns a workplace into a motivating, unified space. On the flip side, ambiguity? Well, that's the fast lane to dysfunction—nothing stirs up fear and confusion quicker. Your role as a leader? Kick ambiguity to the curb with clear, two-way communication, and watch your team thrive!

Clarity doesn't just align your team; it inspires them.

As a leader, one of the coolest things you can do is find the balance between giving your team freedom and keeping them accountable. You might be wondering, "How do I pull that off?" Well, it's all about trust and giving your people the space to flex their creativity while making them feel like they own their work. When folks feel trusted and empowered, they step up, take charge, and crush it. It's like giving them wings—without hovering like a helicopter boss!

Will they trip up sometimes? Probably! But that's where the real magic happens. When they hit a roadblock, you help them dust off, learn from it, and return to the game. Growth happens in those stumble-and-recover moments. Plus, flexibility is key and everyone's got their own work style, needs, and quirks. As a leader, tapping into those differences and embracing them is how you bring out the best in your team.

A workplace full of CARE and camaraderie is like having a team that truly has each other's backs. Forget that "fake it 'til you make it" stuff—being real as a leader builds a strong crew. When you're authentic, it creates a tight-knit team where everyone, introverts and extroverts alike, feels part of something bigger. And here's the kicker: when people feel like they belong, not only does productivity soar, but collaboration and problem-solving hit new heights. Suddenly, you've got a team that tackles challenges together, and they come out even stronger on the other side.

Get to know your team beyond the job titles. Find out what fires them up, keeps them motivated, and even what got them out of bed today (even if the answer's just "rent's due!"). Dig into their interests outside of work and create moments for real connection. Ask for their feedback, and hey, let them get to know you, too! Building these relationships turns your workplace into a dynamic, supportive space where everyone thrives.

And let's talk equity—because fairness across the board is non-negotiable. This isn't just about checking a DEIA (Diversity, Equity, Inclusion, and Accessibility) box or sticking policies in a handbook. It's about recognizing and celebrating the unique needs and backgrounds of everyone on your team. There's no cookie-cutter approach because no two people are the same.

Being a caring leader means creating a space where every voice matters, whether someone's pitching a new idea or raising a concern. It's about ensuring everyone feels heard and respected. Pair that with equal growth opportunities, and you've got a culture where individuals thrive, feel valued, and bring their best to the table. Because when everyone feels respected and supported, that's when the real magic happens!

* * *

Overcoming Challenges in a CARE-ing Culture

Building a CARE-ing culture is like setting off on an epic adventure, but let's be honest—it's not without its fair share of challenges. You might have to slay a few dragons along the way, and by dragons, I mean those emotional reactions from team members who resist change. So, how do you handle that? With a good ol' dose of CARE, of course! Don't get defensive or frustrated when someone pushes back—this is your moment to flex those leadership muscles and turn that negativity into a win. Remember, you catch more flies with honey than vinegar, so show your team how a culture of CARE will benefit them.

Now, let's talk about the skeptics—the ones who seem to find every loophole to stir the pot. We've all met them. The trick is to keep the communication lines wide open and get them involved in the process. If organizational silos are in the way, it's time to knock them down! Encourage collaboration across teams and rally everyone around a shared vision. Show them that a CARE-ing culture isn't just fluffed—it's a win-win for everyone that turns obstacles into stepping stones.

Once you've conquered those initial challenges, consistency becomes your next mission. Lip service? That won't fly here. You can't just slap a "CARE" label on the culture and hand it off to HR. Nope. Great leaders (like you!) roll up their sleeves and lead by example. In a CARE-ing culture, you've got to live those values and weave them into your leadership style every single day. It's that ongoing commitment that takes CARE from just another policy to a way of life everyone can rally around.

* * *

A Step Beyond the CARE-ing Model

A happy workforce is typically a thriving one—there's no secret there. When employees are truly satisfied with their jobs, they tend to crush it at work, show loyalty to the company, and crank out top-notch results. A study from Columbia University showed that companies with a strong culture had a turnover rate of just 13.9%, while in toxic work environments, turnover rates skyrocketed to 48.4%. Talk about a difference!

Many businesses owe their success to having an engaged workforce—people who are not only in the game but also playing to win. When employees are aligned with the company's vision and motivated to work together, it's like magic. Sure, you need that balance between getting things done and having fun (because, let's face it, who doesn't love a good laugh at work?). However, a study from the Wharton School of Business reminds us that employee satisfaction goes beyond the occasional team-building activity or free snacks in the breakroom.

According to the study, employees who felt they worked in a caring culture had higher levels of job satisfaction and were more likely to collaborate with their colleagues. They didn't just show up to work—they showed up with a positive attitude, which even rubbed off on customer relationships! Columbia University's research backed this up, too, showing that leaders who create an emotional culture where employees feel genuinely valued build teams that stick around because they feel appreciated—and even "loved."

As a leader, you already know how important it is to make your employees feel valued. They want to know they matter, and showing recognition is one of the easiest ways. It could be as simple as throwing a small celebration when a team hits a big goal or organizing a fun gathering. But appreciation isn't just about parties; it's about making thoughtful improvements across the company. Maybe it's sprucing up the office, upgrading benefits, or improving communication channels. All these tell your employees, "Hey, we care about you and the experience you're having here."

When employees feel genuinely appreciated and cared for, their engagement and loyalty skyrocket, creating a culture built to last.

- **Make health a priority:** As a leader, it's essential to prioritize health in the workplace. Your employees often spend more time at work than at home, so promoting healthy habits and ensuring they have the time to care for themselves and their families should be a key focus for your business. Encouraging employees to take time off when they're not feeling well, especially during flu season, is a simple yet impactful way to show you care. Allow them the time to recover without fear of punishment or losing wages. Many employees hesitate to take sick leave because they worry about repercussions, which can lead to the spread of illness and even more team members falling ill. This not only affects productivity but also drains motivation from employees who are trying to work through sickness. To create a truly caring culture, it's important to support your employees during these times. Offering flexible schedules and allowing them the time to heal shows that you value their well-being. However, fostering a healthy workplace shouldn't stop with short-term illnesses. It's also about supporting your employees' long-term health. Consider offering discounted gym memberships, providing on-site wellness programs like yoga or meditation, or finding other ways to encourage healthy habits. As a leader, you can model the importance of work-life balance by actively demonstrating your commitment to health. When employees see you prioritizing wellness and encouraging them to do the same, it creates a culture where health and well-being are part of the organization's values.

- **Pay attention to personal lives:** Fun events like company outings or baseball games can certainly boost employee engagement, but true loyalty is built on a more personal level. It's how a company responds to the significant moments in an employee's life—such as the birth of a child, the loss of a loved one, or other major life events—that can shape how they feel about their workplace when they return. Life is full of stressors and emotional challenges, and a company that fosters a strong, caring environment proactively supports employees through those times. Offering additional vacation days during a major life event, sending flowers during a loss, or even a simple text on their birthday can go a long way in showing that you care. It's the small, thoughtful gestures that make employees feel valued and appreciated. As a leader, taking these steps helps build a culture of compassion, where people know they are not just seen as workers but as individuals whose personal well-being matters.

- **Get to know your employees:** I've found that inviting employees to activities like golf outings, theater events, or even casual after-work cocktails can be a great way to build stronger relationships. These informal settings allow me to get to know my team on a more personal level—learning about their interests, goals, and any life changes they're going through. Understanding these aspects of their lives makes me better equipped to support them when significant events arise, whether personal or professional. It's about building trust and creating an environment where employees feel valued, not just for their work, but for who they are.

- **Support open communication:** In today's fast-paced business environment, it can be challenging to ensure that everyone feels truly heard and understood. That's why I maintain an open-door policy, allowing employees to meet with me whenever they need to discuss important matters. It's crucial to remind employees that I care about their well-being, both at work and in their personal lives. When an employee does approach me, I make it a point to ask open-ended questions, give space for thoughtful silence, and focus on key statements. Encouraging them to "say more" about critical ideas or concerns helps to foster deeper conversation and understanding. The cultural health of any organization relies on addressing important issues as they arise, which requires close attention, openness, and measured patience. It's about creating an environment where employees feel valued and supported, both in their work and their overall experience.

Building a caring environment isn't always a walk in the park—it takes more than just you putting in the effort. It's all about getting buy-in from everyone, from the CEO to every teammate, to truly embrace what real work-life balance looks like. A culture of care means employees feel comfortable coming to their leaders with anything, knowing they won't be judged or brushed off when they ask for help. It's about creating a space where openness and trust are the norm, and asking for support is seen as a superpower, not a weakness.

* * *

The Power of Active Listening

Active listening might not get as hype as other leadership skills, but trust me, it's the secret sauce for creating a thriving workplace. When you, as a leader, really tune in to your team, you're not just checking off boxes—you're getting to the heart of their challenges, dreams, and even those unspoken concerns that tend to fly under the radar. It's what separates managing tasks from truly leading people. When you're in active listening mode, you're not just hearing words—you're picking up on the emotions and intentions behind them.

From my experience, leaders who genuinely listen build a sense of safety and trust within their teams. When employees feel heard, they're way more likely to open up about their struggles, give honest feedback, or even share that brilliant idea they've been sitting on. Listening doesn't just break down barriers—it helps you build stronger, deeper connections that make teams more engaged and motivated.

Now, I've seen leaders go full-speed into "problem-solving mode" the moment someone brings up a concern. While their intentions are good, they often miss the chance to get to the real root of the issue. People want to feel acknowledged first. Listening is the key to that acknowledgment, and it's often the most powerful first step.

One of the best ways to show you care as a leader is by being available and present when your team needs you. Employees deal with more than their day-to-day tasks—workload stress, career worries, and even personal stuff that can spill over into work. When you take the time to truly listen, you send a clear message: "I care about you as a person, not just as an employee."

Take Diane, a leader I once worked with. She had a team member named Peter who wasn't hitting his marks. Instead of reprimanding him, Diane asked, "How are you doing? Is something going on that's affecting your work?" That one question cracked things wide open. Peter admitted that personal stress at home was messing with his focus. Diane didn't rush to fix everything or judge him—she listened.

By showing care through active listening, Diane was able to help Peter both at work and in his personal life. She adjusted his workload and connected him with resources to manage his stress. The result? Peter's performance improved, and his loyalty to Diane and the company skyrocketed.

The lesson here? Listening is more than just a leadership tool—it's an act of care. You don't always need to have the perfect solution right away. Sometimes, being present and showing your team that their struggles matter is all it takes to make a lasting impact.

* * *

How to Create a "Listening Culture"

As a business coach, I often advise leaders to embed a culture of listening at all levels of the organization. It's not enough for a leader to listen in isolation. When you create an environment where everyone feels encouraged to listen to one another, you're laying the foundation for a culture of care that permeates the entire organization.

To establish this kind of culture, leaders need to lead by example. Here are a few steps I recommend to leaders looking to create a listening-first culture:

- **Be accessible**: Ensure your team knows that you are available to listen, whether in one-on-one meetings or informal check-ins. Create open-door policies or schedule regular catch-ups to make space for these conversations.

- **Ask thoughtful questions**: Go beyond surface-level inquiries like "How are you?" Instead, ask deeper, open-ended questions such as, "What's something you've been thinking about lately?" or "Is there anything I can do to support you right now?"

- **Encourage feedback**: Foster an environment where giving and receiving feedback is the norm. When employees feel their voices are valued, they're more likely to contribute constructive ideas and provide insights that benefit the team.

- **Listen without interrupting**: Let employees fully express their thoughts before you respond. This shows that you're not just hearing them but genuinely seeking to understand their point of view.

- **Follow-up**: Listening doesn't stop at the end of the conversation. After you've heard your team's concerns or ideas, take action where necessary and follow up. This shows that their words didn't fall on deaf ears, reinforcing that their input truly matters.

One of the coolest parts of adopting a "listening-first" approach is seeing how it improves not just one—on—one relationship but can completely transform the whole team. When employees see their leader truly listening and responding with care, they feel respected and valued. The result? Higher morale, less turnover, and way better collaboration.

Take my receptionist, Lucy (we talked about her earlier). She was super shy and didn't speak up in team meetings. So, I made a point to check in with her regularly and ask how things were going. Slowly but surely, she started opening up, sharing her frustrations, and even throwing out some great ideas to improve how the office ran. Just by listening, I helped her feel more comfortable, and she started shining!

The change was subtle but oh-so-powerful. Lucy went from being that quiet, behind-the-scenes presence to stepping up and taking initiative. She started organizing office meetings and suggesting new ways to streamline our processes, and before I knew it, she was a key player in team decision-making. Listening helped her grow, and in turn, her growth boosted the entire team!

6

Investing in Success

As a business consultant, I've had the chance to observe a wide range of companies. Some soar, and others, well, struggle to stay afloat like a paddleboat with a hole in it, hoping for a lucky break. What I've noticed time and time again is that the real game-changer isn't some magical strategy or the next big innovation—it's how much these companies invest in their employees.

Sure, you can spend all your time crafting the perfect business plan or chasing that elusive next big idea. But here's the thing: even the most brilliant strategies flop if the people behind them aren't fully engaged and ready to bring their best. I've seen it happen—companies that skimp on investing in their teams can't seem to get traction, while those that make employee development and well-being a priority? They're the ones hitting it out of the park every time.

Investing in employee success isn't some fancy luxury—it's the secret sauce for long-term growth. When leaders make it a point to focus on their team's development, the results are clear: employees become more engaged, perform at higher levels, and drive more substantial business outcomes. It's like magic, except it's not—it's just good leadership. I've watched businesses turn around, not because they had groundbreaking ideas but because they created a culture where people felt valued and supported. And trust me, that's where the real breakthroughs happen! (And no, I'm not talking about the break room doughnuts—though those don't hurt either.)

***

Prioritizing Employees for Long-Term Success: The Richard Branson Philosophy

One of the most influential business leaders of our time is Sir Richard Branson, the visionary behind the Virgin Group. From airlines to cruises, cell phones to space exploration, Branson has built a diverse empire, and his immense net worth speaks to his success. However, there's an important insight into his achievements—he didn't accomplish all this alone. Behind him was a team with the right training and mindset to execute his vision. Let's look at one of his more thought-provoking and, at times, controversial quotes.

> *"Clients do not come first. Employees come first. If you take care of your employees, they will take care of the clients."* -Sir Richard Branson

Wait—what? Customers don't come first? I know it sounds wild at first but hang with me for a second. Before you completely dismiss the idea, let's break it down. To consistently deliver that legendary customer service every company dreams about, you need a workforce that's motivated, engaged and cares about making the customer experience great. That makes sense, right?

Here's the thing: many companies love to boast, "We put customers first!" And while that sounds great on paper (or plastered on the office walls), do they live up to it? I mean, what about the employees who start their day diving into a sea of phone calls, dealing with complaints, or scrambling to meet a customer's last-minute "I forgot I needed this yesterday" order?

Richard Branson's point is crystal clear: if you don't take care of your employees, they won't be able to care for your customers. It's pretty simple.

When employees feel valued, appreciated, and empowered, they'll naturally deliver better service. And guess what happens next? Satisfied customers. Do satisfied customers turn into loyal customers and loyal customers? Well, they're the ones who keep your business growing.

Branson nailed it. Taking care of employees isn't just the "nice" thing—it's the smart business move. Happy employees create happy customers, and that's how you build a sustainable, successful business. Plus, who wouldn't want a team that loves what they do? That energy's contagious.

Prioritize employees + provide exceptional training = **loyal customers**

At first glance, it might seem counterintuitive to prioritize employees over clients, especially when customer satisfaction is typically viewed as the cornerstone of business success. But Branson's philosophy doesn't diminish the importance of clients—it's about recognizing a deeper, more sustainable approach to delivering long-term customer satisfaction by empowering, motivating, and valuing employees. After all, happy employees equal happy customers—it's simple math!

Sir Richard Branson's perspective suggests how we treat our employees directly impacts the customer experience. When employees feel supported, heard, and appreciated, they're naturally more motivated to provide exceptional service. It's like the difference between someone who loves their job and counting down the hours until Friday—you can guess which one provides better service!

Companies prioritizing a positive internal culture often find their employees more loyal and willing to go above and beyond for customers. When employees feel valued, they're more engaged in their roles, enthusiastic about their work, and more creative in problem-solving. And a workforce that feels genuinely appreciated? That's the key driver of customer satisfaction, which ultimately boosts the business's bottom line.

In my experience, businesses that put employees first create a ripple effect. Engaged employees lead to loyal customers, and loyal customers lead to growth. It's a win-win all around—plus, you get fewer awkward "Can I speak to the manager?" moments!

***

A Global Payoff - One Sip at a Time

In 2014, Starbucks made a bold move that set it apart from many other companies in the retail industry. Already known for its high-quality coffee and recognizable brand, the company launched the College Achievement Plan, a partnership with Arizona State University (ASU) to provide full tuition coverage for its employees, referred to as "partners." This initiative wasn't just a typical employee benefit. It represented a strategic, long-term investment in the workforce that aligned with Starbucks' core values and commitment to employee development.

The College Achievement Plan is open to any partner working at least 20 hours weekly. It covers full tuition for various online bachelor's degree programs ASU offers. From business and engineering to psychology and the arts, partners can pursue higher education without the burden of student loan debt. This initiative goes beyond immediate financial incentives; it demonstrates Starbucks' belief in the potential of its employees and their capacity to achieve more, both within and beyond the company.

Starbucks' decision to offer this program stems from its understanding of the retail sector's high turnover rates and the importance of employee satisfaction. By investing in education, Starbucks aims to create a loyal, motivated workforce. This long-term view acknowledges that well-supported employees are more engaged, productive, and likely to stay with the company. In an industry where retention is a constant challenge, Starbucks' investment in its partners' futures helps foster stronger relationships between employees and the company.

One of the key outcomes of the College Achievement Plan has been its impact on employee retention. Partners who participate in the program are twice as likely to remain with Starbucks compared to those who do not. This is a significant accomplishment in an industry where employee turnover is often high, and it demonstrates the value employees place on the opportunity to further their education. The stability and continuity this creates within Starbucks locations have a direct impact on customer service. When customers see familiar faces and interact with motivated, knowledgeable partners, it enhances their overall experience, creating a positive feedback loop that benefits employees and the business.

The College Achievement Plan also reflects Starbucks' broader philosophy of treating its employees as partners in its success. By offering such an extensive educational benefit, Starbucks is signaling that it values the long-term personal and professional development of its employees. This is not just about providing a paycheck or standard benefits; it's about investing in the future potential of every partner. Starbucks recognizes that many of its employees may have career aspirations beyond their current roles, and the company sees this as an opportunity to help them achieve those goals.

From a business perspective, this initiative is more than a benefit for employees—it is also a financially sound strategy. Lower turnover means fewer resources spent on recruiting, hiring, and training new employees. Additionally, higher employee engagement often results in better performance and stronger customer interactions, directly contributing to the company's bottom line. The investment Starbucks makes in its employees through the College Achievement Plan not only strengthens individual careers but also enhances the overall stability and success of the business.

The impact of this initiative goes beyond individual Starbucks locations. By helping partners pursue higher education, Starbucks contributes to developing a more educated workforce. Many of the skills and knowledge employees gain through their degree programs are transferable, allowing them to bring new ideas and perspectives to their current roles. This, in turn, encourages innovation and a more dynamic work environment within the company.

* * *

The Importance of Investing in Your Team

Investing in your team is hands down one of the most important things you can do for long-term business success—no question about it! Sure, strategies, tech, and innovation are crucial, but let's be real: the true powerhouse behind any organization's growth is its people. When your team feels valued, supported, and set up to win, they're more engaged, motivated, and ready to crush it at work.

By putting resources into employee development—whether training, education, or initiatives focusing on well-being, you're creating a culture of continuous improvement that naturally leads to loyalty. People stick around when they know the company's got their back! And let's be honest, companies that invest in their employees get the bonus of:

- **Making more money:** Let's be real—who doesn't love seeing positive results? Here's a fun fact: companies with highly engaged employees outperform those without by a whopping 202%! Yes, you read that right—202%! It's like ordering a regular sandwich and finding out they threw in extra bacon for free. When you invest in your team, they level up their performance, and that boost goes straight to your bottom line. Win-win, right?

- **Sky-high employee retention:** One of the sneakiest money pits in business? Employee turnover. Replacing someone can set you back up to 33% of their annual salary—ouch! But when you invest in your team, they feel valued and truly belong. And guess what? They're way less likely to jump ship! That means less scrambling to hire and train new people and more time spent celebrating the awesome, loyal crew you've built—plus fewer headaches.

- **A smarter team:** When your crew is constantly learning, growing, and sharpening their skills, they become total rockstars in their roles. And who wins here? You, the fearless leader! When your team crushes it, you get to bask in the glory. It's like baking cookies—sure, the oven does most of the work, but who gets the compliments? The baker, of course! So, when your team shines, your leadership gets the spotlight.

- **Additional loyalty:** When you invest in your people, you're not just building skills—you're building loyalty. That means fewer mysterious "sick days" after long weekends and more employees who consistently show up ready to crush it. Plus, loyal team members don't just do their jobs; they go the extra mile, tackle new challenges, and help out their coworkers. Heck, they might even volunteer to move the office printer—you know, that one that somehow weighs more than a small car.

- **A strong culture:** When you invest in your team, you build a culture of growth, support, and good vibes. Your crew should feel like they're working in a collaborative, productive space—not some drama-filled battleground where office politics reign supreme. A strong, positive work culture is like glue for your team—it keeps things running smoothly, encourages everyone to work together, and dials down distractions. The result? A happier, more effective team that enjoys showing up to work!

* * *

Investing in an Employee's Well-Being

Prioritizing employees means investing in their well-being, both on and off the clock. And no, it's not just about salaries or benefits (although, let's be real, those definitely matter). It's about building a work culture that understands people have lives outside the office, promotes work-life balance, offers real opportunities for growth, and gives everyone a sense of purpose.

Companies that truly put employees first don't stop at the paycheck. They create awesome programs focused on mental health, flexible work options, continuous learning, and career development. These perks don't just attract top talent—they help keep people around for the long haul, saving businesses from the revolving door of hiring and training. When employees know their company has their back, they're more likely to stick around, bring fresh ideas, and be more productive overall.

Just look at companies like Google or Salesforce. These guys are pros at creating employee-centric cultures. They consistently rank high for employee satisfaction, and surprise, surprise—they also kill it in customer satisfaction. They've cracked the code: take care of your employees first, and those happy, engaged people will turn around and take care of your customers.

* * *

The Balance Between Client and Employee Prioritization

Sir Richard Branson's quote might sound like it's forcing a choice between employees and clients, but here's the secret: taking care of your employees means taking care of your clients. It's not an either/or situation—it's a win-win! When employees are happy and feel valued, they bring that energy into everything they do, from delivering top-notch service to creating better products. The result? Happy customers who keep coming back for more.

But here's the flip side: if you don't prioritize your employees, things can get messy fast. Disengaged employees lead to poor customer service, lower productivity, and a revolving door of turnover. And trust me, customers can tell when an employee is checked out or unhappy—it's like putting a giant "we don't care" sign on your brand.

Conversely, a team that feels supported, appreciated, and empowered is a game-changer. They'll not only reflect the company's values but also go the extra mile for customers. It's like a trickle-down effect: when you make your employees' experience a positive one, it flows right into your customers' experience, proving that when you place employees first, everyone wins.

* * *

The Ripple Effect of Happy Employees

Take a quick trip down memory lane to The Virgin Group's legendary commitment to their employees. Sir Richard Branson's philosophy revolves around one big idea: when you treat your employees well, the ripple effect is real. Give them autonomy, make them feel secure in their roles, and you'll see that positivity shine through in how they treat your customers. It's a simple equation: happy employees = happy customers.

When employees feel good, they naturally build stronger connections with their coworkers. These bonds come in handy during crunch time when tight deadlines and problem-solving are on the menu. From my experience, happy employees fuel engagement, and that engagement is pure rocket fuel for success. IBM even found that employee engagement accounted for two-thirds of its positive client experiences. The takeaway? When employees feel valued, it's like putting success on autopilot.

It's no secret—research backs this up, too. Gallup found that companies with highly engaged employees outperform their competition by 147% in earnings per share. That's no small feat! The bottom line is this: when employees feel empowered and appreciated, they don't just perform better—they become your company's biggest cheerleaders. And let's face it, that kind of loyalty and enthusiasm can't be faked, no matter how good your customer service script is.

* * *

Your Role as a Leader

Implementing an employee-first culture requires more than fancy words—it demands real, intentional leadership. You've got to model the behaviors and attitudes that show you're genuinely committed to your team's well-being. It's about creating a space where people feel safe to express concerns, suggest improvements, and know they're valued for more than just the tasks they complete. Think of it like tending a garden: if you want your plants (employees) to thrive, you can't just water them once and walk away!

Fostering a culture of trust can truly transform an organization. It's about leading with empathy, showing that you understand the human side of business, and making sure your employees feel appreciated not just for what they do but for who they are. Trust me, when your team feels valued, they'll move mountains. And as a leader, there are a few key strategies you can use to bring this employee-first culture to life:

1. **Foster open communication:** Step one in building a connected team. Open, honest communication. Your employees must feel like their voices matter, whether sharing ideas, raising concerns, or giving feedback. Set up regular one-on-ones, team meetings, or even anonymous surveys to make sure everyone has a platform. From my experience, teams that keep communication transparent not only come up with more innovative ideas but also tackle problems before they snowball. Be approachable, listen actively, and respond thoughtfully—this will go a long way in creating an open atmosphere.

2. **Encourage collaboration, not competition:** A little friendly competition is fun, sure, but too much can lead to silos and trust issues. Instead, focus on promoting collaboration. Get employees from different departments to work together on projects or problem-solving sessions. When you bring different perspectives together, you create stronger teams and broader ideas. Want to model collaboration as a leader? Involve others in your decision-making and celebrate

team wins, not just individual achievements.

3. **Provide opportunities for growth:** Your employees are more connected to the team and the company when they see a clear path for growth. Offer them chances to learn and develop through training, mentorship, or challenging new projects. From what I've seen, companies that invest in their people's futures see higher engagement and loyalty. Sit down with your team regularly to talk about their career goals, and offer your support in helping them get there.

4. **Build a sense of purpose:** To engage your team, connect their daily tasks to a larger purpose. People want to feel like what they're doing matters. Your job as a leader is to explain the company's mission in a way that resonates with your team and show them how their work contributes to that mission. Whether sharing customer success stories or connecting individual achievements to broader company goals, helping your employees see the bigger picture fosters a deeper sense of purpose and connection.

5. **Create a supportive and inclusive environment:** A strong team thrives on psychological safety—the belief that it's okay to take risks, voice concerns, or make mistakes without fear of backlash. Start by showing vulnerability yourself: admit when you don't know something, and encourage your team to do the same. Ensure you're also promoting diversity and inclusion by making space for every voice at the table, not just the loudest. Inclusive meeting practices and recognizing contributions from all team members go a long way in building a cohesive, innovative team.

6. **Recognize and celebrate achievements:** A little recognition can go a long way. When people feel appreciated, they're more motivated to keep bringing their A-game. And no, it doesn't always have to be about big bonuses (though those don't hurt). A shout-out in a meeting or a

personal thank-you note can do wonders for morale. Celebrate both individual and team successes, and don't wait until the annual review to do it—regular recognition keeps everyone energized and engaged.

7. **Lead by example:** Lastly, remember that as a leader, you set the tone. If you want a culture of teamwork and connection, you have to model it yourself. Be transparent, empathetic, and accountable, and show your team that you're committed to your growth as much as theirs. When your employees see you walking the talk, they're much more likely to follow your lead and adopt those behaviors.

In the end, building a culture where employees come first is about more than just boosting performance—it's about creating a workplace where people feel like they belong, and that's when they'll truly give their best.

***

Reducing Costly Turnover

Employee turnover is a huge headache for companies that don't invest in their people. I mean, who wants to keep losing great employees and having to shell out cash to replace them? According to the Society for Human Resource Management (SHRM), replacing an employee can cost you six to nine months of their salary—yikes! That's everything from recruiting to training and the drop in productivity while new hires find their footing. But here's the good news: companies that invest in career development see a 34% bump in retention. That's some serious ROI right there!

When employees feel connected to their team and the company's mission, they're less likely to jump ship, especially not just for a bigger paycheck. In my experience, employees who feel truly engaged rarely look at competitor offers, and they're not about to start spilling company secrets either. That kind of loyalty doesn't just create a solid workplace culture—it puts your company on the map as a place where people *want* to work. In today's world, where employees value fairness, social responsibility, and purpose more than just a fat paycheck, that reputation is worth its weight in gold.

Offering growth opportunities, mentoring, and skill-building programs shows your team that you're committed to their future, not just your bottom line. And when employees know you've got their back, they're far less likely to jump at external opportunities. For businesses, that means fewer disruptions, stronger team dynamics, and big savings on turnover costs. Plus, who doesn't love watching their team grow and thrive?

***

Employee Success Investment Formula (ESI)

I'm excited to introduce you to the Employee Success Investment Formula—a ridiculously simple yet game-changing way for leaders to invest in their teams and see the magic unfold. It's super easy to roll out, incredibly effective, and will have your entire organization thriving before you know it! Let's get ready to watch the sparks fly!

Identify + Develop + Support = Employee Success (ES) + Business Growth (BG)

1. **Identify** – Strengths, goals, and potential

- **Evaluate employee strengths**: Regularly assess employees' unique skills, talents, and areas of expertise.

- **Set clear goals**: Have discussions about their career aspirations and align them with business objectives.

- **Assess potential**: Identify areas for growth and untapped potential that align with their personal development and the company's needs.

2. **Develop** – Growth, learning, and mentorship

- **Provide training and upskilling**: Implement ongoing learning opportunities, such as workshops, online courses, or certifications.

- **Offer mentorship**: Pair employees with mentors to guide and help them navigate their career paths.

- **Encourage innovation**: Create a culture where employees are encouraged to contribute ideas and solutions, fostering a sense of ownership and involvement.

3. **Support** – Resources, feedback, and recognition

- **Offer resources**: Ensure employees have access to the tools and resources they need to perform at their best.

- **Provide constructive feedback**: Regularly check in and offer feedback to help them stay on track with their development.

- **Recognize achievements**: Acknowledge accomplishments and celebrate milestones, both big and small, to keep morale high and employees motivated.

The result:

- **Employee success (ES)**: Engaged, skilled, and motivated employees with clear career progression.

- **Business growth (BG)**: Increased productivity, innovation, loyalty, and retention, leading to long-term organizational success.

***

Investing in Disengaged Staff

It's a reality that staff members are not always fully engaged. Whether due to personal challenges, occasional off days, or a loss of connection with the company's mission, disengagement can happen. When this occurs, continuing to invest in your team may seem difficult, but it's crucial for reversing the trend and re-engaging your workforce. There are ten key steps to maintaining momentum in investing in your staff, even when they appear disengaged.

1. **Start with open communication:** Disengagement often stems from feeling unheard or misunderstood. Take time to ask your employees how they're feeling about their work, what challenges they're facing, and what would motivate them to re-engage. Let them express concerns and ideas in a safe environment. Share your perspective and explain that their disengagement is noticed, but you're committed to improving the situation.

2. **Identify the root cause of disengagement:** Use anonymous surveys to understand why employees feel disconnected. Whether it's a lack of recognition, unclear goals, or workload stress, understanding the specific reasons helps you address the issue effectively. Observe patterns and look for commonalities among disengaged employees, such as unclear expectations, lack of growth opportunities, or insufficient support.

3. **Reignite a sense of purpose:** Sometimes, employees lose sight of the bigger picture. Remind them how their role contributes to the organization's goals and success, and show how they can make a meaningful impact. Clarify goals that will help your team set clear,

achievable goals aligned with their strengths and interests. Clear direction can reinvigorate their sense of purpose.

4. **Empower your team:** Give your staff more ownership of projects. When employees feel empowered and trusted to make decisions, they're more likely to re-engage. Ask for their input on solutions to company challenges. When people are part of the problem-solving process, they're more likely to be invested in the outcome.

5. **Provide growth opportunities:** Disengagement often comes from feeling stuck. Provide access to training, mentorship, and leadership opportunities that encourage growth and development. Create individualized career plans for employees to help them see a clear path to advancement.

6. **Recognize effort and achievements:** Sometimes, employees need a morale boost. Regularly recognize hard work and celebrate even small successes. Public recognition can significantly boost motivation. A simple "thank you" can go a long way in making employees feel valued.

7. **Create a positive work environment:** If your team dynamic is off, invest in team-building activities to strengthen relationships and rebuild trust. Encourage a healthy work-life balance by offering flexibility where possible. Overworked employees are often disengaged employees.

8. **Lead by example:** Be enthusiastic, supportive, and involved to show your team what engagement looks like. If they see your commitment, they're more likely to follow suit. Consistency in your actions and support shows employees that you're genuinely invested in their success.

9. **Provide feedback and listen to theirs:** Help your employees improve

and grow by providing regular, constructive feedback. Make sure it's framed positively and focuses on how they can excel. Ask for feedback on your leadership and how you can better support them. Showing vulnerability and openness can bridge gaps in communication and trust.

10. **Keep your patience:** Employee engagement won't shift overnight. Stay patient, keep investing in them, and gradually, you'll start seeing progress. Building a thriving and engaged team is a continuous process, but persistence pays off.

* * *

The High Cost of Not Investing in Your Staff

The financial hit from not investing in staff development? It's no joke. Companies that skimp on growth opportunities or ignore employee well-being aren't just facing sky-high turnover—they're also missing out on innovation and getting stuck in a rut. According to LinkedIn, 94% of employees would stick around longer if their company invested in their learning and development. Yet, somehow, many businesses still treat professional growth like an optional side dish instead of the main course.

And here's the kicker: disengaged employees cost the U.S. economy around $550 billion yearly in lost productivity (thanks, Gallup, for that depressing stat). So, if you're not focusing on keeping your team happy and helping them grow, you're not just hurting your culture—you're taking a direct hit to your wallet. Investing in your team isn't just a feel-good strategy, it's the secret sauce for keeping your business booming.

7

The Art of Retention

Let's talk about employee retention—otherwise known as the fine art of keeping your team from bolting for greener pastures. Trust me, as someone who's been in the trenches as both an entrepreneur and a business consultant, this is one of the trickiest challenges you'll face. Back when I was running my eCommerce ventures, I couldn't help but feel like I was constantly auditioning employees for a role in a show they didn't want to stay in. And after I moved into the nine-to-five world? Same story, different set. The workplace felt like a revolving door—new hires in, then out, and off they went to "pursue other opportunities" (which, let's be real, usually meant better pay, cooler perks, or a boss who didn't accidentally CC the whole company on "confidential" emails).

It was exhausting! So, naturally, I started asking myself: What's really going on here? Why does it feel like I'm playing a never-ending game of employee musical chairs, where the music just won't stop? And let me tell you, this problem isn't just mine—it's everywhere. In today's evolving job market, keeping top talent is like holding on to your last donut at an office party—everyone's got their eye on it.

The truth is, employee retention is way more than just flashing a nice paycheck or hosting the occasional team-building bowling night (which, let's be honest, only half your team even wants to attend). It's about understanding what your people really need—what motivates them, what makes them want to come back tomorrow, and not just because it's Friday and there's free pizza. The companies that nail this are the ones that thrive, while the ones that don't? Well, they're stuck wondering why their productivity and morale are sinking faster than that idea for casual Friday pajamas.

So, buckle up! We're diving into the key elements that drive employee retention, and no, it's not just about compensation (although that does help, obviously). We'll talk about work-life balance, career growth opportunities, and the kind of work culture that makes people say, "Yeah, I think I'll stick around here." Whether you're trying to keep your star performers or just hold on to anyone willing to stay, we've got some solid strategies to explore. Let's get to it!

* * *

Patagonia - Mastering Employee Retention

One company that has consistently excelled in retaining its employees is Patagonia, the outdoor clothing and gear company known not only for its high-quality products but also for its strong values and commitment to its workforce. Patagonia's approach to employee retention is rooted in a deep understanding of what drives employee satisfaction and engagement. By aligning its business strategy with employee well-being, the company has cultivated a loyal workforce with some of the lowest turnover rates in its industry.

Patagonia's success in retaining employees can be attributed to a combination of factors, including its investment in work-life balance, a strong sense of purpose, career development opportunities, and a supportive workplace culture.

One of Patagonia's most celebrated policies is its commitment to work-life balance. The company offers flexible working hours and allows employees to take time off when needed, recognizing that a healthy balance between work and personal life leads to more engaged and productive employees. Patagonia's on-site child care center at its headquarters in Ventura, California, is a prime example of this commitment. The company subsidizes child care for its employees, ensuring that working parents can focus on their jobs while knowing their children are cared for close by.

Their flexible policies extend beyond child care. Employees are encouraged to take time off to pursue outdoor activities, which aligns with the company's mission to connect people with nature. This flexibility has created a workplace culture where employees feel trusted and respected, significantly enhancing job satisfaction and retention.

Patagonia's strong sense of purpose is another key factor in its employee retention strategy. The company is renowned for its environmental activism and commitment to sustainability, and it makes these values a core part of its business operations. Employees at Patagonia are not just working for a company—they are contributing to a mission they believe in.

This sense of purpose fosters a deep connection between the company and its employees. Workers feel that their efforts are making a tangible difference, not just in terms of business success but also in advancing environmental causes. This alignment of personal and company values has been instrumental in keeping employees engaged and invested in the long-term success of the organization.

Patagonia understands the importance of career development in retaining top talent. The company invests heavily in its employees' professional growth by offering opportunities for internal promotions, skill development programs, and mentorship. Patagonia encourages its employees to pursue leadership roles and provides the necessary resources and training to help them succeed.

Additionally, their culture encourages employees to take on new challenges and develop various skills. This commitment to professional growth helps employees feel that they are advancing in their careers, reducing the likelihood that they will seek opportunities elsewhere. The company's low turnover rates are a testament to how effectively it invests in its workforce's long-term career paths.

Patagonia's workplace culture is built on trust, transparency, and collaboration. The company's leadership emphasizes open communication and values employee input at all organizational levels. Patagonia is also known for its inclusive environment, where diversity is celebrated, and employees feel a sense of belonging.

This culture of support and inclusivity has created a workplace where employees are highly engaged and motivated to contribute to the company's mission. Patagonia regularly conducts surveys to gauge employee satisfaction and make improvements where necessary, ensuring that employees feel heard and valued.

The results of Patagonia's employee retention strategy speak for themselves. The company consistently ranks as one of the best workplaces, with retention rates far above the industry average. Patagonia's employees are not only loyal but also deeply engaged with the company's mission, contributing to both the business's success and its broader environmental goals.

By investing in work-life balance, providing career development opportunities, fostering a strong sense of purpose, and cultivating a supportive culture, Patagonia has mastered the art of retention. The company's approach shows that when businesses prioritize their employees' well-being and growth, they are rewarded with a committed and high-performing workforce.

* * *

Retention Rates Across Generations

One of the most intriguing aspects of employee retention is how differently each generation approaches their jobs. Over the years, I've had the pleasure (and sometimes the challenge) of working with organizations that have a workforce ranging from Baby Boomers to Gen Z. Let me tell you, the contrast is nothing short of fascinating. On one hand, you've got the Baby

Boomers who seem to stick with a company longer than most people keep their favorite coffee mug. On the other hand, there's Gen Z, who can juggle multiple jobs in the span it takes to scroll through their TikTok feed.

This generational divide in retention rates has become a hot topic among business leaders and HR pros. And no wonder—if you're trying to figure out why one employee has been at your company since the fax machine was a big deal while another leaves after six months to "explore new opportunities," understanding the generational mindset is key.

In this chapter, we're diving into the drivers behind these differences. Why do older generations tend to stay loyal to one employer for decades, while younger employees are more likely to be "job hopping" their way through their career? Is it about values, motivations, or just changing times? Spoiler alert: it's a mix of all three, with a few twists. But the good news is, once we understand what each generation is looking for, we can tailor retention strategies to keep everyone—from the seasoned pro with years under their belt to the ambitious newcomer fresh out of college—engaged and committed.

Let's start by breaking down the key generational groups in today's workforce. Baby Boomers, Gen X, Millennials, and Gen Z. Each one brings something unique to the table, and understanding what makes them tick will help you figure out how to keep them around. And trust me, it's not as simple as throwing money at the problem—though, if you're dealing with Millennials and Gen Z, a little extra in the paycheck doesn't hurt!

- **Baby Boomers (born 1946-1964):** Typically in their late careers or nearing retirement, this generation is known for its loyalty and long tenure with employers. Many Baby Boomers spent most of their careers with a single company, often seeing long-term employment as a mark of stability and success.

- **Generation X (born 1965-1980):** Often referred to as the "middle child" of generations, Gen Xers value stability and flexibility. While they tend to stay with companies longer than Millennials or Gen Z, they are more open to change than Baby Boomers, especially if they feel undervalued or if career advancement opportunities are lacking.

- **Millennials (born 1981-1996)**: Millennials are known for their desire for personal growth and work-life balance, which often leads them to change jobs more frequently than older generations. Studies have shown that Millennials are more likely to prioritize career development, flexibility, and purpose over long-term loyalty to one employer.

- **Generation Z (born 1997-2012)**: The youngest group in the workforce, Gen Z, is even more likely to embrace frequent job changes. They value flexibility, purpose, and technology-driven workplaces and are not afraid to leave a company that doesn't align with their values or offer growth opportunities.

According to a 2022 Gallup study, Baby Boomers tend to stay with their employers for an average of 10.3 years, while Millennials typically average just 2.8 years. This stark difference in retention rates highlights why employers today need to rethink their retention strategies to meet the needs of a more mobile and opportunity-driven younger workforce.

In my experience working with organizations, I've often seen this pattern play out firsthand. Baby Boomers and Generation X employees usually remain with their employers for much longer periods. This tendency is influenced by a combination of generational values, economic factors, and the traditional structure of career trajectories during their early professional years. Understanding these generational dynamics is essential for developing strategies that effectively retain talent across all age groups.

1. **Loyalty to employers:** Older generations, particularly Baby Boomers, were raised with loyalty. In the post-World War II era, long-term employment with one company was considered the gold standard for career success. Companies often rewarded loyalty with pensions, health benefits, and stability, creating an environment where

employees felt incentivized to stay for the long term. In this context, changing jobs frequently was often seen as risky or indicative of instability. In addition, the hierarchical nature of many organizations in the past provided a clear path for advancement. Employees could "work their way up the ladder," and those who stayed with the company for many years often achieved senior positions. Baby Boomers and Gen Xers, therefore, viewed long-term employment as a way to secure both professional success and financial security.

2. **Economic conditions:** The economic conditions of previous decades also played a significant role in fostering employee retention among older generations. When Baby Boomers entered the workforce, the job market was more stable and large, well-established companies dominated many industries. Working for the same employer for 30 or 40 years wasn't just common—it was the norm. Moreover, during the Baby Boomer era, many companies offered defined benefit pensions, which were contingent on long-term service. This created a powerful financial incentive for employees to stay with their employers until retirement.

3. **Fear of change:** Older generations were often taught to view change as risky. This mindset, combined with the more hierarchical, stable work environments of the past, made employees less likely to jump from one job to another. For Baby Boomers and many Gen Xers, security was a key driver in career decision-making, and staying with one employer was often seen as the safest path.

* * *

Why Younger Generations Job Hop

Millennials and Gen Z approach their careers with a different mindset than previous generations, and I've seen this shift firsthand. In my experience, younger employees are far more likely to move on from a company if it doesn't align with their expectations for growth, work-life balance, or personal values. And let's be honest, they're not shy about it either. If the job isn't giving them what they want, they'll swipe left faster than you can say "annual performance review."

What drives this "job-hopping" tendency? A mix of factors—different economic conditions, evolving social values, and, of course, the fast-paced world of technology. Unlike older generations who may have prioritized job security and stability, Millennials and Gen Z are driven by a desire for meaningful work, flexibility, and opportunities to develop their skills. If they're not finding that where they are, they're not afraid to start looking elsewhere—and fast.

So, as business leaders, the challenge is clear: if we want to retain top talent from these younger generations, we need to rethink the way we structure roles, benefits, and career progression. The days of staying with one company for 30 years are long gone, and let's face it—that might not be such a bad thing.

1. **Focus on career growth:** Millennials and Gen Z place a high value on personal and professional growth. They are eager to acquire new skills, take on challenges, and advance in their careers. Unlike Baby Boomers, who were often content with a slow and steady climb up the corporate ladder, younger employees want to see rapid progress—and if they don't, they're more than willing to seek opportunities elsewhere. A LinkedIn study found that 87% of Millennials consider professional development and career growth opportunities very important in a job. When these opportunities are lacking, younger employees often view job changes as the quickest path to advancement.

2. **Work-life balance and flexibility:** Work-life balance is a critical factor for Millennials and Gen Z, often more than salary. Both generations prioritize flexible work arrangements, such as remote work or flexible hours, and are more likely to leave a company that doesn't provide these options. According to a 2022 survey by FlexJobs, 72% of Millennials would consider leaving their job for better work-life balance. This focus on flexibility is a stark contrast to the values of Baby Boomers, who were often willing to sacrifice personal time for career advancement. Younger generations, however, are less willing to make that trade-off and instead seek employers who offer flexibility as part of their core work culture.

3. **Alignment with personal values:** Younger employees are also more likely to seek out employers who align with their values, particularly when it comes to social responsibility, sustainability, and diversity. If a company doesn't reflect its values or provide a sense of purpose, Millennials and Gen Z employees are more inclined to leave in search of a better cultural fit. In a Deloitte survey, 49% of Millennials said they had made career choices based on the organization's ethics. Gen Z is even more outspoken about the importance of working for companies committed to social causes, further driving the trend toward frequent job changes when companies don't meet their expectations.

4. **Economic and technological shifts:** The economic landscape for Millennials and Gen Z is vastly different from that of older generations. With the rise of the gig economy, the advent of remote work, and the rapid pace of technological advancement, younger generations are accustomed to navigating a fluid job market. They are less concerned with job security and more focused on finding opportunities that provide personal satisfaction, skills growth, and financial stability on their terms.

Millennials and Gen Z came of age during a time of significant economic instability, with events like the 2008 financial crisis leaving a lasting impact on their views toward job loyalty. I've noticed that many in these generations tend to prioritize career advancement and personal growth over long-term loyalty to any one employer. And who can blame them? After watching entire industries get shaken up, it's no wonder they're more focused on building their own career resilience than sticking around for a company gold watch.

In today's job market, loyalty isn't about how long you stay—it's about how well you align with opportunities that match your ambitions. So, if these younger employees aren't getting the growth they're looking for, they're not afraid to explore what's out there. After all, why wait 10 years for a promotion when you can find a better opportunity (with free snacks and unlimited vacation) down the street?

* * *

Understanding the Current Job Market

To really get a handle on employee retention, we need to start by understanding what's happening in the job market today. It's a different world out there compared to even a decade ago. As of 2024, the job market has become increasingly mobile, with employees more willing to switch companies in search of new opportunities. According to the U.S. Bureau of Labor Statistics, the average employee tenure in 2023 was just over four years, with younger workers (ages 25 to 34) averaging a much shorter stint—around 2.8 years at a company. And get this: a Gallup survey found that a whopping 60% of millennials are open to new job opportunities at any given time. In other words, the phrase "always on the lookout" might as well be their motto.

So, what's driving this trend? Well, loyalty isn't quite the currency it used to be in the workplace. Today's employees—especially the younger generations—are focused on personal and professional growth. They're not sticking around just because it's what their parents did. Instead, they're willing to move on if their needs for career advancement, flexibility, or work-life balance aren't being met. It's no longer just about the paycheck (though let's be honest, that doesn't hurt)—it's about whether they feel like they're progressing and maintaining control over their time.

Take a look at some recent stats: in 2023, a report by the Society for Human Resource Management (SHRM) found that 47% of workers who left their jobs did so to pursue better career advancement opportunities. Meanwhile, FlexJobs reported that 52% of employees left their positions due to a lack of flexibility or poor work-life balance. These numbers aren't just stats—they're flashing neon signs that say, "People want more than just a desk and a salary." If companies aren't offering growth or flexibility, employees will pack up faster than you can say, "exit interview."

Looking ahead, the next decade promises even more change. With the rise of remote work, automation, and technological advancements, we're going to see employees demanding even greater flexibility and a more personalized approach to work. Companies will need to adapt to this shift by offering not just competitive pay but also opportunities for continuous learning and a better work-life balance. The workforce of the future is going to expect—and demand—environments where they can grow, be challenged, and still make it home in time for dinner (or log off their laptop from the couch).

As business leaders, it's time to recognize that the job market isn't just evolving—it's transforming. If we want to retain top talent in this new landscape, we've got to think beyond traditional incentives and start focusing on what really matters to employees: growth, flexibility, and a sense of purpose. After all, the days of the 30-year career at one company are long gone, and we'd better be ready to keep up with the change.

***

The Impact of Competitive Compensation on Retention

When it comes to employee retention, you can't ignore the elephant in the room: compensation. Let's be real—competitive salaries and benefits have always been crucial to attracting and keeping talent. But in today's job market, offering a competitive compensation package is no longer just important; it's essential. According to a 2022 PayScale survey, 63% of employees who left their jobs said low pay was the main reason for their departure. So, while salary may not be the only thing on an employee's mind, it's certainly one of the louder voices in the room.

Over the past few years, I've seen a growing shift in expectations when it comes to compensation. Employees today are looking for more than just a solid base salary—they want the full package. Think health benefits, retirement contributions, stock options, and performance bonuses. And if you want to stand out as an employer, throw in some more modern perks like wellness programs, paid parental leave, and mental health support. Trust me, the days of just offering a paycheck and calling it a day are long gone. You've got to bring a little more to the table.

But here's the thing: while competitive compensation can keep employees happy in the short term, it's not a magic bullet for long-term retention. Sure, people may leave for higher pay, but those who stay? They're doing it for more than just the money. Studies have shown that employees who stick around are usually motivated by factors like job satisfaction, opportunities for career growth, and a positive work environment. And let's face it, you can only throw so many bonuses at someone before they start asking, "But what about my work-life balance?"

So, while compensation is a critical piece of the puzzle, it's not the whole picture. Offering a great salary and benefits package is a good start, but if you want to retain your top talent, you've got to think beyond the numbers. After all, nobody ever stayed at a job they hated just because the dental plan was good.

* * *

The Role of Work-Life Balance in Retention

One of the biggest trends shaping today's workforce is the increasing demand for better work-life balance. In a world where remote work, flexible hours, and mental health awareness have taken center stage, employees are looking for more than just a paycheck—they want a job that lets them maintain a healthy balance between their professional and personal lives. And the numbers back this up. According to a 2022 Deloitte survey, 77% of employees said they'd experienced burnout at their current job, and 42% of them pointed directly to a lack of work-life balance as the culprit. That's a pretty eye-opening statistic and a clear reminder that work-life balance isn't just a "nice-to-have" anymore—it's essential for retaining talent.

In my experience working with companies across various industries, one thing has become clear: those that prioritize flexibility tend to keep their employees longer. Whether it's offering remote work options, flexible hours, or a company culture that actually encourages people to use their vacation days (and not just *say* they offer unlimited PTO), these organizations understand that employees need balance to stay productive, engaged, and—most importantly—happy. On the flip side, companies that don't offer this flexibility? Well, they're usually the ones struggling with burnout, high turnover rates, and employees constantly eyeing the door, wondering where they can find a more balanced life.

Now, here's the catch: work-life balance isn't a one-size-fits-all solution. For one employee, balance might mean being able to pick up their kids from school in the middle of the day. For another, it might be the freedom to work remotely and avoid the soul-sucking daily commute. And then some just want to be able to clock out at 5 p.m. sharp without feeling guilty. The key as a leader is understanding these individual needs and creating policies that support a wide range of preferences.

So, if you're serious about keeping your top talent around, you've got to think beyond the usual perks and pay attention to what really matters: giving your employees the flexibility to live their lives while doing great work. After all, nobody wants to feel like they're living to work when they should be working to live—unless, of course, you've got some *really* exciting Zoom meetings planned!

* * *

Career Advancement Opportunities

One of the biggest factors that keeps employees around is the opportunity for career growth. Let's face it—nobody wants to feel like they're stuck in a dead-end job, no matter how good the coffee is in the breakroom. In today's fast-paced job market, people are constantly looking for ways to develop their skills and move up the ladder. Companies that don't provide these opportunities? Well, they often find themselves with high turnover rates and a revolving door of talent. According to LinkedIn's 2022 Workforce Learning Report, 94% of employees said they'd stick around longer if their company invested in their career development. That's a pretty strong signal that growth matters.

In my experience, companies that lay out clear paths for advancement—whether through internal promotions, professional development programs, or mentorship—tend to hold on to their best people. Employees want to know that they're making progress, that they're on a trajectory to something bigger, and that their employer sees a future for them within the organization. If they don't feel that sense of forward motion, they're likely to start looking for greener (or at least more upwardly mobile) pastures.

As leaders, we need to regularly check in with our team members about their career goals. It's not enough to assume that people are happy where they are—most want new challenges, opportunities to learn, and the chance to move into higher-level roles. Offering them these opportunities is one of the best ways to build loyalty and commitment. Plus, it shows you're invested in their success, not just the success of the company.

Don't forget about continuous learning, either. Workshops, training programs, and even tuition reimbursement can go a long way in showing employees that you're committed to their professional growth. And let's be real—no one ever left a company because they were learning too much. If anything, they'll stick around longer, if only to avoid another "onboarding process" elsewhere.

***

Positive Work Environment

While we often focus on compensation, work-life balance, and career advancement when discussing employee retention, there's one factor that's just as crucial—but sometimes gets overlooked: the overall work environment. Let's face it, people want to work in a place where they feel valued, respected, and supported. A toxic work culture? That'll have even your most dedicated employees running for the exits faster than you can say "exit interview."

A 2021 study by MIT Sloan Management Review found that toxic corporate culture was the number one predictor of employee turnover, even more significant than compensation. That's right—people would rather take a pay cut than stick around in a toxic environment. This goes to show just how important it is to create a workplace culture rooted in inclusivity, respect, and collaboration. Employees who feel like they're part of a supportive team are much more likely to stick it out—even when the going gets tough or when another company tries to lure them away with shiny new offers.

As leaders, we set the tone for the work environment. It's on us to foster open communication, promote diversity and inclusion, recognize and reward contributions, and make sure our employees feel safe sharing their ideas and concerns. In my consulting work, I've seen firsthand how a positive work culture can do wonders for retention rates. On the flip side, a negative culture leads to disengagement and turnover faster than a company-wide email with the subject line "Mandatory Fun Event."

Speaking of recognition, it plays a huge role in keeping people happy. According to Gallup, employees who feel adequately recognized are five times more likely to stay with their employer. Meanwhile, those who feel unappreciated are likely to update their resumes. Recognition doesn't always have to come in the form of bonuses (though I'm sure no one would turn them down). Simple things like public acknowledgments, personalized thank-you notes, or even giving someone new growth opportunities can make a big difference.

In my experience, companies that build a culture of recognition—whether through formal programs or just regular shout-outs—tend to have employees who are more motivated, engaged, and loyal. The trick is to make sure recognition is genuine and consistent, not something reserved for the annual review or just when someone hits a major milestone.

But perhaps the most powerful tool in the retention toolbox is creating a culture of solidarity. When employees feel like they're part of a team that shares common goals, values, and a sense of purpose, they're far less likely to leave—even when faced with external offers or tough working conditions. Building that sense of belonging takes time and effort, but the payoff is huge in terms of satisfaction and loyalty.

Creating a culture of solidarity means fostering trust, collaboration, and shared success. As leaders, it's up to us to create opportunities for team bonding—whether through cross-departmental projects, team-building exercises, or even just regular social events. It's about encouraging people to support each other and work together toward common objectives. When employees feel connected to their team and the organization, they're more likely to stay, even during challenging times.

In my work with companies, I've seen just how impactful building a positive, inclusive, and supportive work culture can be. Sure, it takes effort and intentionality, but the results speak for themselves: more engaged employees, higher retention rates, and a team that's not just working together but thriving together. And hey, isn't that what we're all aiming for?

* * *

Recognition & Retention

Recognition and retention go hand in hand, and if there's one thing I've learned as a leader, it's that recognizing employees is fundamental to keeping them engaged and motivated. It's not just about the occasional pat on the back when something goes right—it's about making sure your team feels seen, valued, and supported every single day. In my experience, recognition can take many forms, from simple words of encouragement to more formal recognition programs. But no matter how you do it, the impact of genuine recognition on employee retention is undeniable.

I'll never forget an experience I had with an employee who was struggling in their role. On paper, they were fully capable, but their performance just wasn't matching up to expectations. It was frustrating—for both of us, to be honest. Instead of writing them off, I decided to invest in their growth. I took the time to coach them and offered opportunities for professional development, even sending them to a training seminar tailored to the skills they were missing.

The transformation was remarkable. As they started to grasp their job better, their confidence skyrocketed. I made a point to recognize their progress every step of the way—not just waiting for big wins but celebrating the small, everyday victories that might otherwise go unnoticed. And that's when I realized something important: recognition isn't just about the major milestones; it's about appreciating the journey and the little steps that lead to those bigger successes.

Over time, this employee's performance improved dramatically. Not only did they excel at their tasks, but they also became more engaged and confident. The simple act of recognizing their growth reinforced the behaviors and outcomes we wanted to see, and it also taught me a valuable leadership lesson—recognition builds confidence, and confidence leads to retention.

Now, I'll be the first to admit that recognition is often underutilized in the workplace. Yet, it's one of the most effective tools for retaining talent. When employees feel appreciated, they are more likely to find job satisfaction and less likely to start daydreaming about their next opportunity. And here's the good news—recognition doesn't have to be grand or costly. Sometimes, a sincere "thank you" or a quick note of appreciation can go a long way. What matters most is that it's genuine and consistent.

Research backs this up, too. Studies show that companies with strong recognition practices are three times more likely to see an increase in employee retention. That's not just anecdotal evidence—the numbers don't lie. When people feel valued, they stick around. Organizations that invest in recognition programs also see other benefits, like increased internal mobility and enhanced agility, as employees become more engaged with the company's goals and vision.

Beyond improving retention, recognition helps create a positive work environment. When employees feel their contributions are appreciated, they develop a stronger sense of belonging within the team. And let's be honest, a little praise can go a long way toward making the Monday morning grind a bit more bearable! When employees know their efforts matter, they're not just motivated—they're committed. This deepened engagement translates into better performance and greater loyalty to the organization.

Here's the thing: recognition shouldn't be confined to the annual performance review or the occasional shout-out at the team meeting. It should be an ongoing practice, woven into the fabric of your daily interactions. I've seen firsthand how regularly celebrating small achievements can have a huge impact on an employee's motivation. The employee I coached flourished because they knew that their day-to-day progress was valued—and that built the confidence they needed to succeed.

When employees feel supported in their daily work, they take more ownership of their tasks and consistently perform at a higher level. They know their efforts won't go unnoticed, which fuels their drive to excel. Recognition, in this sense, becomes a powerful cycle: the more employees feel appreciated, the more engaged they become, leading to better performance—and more opportunities for recognition.

So, if you're looking for a simple, effective way to boost retention, start by recognizing your team for the great work they're already doing. Trust me, a little recognition goes a long way!

***

The "Golden Rule"

Let's take it back to the basics: *Treat others as you would want to be treated.* It's one of the first life lessons we learn as kids, and it's amazing how relevant that little nugget of wisdom becomes in the workplace. The Golden Rule, at its core, is about respect and compassion, two values that are essential to creating a healthy work environment. Without them, we're just setting ourselves up for high turnover, disengaged employees, and a workplace culture that feels like more of a battlefield than a place of collaboration.

Respect in the workplace isn't just a "nice-to-have." It's critical, especially when it comes to retention. Employees want to work where they feel valued, where their contributions are respected, and where they can trust their colleagues and leadership. When people feel respected, they stick around. When they don't, well, they start shopping around with their resumes like it's Black Friday.

In my experience working with companies, I've noticed one thing time and time again: employees who feel respected are far more likely to stay with their employer, even when a more competitive offer comes along. Why? Because feeling respected isn't something you can put a dollar amount on. It's a sense of value, of belonging, and it's not easily replaced.

A workplace where respect and compassion are prioritized sees higher levels of employee engagement and commitment. People want to stay where they feel they're part of something meaningful. On the flip side, a lack of respect can be a one-way ticket to high turnover, low morale, and poor productivity. And it's not always about grand gestures—sometimes respect comes in the form of a simple "thank you," or listening when someone needs to voice a concern. The small things add up.

But let me tell you about a time when I saw the exact opposite of respect in action. I was working with a company, and I overheard one of the high-level managers talking, loudly and carelessly, about an employee's work. We're not talking constructive feedback here—this was full-on criticism, and it wasn't behind closed doors. The manager was just blurting it out for everyone within earshot to hear, as if it were office gossip. The employee in question wasn't present, but that didn't seem to matter to this leader. There was no respect for confidentiality, no consideration for the employee's hard work, and frankly, no professionalism.

What struck me wasn't just that the criticism was harsh—it was that the manager showed a complete disregard for how this would affect the team. Everyone within a few feet of this manager heard the rant, and you could practically feel the morale drop as they listened. It was one of those moments that reminded me just how important it is for leaders to lead by example, and how quickly things can go downhill when respect is tossed out the window.

As leaders, it's our job to set the tone. Respect is something we demonstrate in our actions, in how we communicate, and how we make decisions. Here are a few key ways leaders can show respect to their coworkers:

1. **Communicate with intention**: Whether you're offering praise or delivering feedback, the way you communicate matters. Avoid public criticism—especially the kind that I overheard that day—and instead, handle issues privately, with respect for the individual and their contributions.

2. **Respect confidentiality**: This might seem obvious, but I've seen too many examples of leaders forgetting that not everything is for public consumption. Discuss performance issues or sensitive matters behind closed doors, not over coffee in the breakroom where everyone else can hear.

3. **Show empathy**: Everyone has bad days, but as leaders, it's important

to approach others with empathy and understanding. Sometimes, simply recognizing when someone's having a tough time and offering support can go a long way in building respect and trust.

4. **Be inclusive**: Treat everyone with the same level of respect, regardless of their role. Too often, I see leaders who only focus on upper management, while overlooking the efforts of the rest of the team. It's the little things—greeting your employees by name, asking for their input, and acknowledging their efforts—that build a respectful, cohesive team environment.

5. **Offer recognition**: Employees thrive when their hard work is recognized. It doesn't have to be an elaborate awards ceremony; sometimes, just a simple, sincere "great job" can make all the difference. Recognition shows that you respect and appreciate the work your team is putting in.

But what happens when respect goes out the window? When an employee feels they've been disrespected, or when a leader's actions undermine the culture of respect? First things first: take it seriously. When someone raises a complaint about being treated disrespectfully, it's not something to brush off. It can be a sign of deeper issues in the workplace, and the worst thing a leader can do is dismiss it.

Here's how I'd recommend handling it:

1. **Listen without judgment**: The first step is to listen—really listen. Let the employee explain the situation fully, without interrupting or jumping to conclusions. Listening with respect shows that you take their concerns seriously and value their perspective.

2. **Stay neutral**: It's easy to let your emotions or personal biases come into play, but it's important to remain neutral as you assess the situation. Your goal is to understand the facts and handle the complaint

objectively.

3. **Take action**: After investigating the situation, you need to take appropriate steps to address it. This could mean having a conversation with the individual involved, setting clearer expectations, or providing training on workplace respect. The key is to act—not just listen and then sweep it under the rug.

4. **Follow up**: After resolving the issue, follow up with the employee to make sure the situation has improved. This not only shows you're committed to fostering a respectful workplace, but it also reinforces trust between you and your team.

At the end of the day, the Golden Rule applies to the workplace just as much as it does anywhere else: *treat others as you'd want to be treated.* Respect isn't just a nice idea—it's a key factor in creating a positive work culture and keeping employees engaged and committed. And while I've seen firsthand how a lack of respect can damage a workplace, I've also seen how showing respect can strengthen relationships, boost morale, and improve retention.

8

Creating a Shared Vision

Creating a shared vision is one of the most critical elements for achieving long-term success in any organization. Without it, even the most talented teams can find themselves heading in different directions, causing confusion, missed opportunities, and, quite frankly, a lot of unnecessary headaches. I learned this firsthand when I was asked to chair our company's DEIA (Diversity, Equity, Inclusion & Accessibility) committee and tasked with developing a strategic plan for the next decade. Sounds simple, right? Well, not exactly.

From day one, I realized I had a big challenge ahead of me: the leadership team had vastly different ideas about what diversity and inclusion should look like. Picture a boardroom full of passionate leaders, all pulling in different directions. It was like trying to conduct an orchestra where everyone was playing a different tune. Not exactly music to my ears!

To get us aligned, I decided to take a straightforward approach. I asked each leader to write down their top 10 goals for the next ten years. This wasn't a trick question or an overly complicated exercise—it was just about getting everyone to think seriously about what truly mattered for the company's future. Once I collected everyone's lists, I laid them all out side by side.

Seeing everyone's goals in one place was an eye-opener. Suddenly, it was easy to spot the common threads. There was more overlap than anyone had anticipated, and we began to see the shared priorities emerging. This moment was a turning point. Once we identified our shared goals, the energy in the room shifted. Instead of competing ideas pulling us apart, we now had a unified vision pulling us together.

With this clarity, everything else started to fall into place. We were able to develop specific strategies aligned with our shared vision, and everyone felt a sense of ownership and commitment to the direction we were heading. The process of building that strategic plan became less about managing competing priorities and more about collaborating from a common perspective.

The biggest lesson I took away from this experience is simple: before you can work toward a goal, everyone needs to agree on what that goal actually is. If people aren't aligned on the destination, you'll waste a lot of time, energy, and resources getting nowhere. But once you establish a shared vision, decision-making, collaboration, and unity all become so much easier. It's like getting everyone in the orchestra to play the same sheet of music—now, we've got harmony.

A shared vision doesn't just help with planning—it's one of the most powerful tools any organization can use to drive growth and success. It brings clarity, focus, and a renewed sense of purpose. When a team is aligned around a common goal, they can achieve far more together than they ever could working in silos. So, the next time you're leading a project or team, make sure everyone is on the same page before you start—trust me, it'll save you a lot of headaches down the road!

***

A New Direction at Microsoft

One company that has excelled in creating a shared vision is Microsoft. Under the leadership of CEO Satya Nadella, Microsoft underwent a cultural transformation that reinvigorated the organization and set a new course for its future. By fostering a shared vision built around collaboration, innovation, and inclusivity, Nadella was able to unite Microsoft's vast global workforce, resulting in a dramatic boost to morale, productivity, and overall company performance.

In this chapter, we will explore how Microsoft successfully created and implemented a shared vision and why it was so effective. We will examine the specific steps the company took to get all team members on the same page and discuss the impact this had on the organization's culture and success.

When Satya Nadella took over as CEO of Microsoft in 2014, the company faced significant challenges. While still a dominant force in the technology industry, Microsoft had become stagnant, with a hierarchical culture that stifled innovation and collaboration. Employee morale was low, and the company was losing ground to competitors like Apple and Google, particularly in key areas like cloud computing and mobile technology.

Recognizing the need for change, Nadella knew that Microsoft's success would depend on more than product innovation—it required a cultural shift. Employees needed to be aligned around a shared vision that was forward-thinking, inclusive, and built on collaboration. Nadella's vision was to turn Microsoft into a "learn-it-all" company that embraced growth, curiosity, and continuous learning, moving away from its previous "know-it-all" culture.

The cornerstone of Nadella's shared vision for Microsoft was the idea of empowerment. He articulated a clear and straightforward mission: "To empower every person and every organization on the planet to achieve more." This vision resonated deeply with employees because it connected the company's purpose with the work each individual was doing daily.

This new vision wasn't just a corporate slogan—it became the guiding principle for every decision, project, and strategic move the company made. Nadella knew that for the vision to be successful, it had to be embraced by every employee, from engineers to sales teams to executives. To achieve this, the company focused on three key elements:

1. **Communication and transparency**: Nadella made a concerted effort to communicate the new vision to every level of the organization. He held frequent town halls, sent open letters to employees, and ensured that leaders across the company consistently reinforced the message. This transparency helped employees understand the why behind the vision, making it easier for them to align their work with the company's goals.

2. **Shifting the culture to collaboration**: One of the critical aspects of the shared vision was a focus on collaboration over competition, both internally and externally. Microsoft had long been known for its siloed departments and competitive culture. Nadella changed this by fostering a growth mindset throughout the company. Employees were encouraged to share ideas, experiment, and learn from failures. This cultural shift not only created more innovation but also built stronger connections among teams.

3. **Inclusive leadership**: Nadella understood that a shared vision would only work if leaders fully embraced it. He placed a strong emphasis on inclusive leadership, ensuring that leaders at all levels embodied the values of empathy, inclusivity, and collaboration. By training leaders to support their teams in this new culture, Microsoft created a ripple effect where the shared vision was reinforced at every company layer.

The results of Microsoft's cultural transformation and shared vision have been profound. By 2020, Microsoft's market value had more than tripled under Nadella's leadership, reaching over $1.6 trillion. But beyond the financial success, the cultural changes were evident in the company's day-to-day operations and employee satisfaction.

One of the most significant impacts of Microsoft's shared vision was a dramatic improvement in employee morale. A survey conducted within the company in 2019 showed that 88% of employees felt aligned with the company's mission, a sharp increase from prior years. Employees reported feeling more connected to their work and more empowered to contribute to the company's success.

This boost in morale was also reflected in Microsoft's ranking on the Great Place to Work survey, where the company consistently improved year-over-year under Nadella's leadership. The cultural shift towards collaboration, learning, and inclusivity created an environment where employees felt valued, respected, and motivated to do their best work.

With a shared vision, Microsoft also saw significant improvements in productivity and innovation. By fostering a culture of collaboration, the company broke down silos that had previously hindered progress. Teams across different departments began working together more seamlessly, leading to faster product development and more innovative solutions.

For example, the success of Microsoft's cloud computing platform, Azure, can be directly linked to this new collaborative culture. Teams from different divisions, including engineering, marketing, and sales, worked closely together to create a product that quickly became a market leader. Today, Azure generates over $50 billion in annual revenue and is a key driver of Microsoft's growth.

The shared vision also helped Microsoft streamline its workflow and increase organizational agility. By aligning all employees around a common purpose, the company was able to reduce bureaucracy and decision-making bottlenecks. Teams were empowered to make decisions more quickly, knowing that their work was contributing to the broader vision of empowering people and organizations globally.

This increased agility was particularly evident during the COVID-19 pandemic when Microsoft quickly adapted to the new remote work environment. The company's ability to pivot and roll out new solutions, like Microsoft Teams, at scale was a testament to the strength of its shared vision and collaborative culture.

There are several key reasons why Microsoft's approach to creating a shared vision was so successful:

1. **Simplicity and clarity**: Nadella's vision was clear and easy to un-

derstand. By focusing on a single, powerful idea—empowerment—he ensured that every employee, regardless of their role, could see how their work contributed to the company's mission.

2. **Inclusive and collaborative culture**: By fostering a culture of inclusivity and collaboration, Nadella broke down the barriers that had previously held the company back. This shift allowed employees to feel more engaged with their work and more connected to their colleagues, which in turn drove innovation and productivity.

3. **Commitment from leadership**: Microsoft's leaders fully embraced the shared vision and set an example for the rest of the company. This top-down commitment was critical in ensuring that the vision was not just a statement but a guiding principle that influenced every aspect of the company's operations.

4. **Ongoing communication**: Nadella's consistent communication of the shared vision helped to reinforce its importance. By regularly sharing updates, stories of success, and lessons learned, he kept the vision alive.

***

The Shared Vision Formula

Creating a shared vision formula is about establishing a structured and clear framework that aligns individual perspectives and goals toward a unified direction. In my experience, when a team lacks a shared vision, you end up with a lot of fragmented efforts—people and departments working in silos, sometimes even at cross-purposes. It's like rowing a boat, but everyone's paddling in different directions. Spoiler alert: that boat isn't going anywhere fast.

By developing a shared vision formula, I help bring clarity and focus to the team's efforts. It ensures that everyone's not only contributing their ideas but also working cohesively toward the same, mutually agreed-upon goals. This process fosters collaboration, encourages shared ownership, and motivates the team by giving them a clear roadmap of where the organization or project is headed.

And trust me, when the whole team is aligned, it's like shifting from rowing with random paddles to turning on the engine. Here's the structure of my shared vision formula:

(Individual Goals + Common Ground) x Clear Communication = **Shared vision**

Here is the formula in more detail:

- **Individual goals**: Start by identifying each team member's individual goals and perspectives. This ensures that everyone's ideas and priorities are heard and considered. It also helps you see the full range of visions and objectives within the team.

  How to implement: Have each team member write down their top goals for the business or project, focusing on where they see the team or company in the future (e.g., 5-10 years). This exercise should allow for independent thinking without immediate influence from other team members.

- **Common ground**: Once the individual goals are gathered, identify their commonalities. This is where alignment begins. Look for patterns, shared themes, or mutual priorities that resonate with multiple team members.

  How to implement: Compile the goals and facilitate a discussion among the team to highlight which ideas overlap or are shared by multiple members. Create a list of these common goals to serve as the foundation of the shared vision. I suggest using a Venn Diagram to find similarities in leadership vision:

The result: The final output is a shared vision that is both inclusive and strategic. It unites the team around a common purpose while respecting individual perspectives. A shared vision clarifies the organization's direction and helps align efforts, resources, and strategies toward achieving that future state.

* * *

Implementing the Shared Vision Formula

Let's say you're working with a marketing team to develop a shared vision for the next five years. The first step? Get everyone's ideas on the table. I'd ask each team member to submit their top goals for the department over the next few years. Naturally, you'll get a variety of responses. One person might prioritize expanding the company's social media presence, another might focus on improving customer acquisition, and yet another might want to invest in brand partnerships. At this stage, the ideas can seem all over the place, but that's okay—this is where the magic happens.

Once I've gathered all the goals, the next step is to analyze them and find common ground. You might notice a theme emerging, like several team members focusing on improving brand visibility. Some see social media as the best route, others lean toward brand partnerships, but at the core, everyone's aiming for the same thing: making sure more people know about and engage with the company. That shared focus on "brand visibility" becomes a central element of the shared vision.

From there, it's all about communicating this common goal back to the team and using it as the cornerstone of the strategic vision. This is the part where you might need to pull the group together to clarify how social media efforts and partnerships will complement each other in achieving brand visibility. It's critical to ensure everyone understands their role in making this vision a reality. After all, if someone's rowing a boat in the wrong direction, you're still going in circles. Let's get everyone rowing in sync!

The key here is not just to create the shared vision, but to show the team how their contributions fit into the bigger picture. Whether it's through social media campaigns, customer acquisition, or partnerships, each team member needs to feel like their work directly impacts the collective goal. When people see how their efforts contribute to the larger vision, engagement skyrockets—and that's where the real momentum comes from. Plus, it's a lot easier to work toward a goal when everyone's on the same page and not pulling in different directions.

***

Applying the Shared Vision Formula

Now that we've covered how to implement the shared vision formula, the next step is learning how to apply it effectively in day-to-day operations. After all, it's one thing to create a shared vision, but it's another to make sure it doesn't gather dust in a slide deck somewhere. The real challenge is turning that vision into action.

The beauty of a shared vision is that it serves as your team's North Star. Every decision, strategy, and task should point toward that direction. The key to applying the shared vision is keeping it front and center in everything you do. Whether you're developing a marketing campaign, setting quarterly goals, or just planning the weekly team meeting, you should always ask yourself and your team: *How does this align with our shared vision?* If it doesn't, you may be steering off course.

Here's a simple way to apply it:

CREATING A SHARED VISION

1. **Start with individual contributions**: Gather input from each team member. Ensure everyone's ideas matter and will be factored into the final vision.

2. **Identify and focus on common goals**: Look for shared themes and ideas that multiple people are passionate about. These elements will form the basis of your shared vision.

3. **Engage in open communication**: Share the common goals with the team and ensure everyone is aligned on the key objectives. Continue to communicate and adjust the vision as needed.

4. **Reinforce the shared vision**: Embed it into team meetings, decision-making processes, and long-term strategies to keep it in mind. Regularly revisit and refine the vision to keep it relevant and aligned with any changes in the organization or market.

This process enables you to incorporate all perspectives, narrow the focus to a unified direction, and establish a foundation of clarity and collaboration. It is adaptable to teams of any size and applicable across departments, ensuring that everyone is aligned and working toward the same future.

***

The Benefit of Having a Shared Vision

Having a shared vision is like giving your team a North Star—something to guide them, keep them on track, and ultimately lead to long-term success. From my experience, when a team is working with a clear, well-defined vision, everything runs smoother. They're not just more productive; they're more motivated, and they collaborate better. A strong shared vision brings three key benefits: clarity, alignment, and motivation.

The first benefit is *clarity*. When everyone knows what the goal is, it clears up confusion and minimizes misunderstandings. Each team member understands how their specific role fits into the broader strategy. This clarity streamlines decision-making and helps everyone stay focused on what really matters, avoiding wasted time on distractions that don't contribute to the ultimate objective.

Next is *alignment*. Without a shared vision, teams can end up working on their own priorities, sometimes unintentionally pulling in different directions. A shared vision brings everyone together under the same mission. It ensures that all efforts are aligned, boosting collaboration and minimizing friction. When everyone is rowing in the same direction, the boat moves a lot faster—and no one's left wondering why their paddle isn't making a difference.

Finally, the secret ingredient is *motivation*. When people see how their work contributes to something bigger and meaningful, they naturally become more engaged and driven. A shared vision provides purpose. It gives team members a reason to push a little harder and get creative when solving problems. It's also a huge source of resilience. When challenges arise—and they always do—the shared vision serves as a reminder of why the hard work is worth it, keeping the team inspired to push through the tough times.

In short, a shared vision is the glue that holds a team together. It provides clarity about what needs to be done, aligns efforts across the organization, and keeps everyone motivated and invested in the bigger picture. When a team has this kind of unity and purpose, they're practically unstoppable.

***

Uniting Teams & Building a Collaborative Culture

Building a collaborative culture is a lot like planting a garden—it requires time, care, and just the right conditions to help it grow. When a team collaborates effectively, it can accomplish far more than even the most talented individuals working in isolation. From my experience, fostering collaboration not only boosts productivity but also sparks innovation and strengthens team relationships. And let's be honest, who wouldn't want a team where the whole is greater than the sum of its parts?

The first step to creating this culture is straightforward: establish an environment where open communication thrives. Communication is the lifeblood of teamwork. Without it, people retreat into silos and lose sight of the bigger picture. I make sure there are regular opportunities for dialogue—whether it's through team meetings, project debriefs, or even informal chats over coffee. When people feel heard and valued, collaboration becomes a natural part of the workflow.

But let's be clear—collaboration doesn't happen by accident. It's built on trust, and trust takes effort. Teams that trust each other are more willing to share ideas, give constructive feedback, and take risks. As a leader, I've found that setting an example of transparency and vulnerability helps build that trust. People need to see that collaboration isn't just about divvying up tasks; it's about working together to find the best solutions. And yes, sometimes that means admitting when you don't have all the answers. (Which, I can assure you, happens more often than you'd think!)

One of the simplest ways to unite a team is by rallying them around a common goal. When everyone knows they're working toward the same outcome, collaboration becomes second nature. I make a point of clarifying the team's vision and goals, ensuring each person understands how their work contributes to the big picture. It's like giving everyone a map with the destination clearly marked—much easier to get there when we're all heading in the same direction.

Breaking down barriers between departments is another essential step in building a collaborative culture. Silos can stifle creativity and slow progress, and nothing kills innovation faster than a team working in isolation. I encourage cross-functional projects, bringing fresh perspectives and new ideas to the table. In my experience, working on joint initiatives can break those silos and build stronger relationships across teams. Plus, there's something energizing about seeing how another department approaches a challenge—it's like looking at a problem with new eyes.

Creating a space where everyone feels safe to contribute is crucial for true collaboration to flourish. When team members know they can share ideas, ask questions, and make mistakes without fear of judgment, that's when the real magic happens. I make it clear that every voice matters, and I work hard to ensure all team members feel comfortable speaking up. After all, it's not collaboration if only the loudest voices in the room get heard.

And let's not forget the importance of recognizing and celebrating collaboration. Whether it's through a formal recognition program or just a quick shout-out in a meeting, acknowledging team efforts can make a big difference. People are much more likely to continue working together when they know their collaborative efforts are seen and appreciated. (Besides, who doesn't like a little pat on the back now and then?)

Finally, collaboration requires flexibility. Not every project or team needs the same level of collaboration, and sometimes too much can actually slow things down. Knowing when to collaborate and when to let individuals work independently is essential. I've learned that teams appreciate leaders who can strike the right balance—creating the conditions for collaboration without forcing it where it's not needed.

In the end, building a collaborative culture comes down to fostering trust, encouraging open communication, and creating a safe space for teamwork to thrive. By recognizing the value of collaboration and knowing when to nurture it, leaders can create a culture where collaboration isn't just an ideal—it's the way things get done.

* * *

An Evolving Vision

A shared vision is not a static concept—it should evolve as the company grows and the market shifts. In my experience, a vision that remains unchanged for too long can become outdated and lose its relevance. As businesses reach new milestones or encounter fresh challenges, it's often necessary to adjust the vision to ensure it continues to inspire and guide the organization.

What's important is that the vision remains clear and compelling, no matter how it evolves. It should always provide direction, keeping the team aligned and focused on the future. Regularly revisiting and refining the vision allows a company to stay adaptable, responsive to changes, and better prepared for whatever comes next.

Companies that make a habit of reassessing their vision are often more flexible and better equipped to navigate market shifts. By keeping the vision at the forefront, leaders can ensure the organization stays cohesive, even in the face of uncertainty. This flexibility isn't just a benefit—it's crucial for staying competitive and driving long-term success.

***

Communicating to Inspire

Inspiring others through communication is one of the most important skills a leader can have. It's not just about having a great vision—it's about getting your team excited and fully on board. Over the years, I've learned that simply presenting information isn't enough; you have to make a real connection and show people why your vision matters. When done right, communication can transform a group of individuals into a motivated, unified team all heading in the same direction.

The first key to inspiring communication is *clarity*. If your message is buried in jargon or too many details, it's like trying to navigate through a fog—nobody's going to see the destination. I've found it's crucial to boil things down to the essentials: What's the big picture, and what are the key steps to get there? Make sure your team not only understands the *what* but also the *why*—why this vision is important, how it benefits the team, and how it drives the organization forward. Trust me, if you're getting nods but not questions, it might be time to simplify.

Another major part of inspiring communication is connecting your vision to the team's values. People are far more likely to get behind an idea when they feel personally invested. So when I present a new direction, I always consider what the team values most. If innovation is their driving force, I emphasize how the vision will fuel creativity. If they thrive on collaboration, I focus on how this plan will strengthen teamwork. It's not just about selling the idea—it's about aligning it with what matters most to them.

And of course, *storytelling*. Facts and figures are great, but stories? They resonate on a much deeper level. When I need to make a vision feel real, I use stories—whether personal experiences or examples from other companies. Stories make abstract ideas tangible and relatable. After all, who doesn't love a good story? Especially if it involves an underdog triumph or a clever solution. Just make sure your story's point isn't lost in translation, or else you'll get more confused stares than enthusiasm!

Now, let's be real—not everyone's going to jump on board right away, and that's okay. Skepticism is part of the process. Instead of bulldozing over concerns, I invite open dialogue. I ask for feedback, listen carefully, and build trust through these conversations. Oftentimes, the feedback leads to an even better version of the vision. When people feel heard, they're much more likely to support the plan—especially when they've contributed to shaping it.

One trick I've found helpful is involving the team early on. I don't just unveil a vision; I bring people into the process. Whether it's brainstorming sessions or workshops, the more ownership people feel, the more committed they become. Suddenly, it's *our* plan, not just *my* idea, and that makes all the difference.

Small wins are another great motivator. When you're working toward a long-term goal, celebrating the early successes keeps the momentum going. Acknowledge progress, even the small stuff—it builds confidence and shows that the plan is moving in the right direction. Plus, who doesn't love an excuse for a quick team celebration? (Pro tip: bring snacks.)

Don't forget about *transparency*. Teams appreciate honesty, especially when it comes to the challenges ahead. If there are roadblocks or tough decisions to be made, I make sure to communicate them upfront. Being transparent about the hurdles not only builds trust but also strengthens the team's resolve to push through together.

And finally—*enthusiasm*. If you're not excited about the vision, why should anyone else be? I've found that enthusiasm is contagious. If you show you're genuinely passionate about the direction the team is heading, that energy spreads. People are far more likely to get behind a vision when they see their leader is all-in, committed, and, yes, excited to take on the challenge.

* * *

Keeping Your Vision Alive

Creating a strong company vision is essential, but the real challenge comes with keeping that vision alive over the long haul, especially when you're looking at strategic plans that stretch over years—or even decades. It's easy to kick things off with enthusiasm, but as time passes, the excitement can fade, and the vision can start to feel like something distant, sitting on a shelf. So, how do you keep it alive and ensure your team stays motivated and aligned with those long-term goals?

First, you have to revisit and reaffirm the vision regularly. A vision isn't something you introduce at the beginning of the year and then forget about until the next annual meeting. It needs to be a living guide that's embedded in your day-to-day operations. I make a point of having regular check-ins—quarterly or semi-annually—to keep the vision front and center. These check-ins aren't just about going over numbers; they're about showing the team how their work fits into the broader strategy. It's a moment to reflect, adjust, and celebrate progress. And yes, it's also a good time to remind everyone, "Hey, remember that exciting vision we all agreed on?"

Speaking of progress, breaking the vision into smaller, manageable milestones is key to keeping momentum alive. A long-term vision can feel overwhelming, so setting mini-goals along the way gives the team a sense of accomplishment. Every time we hit one of these milestones, I make sure we pause to celebrate, whether it's with a formal recognition or just a simple team shout-out. These small wins reinforce the idea that we're moving forward—even if the final destination is still a ways off. Plus, who doesn't love a good reason to celebrate? Progress should never go unnoticed.

Another important factor is *flexibility*. As the business landscape shifts, so too should your vision. Now, that doesn't mean you throw out everything you've built, but you have to be open to refining it. Successful companies are the ones that tweak their vision to stay relevant, adapting to new opportunities and challenges without losing sight of the core goals. It's like keeping a sailboat on course—sometimes you need to adjust the sails when the wind changes, but the destination remains the same.

One of the best ways to keep the vision alive is to involve everyone in the process. When people feel a sense of ownership over the vision, they're far more invested in making it a reality. I always seek input from the team and help them see how their individual roles contribute to the bigger picture. It's not just *my* vision—it's *our* vision. This sense of connection makes the vision feel personal and relevant to each person, keeping it meaningful across the organization.

Finally, the most effective way to keep a vision alive is to embed it into your company's culture. The vision should be reflected in how people talk, think, and work every single day. This is where regular communication, storytelling, and recognition come into play. When the vision becomes ingrained in the culture, you don't have to constantly remind people of it—it's just part of how things get done. I've seen the difference it makes when the vision is not just a statement on the wall but an active part of the company's DNA. It stops being a concept and becomes second nature.

So, if you want to keep your vision alive, keep it flexible, celebrate the small wins, and make it part of everything you do. When you do that, the vision doesn't just survive—it thrives. And in case you need a little extra motivation: remember, a living vision is a lot easier to manage than dusting off that strategic plan every few years and wondering what happened!

9

Building a Community

Building a strong community in the workplace is one of the most rewarding ways to turn an ordinary office into a vibrant, positive, and productive space. When people feel genuinely connected to each other, work becomes more than just a place to clock in and out—it transforms into a hub where trust, support, and collaboration thrive. A strong workplace community doesn't just boost team morale; it creates deeper engagement and a shared commitment to common goals, driving long-term success.

At the heart of any great workplace community are the social connections between team members. These relationships go beyond task lists and project deadlines. They're built through shared experiences, meaningful interactions, and mutual respect. But, let's be honest—these connections don't just magically happen. They take effort and a bit of intention. Whether it's grabbing lunch together, checking in on a colleague's day, or organizing the occasional team-building activity, these little interactions are the glue that holds a team together. And yes, even those awkward icebreaker games can serve a purpose. I mean, who doesn't love sharing *two truths and a lie* over coffee, right?

The real foundation of any workplace community, however, boils down to communication. Without open, honest, and regular conversations, even the most talented teams can end up feeling disconnected. For a true sense of community to thrive, everyone needs to feel comfortable sharing ideas, asking questions, and offering feedback. This is where leadership plays a huge role—setting the tone and creating an environment where communication flows freely. Whether through team meetings, informal catch-ups, or just keeping an open-door policy, communication is key. Prioritizing this helps build trust, encourages collaboration, and makes everyone feel like they're part of something bigger than just their job description.

In this chapter, we'll dive into the essential ingredients of building a workplace community. We'll talk about fostering those all-important social connections and highlight just how critical communication is to the process. By creating a true sense of belonging, you can transform your workplace into a community where every team member feels valued, engaged, and ready to bring their best. And let's be real—when work feels like a community, it's just a lot more fun!

There are several examples of companies that have successfully built an internal culture of inclusion and community, but one sticks out for me: Zappos. You've probably heard of them, the online shoe retailer that became famous not just for selling shoes but for their over-the-top customer service and unique workplace culture. But here's the fun part—they didn't just stumble into success by focusing on customers alone. Zappos intentionally built a sense of community within their team, which helped grow their business into the powerhouse it is today.

From the very beginning, Zappos and its founder and CEO, Tony Hsieh, made a conscious decision to prioritize their employees as much as their customers. They believed that happy employees would lead to happy customers, and they were right. But they didn't just stop at the basic perks or office parties—they created a true sense of community that made people excited to come to work.

One way Mr. Hsieh did this was by fostering deep social connections. The company built an environment where team members were encouraged to get to know each other beyond their job titles. Zappos' office wasn't a sea of cubicles with people minding their business. It was an open, vibrant space filled with personality—think-themed workstations, friendly chats in the hallways, and regular team events that brought everyone together. They even had a "Culture Team" whose sole job was to create opportunities for employees to bond and have fun. Team-building wasn't something that happened once a year at a retreat—it was a daily occurrence.

This wasn't just about making the office more fun, though. Tony Hsieh knew that these social connections were crucial to motivating their team. Despite his $840 million net worth, Tony would still spend his evenings gathered around a campfire, connecting with neighbors in his mobile home park. When people feel like they're part of something bigger, that they belong, they work harder and are more likely to stick around. It's hard to be motivated when you feel like just another cog in the machine, but Zappos flipped that script. Employees felt seen, heard, and valued—and as a result, they were deeply invested in the company's success.

The company also went all-in on communication. They had an open-door policy, not just in theory but in practice. Leaders were always available to listen to employees' concerns and ideas and even just chat about life. Team meetings weren't dry, checkbox activities—they were lively, inclusive, and encouraged participation from everyone. And here's the kicker: Zappos didn't just communicate top-down. They made sure communication flowed in all directions. Employees were empowered to speak up, share ideas, and collaborate across departments. This created a strong sense of ownership and commitment to the company's goals.

As Zappos grew, this sense of community didn't wane—it strengthened. Instead of letting rapid growth turn them into a faceless corporation, they doubled down on their culture. Even during periods of intense business scaling, they made it a priority to keep that feeling of connection alive. This wasn't just good for employee morale; it was good for business. Motivated employees delivered exceptional customer service, which in turn helped Zappos build its reputation for going above and beyond for customers.

The result? Zappos didn't just grow—they thrived. Their focus on building a community in the workplace turned them into a company where people wanted to work, and customers loved to shop. It's no coincidence that they went from being a small startup to being acquired by Amazon for over a billion dollars. And through it all, the sense of belonging and community they built remained at the core of their success.

So, the next time you think about how to grow a business, remember: it's not just about strategy or product. It's about the people. When you build a community where people feel connected, motivated, and part of something meaningful, amazing things can happen. Just ask Zappos.

**

A Memorial Dedication to Tony Hsieh

Tony Hsieh
1973 - 2020

In memory of Tony Hsieh, a visionary leader whose passion for innovation and community transformed the world of business. As the CEO of Zappos, Tony didn't just build an eCommerce empire—he built a culture of kindness, creativity, and connection that redefined what it means to be successful in business. His revolutionary approach, which put people at the heart of everything, inspired countless entrepreneurs and leaders to think differently about leadership, happiness, and the workplace.

Tony's legacy goes far beyond the company he grew; it lives in the countless lives he touched through his generosity, ideas, and relentless pursuit of building meaningful relationships. He believed in creating spaces where employees could thrive, where happiness was a measure of success, and where work felt like more than just a job—it felt like a community.

His tragic passing on November 27, 2020, in a Connecticut house fire, left a void in the hearts of those who knew him, but his legacy will endure. Tony was more than a business leader; he was a pioneer who believed in the power of human potential and the strength of community. The vision he shared with the world continues to inspire and shape future generations of innovators.

We remember Tony not just for his brilliance as an eCommerce trailblazer but for his kindness, his curiosity, and his deep commitment to making the world a better place, one pair of shoes at a time. His spirit will forever live on through the values he championed and the people he inspired.

Thank you, Tony, for showing us what's possible when you lead with heart.

* * *

The Foundation of Trust

Creating a foundation of trust in the workplace is like building the engine that keeps everything running smoothly. Without it, even the most talented teams can veer off course—communication stalls, collaboration sputters, and everything just feels... stuck. But when trust is solid, it's the glue that holds everyone together, making teamwork easier, conversations more open, and productivity higher. As a leader, building trust isn't just a "nice-to-have"—it's essential for long-term success. But here's the tricky part: trust takes time to build, yet it can be shattered in the blink of an eye if you're not careful.

As a leader, your team looks to you for guidance, support, and decision-making. When employees genuinely trust their leaders, they're more engaged, motivated, and committed to reaching those big company goals. Trust gives people the confidence to take risks, share ideas, and collaborate without fear of judgment. But the flip side? If trust is broken, it breeds suspicion, disengagement, and hesitation. And once that happens, rebuilding trust can feel like climbing a mountain.

So, how can leaders build trust within their teams? First, you've got to walk the walk. Trust isn't handed out—it's earned, and it starts with leading by example. That means being consistent, transparent, and fair. Your team is always watching how you handle tough situations. If you stay steady, make smart decisions, and treat everyone respectfully, you're laying the foundation for trust. But if you're inconsistent, secretive, or play favorites, you'll see trust disappear faster than you can schedule the next "emergency meeting."

Next, communication is your best friend when it comes to building trust. Keep your team in the loop—about both the good stuff *and* the challenges. When employees feel informed, they're much more likely to trust leadership, even when times are tough. Regular, honest communication not only keeps everyone on the same page but also makes your team feel secure in their roles and connected to the bigger picture. Plus, when people see that transparency is valued, they're more likely to speak up without fear of judgment. That kind of open communication is the backbone of trust.

Then there's listening—what I like to call the secret weapon of leadership. If you want to gain the trust of your team, you've got to show them that what they say matters. This means creating a space where people feel comfortable speaking up, knowing they won't be judged or dismissed. When leaders take the time to actively listen and respond to feedback, employees feel heard, respected, and valued. And guess what? That's when trust starts to grow.

Let's talk about consistency—because trust isn't built in a day. It takes time and repeated actions to show your team you're reliable. When you follow through on your promises, make fair decisions, and treat everyone consistently, you're laying down the bricks of trust, one action at a time. Inconsistency, on the other hand, is like hitting the trust brakes. People get confused and uncertain, and before you know it, trust is out the window.

Fairness is another major piece of the trust puzzle. When your team believes you'll treat everyone fairly—regardless of rank, seniority, or personal relationships—they'll trust your judgment. But if they see favoritism or double standards, that's when things start to fall apart. Fairness doesn't mean treating everyone the same; it means applying the same principles to everyone. When you're transparent about your decision-making and show that fairness guides you, trust naturally follows.

Here's a fun one: empowerment. When you delegate responsibility and allow your team to make decisions, you're sending a clear message: "I trust you." And when people feel trusted, they're more likely to trust you back. It's like a trust boomerang! Empowerment also gives employees a sense of ownership and accountability, which only strengthens trust. Just be sure to give them the tools and support they need—nobody likes being set up to fail.

But here's the kicker: while trust takes time to build, it can be broken in an instant. One broken promise, one act of dishonesty, or one lapse in transparency can undo years of trust-building. And when trust breaks, things get messy. Employees start holding back ideas, avoiding risks, and feeling disengaged. Keeping trust alive requires daily effort. As a leader, you've got to be intentional about maintaining it because even the small stuff counts.

Take Patagonia as an example. This outdoor clothing company built its entire business on trust. Founder Yvon Chouinard created a culture where employees manage their own time and are encouraged to take paid time off to get outside and enjoy nature. This trust has led to high employee loyalty and low turnover. Externally, Patagonia's transparency about its environmental impact has earned its customer trust as well. By staying true to their values and being open about their efforts, Patagonia has built a loyal following that trusts them to do the right thing. It's a great example of how trust isn't just a feel-good value—it's a serious competitive advantage.

Building trust takes consistent effort, but it's worth every bit. When leaders lead with integrity, communicate openly, listen to their team, and treat everyone fairly, they create a culture of trust that benefits the entire organization. Trust is the foundation for collaboration, innovation, and engagement. When it's there, teams thrive, and the whole company wins.

So, let's keep building that engine of trust—because when it's running smoothly, everything else falls into place. And remember, trust isn't built in a day, but it can be shattered in a minute. Keep the transparency high and the favorites low, and you'll have a team that's ready to tackle anything.

* * *

Shared Value, Shared Purpose: Finding Common Goals

In the last chapter, we talked about creating a shared vision—a big, bold picture of where your team or company is heading. But let's be honest: even the most inspiring vision falls flat if your team isn't all rowing in the same direction. So how do you get everyone on the same page, moving forward together? That's what we're diving into now—*aligning your team around common goals.*

First off, alignment doesn't mean everyone's doing the same thing as robots—it's about making sure everyone's efforts contribute to the shared mission. Think of it like a band: each musician has their part to play, but they've got to come together to create one epic jam. The key is ensuring that everyone knows how their role supports the big picture and—this part is crucial—that they're excited to be part of it.

To get started, you've got to set clear, specific goals. If your goals are vague or too high-level, even the most well-meaning team members can end up pulling in different directions. Instead, break the goals down into bite-sized, actionable steps. The more clarity you provide, the easier it is for each person to see how their work fits into the larger puzzle—and let's be honest, we all love it when the pieces of a puzzle click together perfectly.

Next up: communication. And no, I don't mean sending out a monthly "everything is fine" email blast. I'm talking about real, consistent, open communication, where everyone feels comfortable asking questions, tossing around ideas, and raising challenges without fear of judgment. Regular check-ins are your secret weapon here. Use them to review progress, address roadblocks, and, of course, celebrate wins. These touchpoints keep everyone aligned and ensure that if someone starts veering off course, you can steer them back early before things go sideways.

Another big factor in getting your team aligned is creating a sense of *shared ownership*. When people feel like they've got skin in the game, they're much more likely to stay engaged and focused. One of the best ways to achieve this? Involve your team in setting the goals. Ask for their input. What do they think the priorities should be? How do they see their work contributing to the bigger picture? When the team has a hand in shaping the plan, they'll be far more invested in making sure it succeeds.

Let's not forget about collaboration. Encouraging cross-functional teams to work together is a fantastic way to ensure alignment. Fresh perspectives lead to more creative problem-solving, and it reminds everyone they're working toward a common goal. It's like one big "we're all in this together" moment, boosting team spirit and motivation.

Here's a curveball—*storytelling*. Yep, you heard me. Storytelling is a sneaky-good way to align your team. People connect with stories on a personal level. Share examples of past projects where everyone was on the same page and knocked it out of the park, or tell a story about how someone's work directly impacted the company's success. Stories help people connect the dots between their daily tasks and the larger goal, making everything feel more meaningful.

Recognition is another powerful tool in your alignment toolbox. When you celebrate work that aligns with your team's goals, you reinforce the behaviors you want to see more of. Whether it's a shout-out in a meeting, a team-wide email, or a formal recognition program, acknowledging achievements boosts morale and keeps everyone focused on the ultimate prize.

Now, let's talk flexibility—because even alignment needs a little room to breathe. Things change. Maybe a new opportunity pops up, or perhaps there's an unexpected roadblock. When that happens, you need to adjust the plan, re-align, and make sure everyone's on board with the new direction. Think of it like adjusting the sails when the wind shifts. You don't abandon the ship, you just tweak the course to keep moving forward.

Finally, make sure alignment is fun. Teams that enjoy working together naturally align better. Whether it's through team-building activities, friendly competitions, or just sharing some laughs during meetings, creating a positive environment makes it easier for everyone to stay connected to the goal and to each other.

At the end of the day, aligning your team is all about shared purpose, open communication, and making sure everyone feels like they're part of something bigger. When that happens, alignment doesn't feel forced—it just flows. And when alignment flows, so does success.

* * *

Celebrating Wins Together

There's nothing quite like the energy in a room when a team wins together. It's that electric feeling when a project wraps up successfully, a milestone is hit, or a tough goal is finally conquered. The joy, the high-fives, the collective sigh of relief—it's a moment worth savoring. But celebrating team wins goes beyond just the fun. It's a powerful way to boost morale, reinforce positive behaviors, and motivate everyone for the next challenge.

Now, let me tell you, celebrating success isn't just about ordering a pizza or firing off a congratulatory email (although, let's be honest, who doesn't love pizza?). While those gestures are great, meaningful celebration goes deeper. It's about acknowledging the hard work, dedication, and teamwork that made the success possible. When leaders take the time to celebrate in a thoughtful way, they send a clear message to the team: *I see your effort, I recognize what you've accomplished, and it matters.*

So, how can leaders celebrate in a way that truly resonates with the team? Well, first off, it's about personalization. Not everyone is a fan of public praise or big celebrations. Some people prefer a quiet "thank you," while others might love being in the spotlight. As a leader, knowing your team well enough to tailor celebrations to their preferences is key. Whether it's a shout-out in a meeting, a handwritten note, or even a small, thoughtful gift that shows you've been paying attention, the way you recognize success matters.

Another great approach is to make it a collective celebration. It's one thing to say, "Great job, everyone!" but it's something else entirely to gather the team, reflect on what worked, and celebrate together. I've seen teams hold mini-celebrations at the end of a project, where they do a quick retrospective, highlight key contributions, and then break out the cake (or cupcakes, if you're feeling fancy). It's simple, but it's a great way to let everyone share in the moment.

Here's where you can have some fun: sometimes, the celebration itself can be unexpected and memorable. I once knew a team leader who, after a particularly grueling project, surprised the team with an ice cream truck. Another leader gave their team a half-day off after pulling off a major win. These moments stick with people because they're not just about success— they create memories and build camaraderie. It's the kind of thing people remember and talk about long after the project is over.

But what about when things don't go according to plan? Should you still celebrate? Absolutely. When a team falls short of a goal, it's tempting to skip the celebration, but that's when recognition is most important. Celebrating the effort, even when the outcome isn't perfect, reminds the team that growth happens in the process, not just in the results. It's a way of saying, *We gave it our best, and we're learning from this.*

This is where leaders can really shine. Instead of brushing off failures, take the opportunity to highlight what went right. Did the team try something new? Did they take a calculated risk that could pay off in the future? Even when the outcome isn't what you hoped for, there's always something to celebrate—the lessons learned, the bold attempts, or the fact that the team pushed their boundaries.

One of my favorite approaches is embracing what I call the "Fail Forward" moment. Some companies even host "failure parties," where the team gathers to acknowledge what didn't go well, what they learned, and how they'll apply those lessons moving forward. It turns what could be a negative experience into something constructive and forward-looking. Plus, it shows that failure isn't the end of the road—it's a stepping stone to future success.

Now, why does all this celebrating matter? Recognizing success doesn't just make people feel good at the moment—it builds a culture of appreciation. It tells the team that their hard work is seen, valued, and important. This kind of positive reinforcement encourages people to keep striving for more. It creates an environment where people want to go the extra mile because they know their efforts will be recognized, even if things don't always go perfectly.

Celebrating wins also helps sustain momentum. After hitting a big goal, it's easy for teams to experience a bit of a lull. But by taking time to acknowledge the hard work, you give everyone a boost and remind them of the progress they've made, getting them excited for the next challenge.

And finally, celebrating together builds stronger bonds. When you share in each other's successes, you're not just coworkers—you become a team that's truly in it together. That sense of unity can be a game changer. When a team feels connected, they work harder for each other, trust each other more, and are more resilient when facing the next hurdle.

So, whether it's a well-earned pizza party, an unexpected surprise, or a moment of reflection after a failure, celebrating wins together isn't just a nice-to-have—it's essential. It keeps the energy up, strengthens the team, and sets the stage for even greater achievements ahead. And hey, who doesn't love an excuse for cake?

***

Embracing Diversity on Your Team

As a member of the LGBTQ+ community, I know firsthand how powerful it is to feel truly seen and valued in the workplace. Celebrating diversity isn't just about doing the "right thing"—it's essential to building a strong, inclusive, and thriving team. To me, diversity is like being invited to a party, but inclusion is when someone grabs your hand and pulls you onto the dance floor. It's one thing to have different voices in the room, but it's another to ensure those voices are heard, respected, and fully included in decision-making and team dynamics.

Let's break it down: diversity is about representation. It means ensuring people from different backgrounds, cultures, identities, and experiences are part of the team. But simply having diversity doesn't guarantee inclusion. Inclusion is about the experience those diverse individuals have once they're in the room. Are their ideas valued? Do they feel comfortable sharing their perspectives? Are their contributions respected? Inclusion is the active process of making sure everyone feels like they belong and can fully participate.

Why is it crucial to have both diversity and inclusion in the workplace? Because diversity without inclusion leads to disengagement. You can hire a wide range of people with different experiences, but if they don't feel welcomed, involved, or respected, you're not going to reap the full benefits of that diversity. The result? Those team members may feel like outsiders, and that sense of exclusion can hurt morale, creativity, and collaboration. On the flip side, when you actively foster inclusion, people feel valued for who they are and are more likely to bring their authentic selves to work. That not only builds a sense of community but also fuels innovation and engagement.

Embracing diversity and inclusion isn't just a "nice to have"—it's a business imperative. Studies show that teams with diverse perspectives solve problems faster and develop more creative solutions. It's no surprise: when you bring different life experiences and viewpoints to the table, you expand the range of ideas and approaches. But here's the kicker—without inclusion, those diverse perspectives won't surface. People need to feel safe to speak up, challenge the status quo, and offer new ideas. That's where inclusion plays a key role, and we need both diversity *and* inclusion to thrive.

Now, as leaders, we sometimes face a tough reality: not everyone may be on board with celebrating diversity or valuing inclusion. Some team members might not believe in the importance of diversity due to personal, religious, or cultural beliefs. This can be one of the most challenging parts of leadership. How do you lead a team where not everyone agrees on the value of diversity or sees its relevance?

The first step is understanding that diversity of thought also includes respecting differences in opinions and belief systems. But as a leader, it's critical to establish that while individuals are entitled to their beliefs, the workplace must be a space where all team members are respected and treated equitably. This means making it clear that discriminatory attitudes or behaviors will not be tolerated, even if they stem from personal or religious beliefs.

It's about setting a standard for the team. I've had to navigate these situations before, and while it's never easy, it starts with open, honest conversations. I've found it helpful to frame these discussions around the company's values rather than making them personal. Remind the team that diversity and inclusion are core to the organization's success. It's not about asking anyone to change their beliefs but about ensuring that everyone on the team feels respected and valued.

For those who may be resistant to embracing diversity, education and support are key. Sometimes resistance comes from a lack of understanding. Hosting diversity and inclusion training can open people's eyes to the experiences of others and help foster empathy. It's about creating opportunities for learning and growth—helping those who may not yet see the value of diversity understand how it positively impacts both the team and the business.

As leaders, we have to balance respecting individual beliefs with ensuring that the workplace is one where everyone can thrive. If someone refuses to create an inclusive environment, it's essential to address that behavior directly but constructively. There's a difference between not fully understanding or embracing diversity and actively creating a hostile or unwelcoming environment. The latter cannot be tolerated, and it's the responsibility of leadership to make that clear.

Ultimately, building a sense of community on your team requires both diversity and inclusion. It's about more than hiring people from different backgrounds—it's about creating an environment where those differences are celebrated, where people feel they belong, and where everyone has a seat at the table and a voice in the conversation. I've been on many diverse teams, and I've seen firsthand how powerful it can be when people are embraced for who they are. That sense of belonging builds a foundation of trust, collaboration, and shared purpose that can transform a team.

To foster that environment, leaders must be intentional in their efforts, willing to have difficult conversations, and committed to creating a culture where everyone feels valued. When we embrace diversity and prioritize inclusion, we create workplaces where people aren't just invited to the party—they're fully part of the celebration. And that's where real community is built.

So, let's be leaders who actively pull everyone onto the dance floor and make sure every voice is heard. The more we do, the more we'll see that diversity and inclusion aren't just feel-good principles—they're the driving forces behind innovation, engagement, and lasting success.

***

Turning Silos Into Energy

Let's talk about the importance of breaking down workplace silos. No, not the ones you see on farms storing grain—I'm talking about the kind we find in the office. In a company, a "silo" happens when departments or teams work in isolation, cut off from the rest of the organization. Each department does its own thing, with little communication between teams. While that might sound harmless, trust me, from experience, I can tell you that silos can wreak havoc not just on a single department, but on the entire organization.

I had a front-row seat to a classic silo disaster while consulting for an eCommerce startup. The company was fresh, exciting, and full of potential, but one thing was holding it back: its departments were completely siloed. Marketing didn't talk to Product Development, Customer Service wasn't communicating with Operations, and Finance seemed to be operating on a different planet altogether. I'd never seen anything like it. The lack of communication was staggering, and it was dragging the entire company down. Decisions were being made in isolation, and nobody had any clue what the other teams were doing. It wasn't just frustrating—it was leading the company straight into the ground.

The leadership team couldn't figure out why things weren't working. Sales were flat, customers were frustrated, and deadlines were being missed left and right. They were doing everything they thought they should be doing, but nothing was clicking. It became clear to me that the issue wasn't a lack of talent or drive—the issue was the silos. The departments were so disconnected they might as well have been working for different companies.

Priority number one became breaking down those silos. The first thing I did was bring everyone to the table—literally. We held a series of cross-department meetings, but instead of diving right into tasks or projects, we started by simply having each department explain what they did and how their work fit into the bigger picture. I wanted everyone to see that, despite being in different departments, they were all working toward the same overall goals. Once people saw that collaboration wasn't just a nice idea but a necessity for survival, things started to click. A lightbulb went off for many of them, and they realized how much more effective they could be by working together.

Next, we established clear channels for communication between departments. Previously, they had been using different tools and platforms for everything, which made it nearly impossible to share information. I helped streamline their communication tools, putting everyone on the same platform. We introduced project management software that allowed teams to see what others were working on in real-time. That transparency made a world of difference—suddenly, departments could track progress, share updates, and, most importantly, communicate easily.

But it wasn't just about technology. Leadership had to step up as well. I worked with the company's leaders to shift their mindset from managing individual departments to thinking holistically about the company's success. We started holding regular cross-functional leadership meetings, where department heads were encouraged to collaborate on strategies and share insights. Leaders began to understand that working in silos wasn't just inefficient—it was actively counterproductive. When they started working together, they created synergy, and that energy began to ripple through the entire company.

So, why is it so important to break down silos and promote collaboration across departments? For starters, it keeps everyone aligned. When departments don't communicate, they often end up working at cross-purposes. One team might be pushing a product feature that another department isn't prepared to support. This leads to delays, frustration, and wasted effort. However, when teams collaborate, they can align their goals, work toward common objectives, and share resources more efficiently.

Collaboration across departments also fosters a sense of community. When people from different parts of the company work together, they build relationships and trust. They begin to see themselves as part of something bigger than their department. This sense of community drives engagement and loyalty because employees feel connected to the larger mission. It's no longer "Marketing vs. Product Development" or "Operations vs.

Finance"—it's one unified team working together.

Now, let's consider what happens when silos are allowed to thrive. Departments operating in isolation can lead to duplicated efforts, missed opportunities, and wasted resources. For example, a marketing campaign might go live without the product team knowing, resulting in poor customer experiences. Customer Service might receive valuable feedback that never reaches Product Development, meaning critical insights are lost. When departments don't communicate, the whole organization suffers. It creates inefficiency, misalignment, and, ultimately, failure to meet company goals.

Breaking down silos requires intentional effort. Technology can be a great enabler. Tools like Slack, Microsoft Teams, and project management platforms like Asana or Trello can help keep everyone connected. These platforms allow for real-time communication and make it easy to share information and updates. But technology alone isn't enough. Leaders have to create a culture that prioritizes collaboration.

Leaders can foster this culture by encouraging openness, where people are comfortable sharing ideas, asking questions, and working across departments. Setting up cross-functional teams to tackle specific projects or problems is a great way to promote collaboration and help employees develop a better understanding of what other departments do. Regular cross-department meetings where everyone discusses what they're working on and how it aligns with overall company goals can also be incredibly effective. When people see how their work fits into the big picture, they're more likely to collaborate and support one another.

Ultimately, breaking down silos is about creating energy. It's about taking the potential within each department and combining it into something far more powerful. When departments collaborate, they generate momentum that propels the company forward. Silos? They drain that energy. But collaboration? That's what drives growth and innovation.

In that eCommerce startup I mentioned, once we broke down the silos and got everyone working together, things turned around quickly. Sales picked up, projects were completed on time, and customer satisfaction improved dramatically. The team wasn't just functioning—they were thriving. It was a complete transformation, all because we turned those silos into energy.

So, here's my advice: break down those walls. Get your team talking, collaborating, and sharing. You'll soon realize that the energy and creativity you've been missing were there all along—just waiting to be unleashed.

***

Fostering a Growing Mindset

There's something truly special about watching a team go from "just getting by" to "constantly leveling up." The secret sauce? A growth mindset. When you foster that mindset in the workplace, people start thinking bigger, acting bolder, and embracing new challenges like they've got nothing to lose. But here's the real magic: it's not just about individual growth—it's about lifting each other up along the way. That's when you see the real transformation happen.

When coworkers truly have each other's backs, you create an electric environment where people aren't afraid to throw out new ideas, tackle challenges, or even fail spectacularly. Instead of playing it safe, they take smart risks because they know their teammates are there to catch them if they fall. That atmosphere builds trust and camaraderie and, frankly, does wonders for the company's success. When one person grows, the whole team rises.

I've seen this dynamic in action. In workplaces where growth is encouraged and people are empowered to push boundaries, there's a buzz in the air. Everyone feeds off each other's enthusiasm, and the company benefits from creativity, efficiency, and overall positivity. But when people feel unsupported—or worse, like their ideas will get shot down—they retreat. Innovation stalls, risks aren't taken, and the whole place starts to feel stuck in a rut.

So, how do you create an environment where people support each other's development? It all starts with building a culture of encouragement. When someone pitches a new idea—whether it's a groundbreaking innovation or a fresh spin on an old process—the response should be "Tell me more," not "That'll never work." Even if the idea isn't perfect, encouraging people to speak up sends a clear message: *Your contributions matter.*

One simple way to do this is through positive feedback loops. When a teammate suggests something, listen with genuine interest and find something to build on. Even if the idea is a little rough, there's almost always a nugget of brilliance in there. By adding your thoughts or suggesting ways to expand the idea, you're not only helping that person grow but also showing them their ideas are valued.

And don't underestimate the power of peer mentoring. It doesn't have to be formal—just creating opportunities for coworkers to ask each other for advice, collaborate, or brainstorm together can work wonders. When people stop seeing each other as competition and start seeing each other as partners in growth, incredible things happen. I've seen teams go from struggling to excelling, simply because someone said, "Hey, I'd love your input on this," and suddenly the whole team was working together in ways they hadn't before.

One of my favorite ways to support a growth mindset is by celebrating learning—even when it comes from failure. When someone takes a risk and misses the mark, the response shouldn't be "You blew it." Instead, ask, "What did we learn from this?" Shifting the focus from blame to growth shows that the company values effort and innovation, even if not every idea hits it out of the park.

Let's not forget the power of sharing knowledge. One of the best ways to support your coworkers is by passing on what you know. Find a tool that makes life easier. Share it. Discovered a trick that saves time? Spread the love! It's not about hoarding knowledge; it's about lifting each other up. The more you share, the more everyone grows, and that growth ripples throughout the company.

Here's a fun twist—asking for help can actually be a way to support growth. Sounds counterintuitive, right? But think about it—when you ask someone for help, you're giving them a chance to shine. It's like saying, "I trust your skills and expertise." That kind of mutual respect builds confidence and reinforces the idea that everyone's contributions are valuable.

Speaking of working together, collaboration is a secret weapon for growth. When teammates join forces on a project, they're not just working toward a goal—they're learning from each other's ideas and approaches. Collaboration pushes people out of their comfort zones and opens up new ways of thinking. It's like being in a continuous innovation workshop where everyone's learning and growing together.

Recognition also plays a huge role in keeping a growth mindset alive. When someone steps out of their comfort zone, takes a risk, or helps a teammate develop an idea, give them a shout-out! It doesn't have to be grand—a quick thank-you or a mention during a meeting can make a big impact. Recognition tells people, *You're doing great, keep it up*, and that kind of encouragement fuels even more growth.

When coworkers genuinely support each other, the entire company wins. People aren't just showing up to punch the clock; they're invested in their work and each other. They're constantly looking for ways to improve, grow, and make things better. That kind of energy is contagious, and before you know it, you've created a culture where people feel empowered to dream big and chase those dreams—knowing their team has their back.

So, encourage each other, collaborate like pros, share your knowledge, and most importantly, lift each other up. The more you support your coworkers' growth, the stronger the whole team becomes. And that's where the real magic happens. Growth isn't just about individual wins—it's about pushing the entire company forward, together.

* * *

The Benefits of Growing Social Connections

Building social connections outside of the workday is one of the most rewarding aspects of any job. Let's be honest—we spend a huge chunk of our lives at work, so why not go beyond just talking spreadsheets and deadlines? Forming genuine connections with coworkers outside the 9-to-5 not only strengthens the sense of community within the team, but also leads to smoother collaboration, better communication, and ultimately, a more successful—and fun—workplace.

Now, don't get me wrong—some people like to keep work and personal life separate, and that's completely okay. I'm not saying everyone has to be BFFs or hit up happy hour every night. But even fostering a bit of social connection beyond work can be both enjoyable and beneficial. When you get to know your coworkers as real people—not just as "the person from accounting"—you start communicating better, collaborating more easily, and generally vibing in a way that makes working together smoother and more productive.

So, how do you build those connections? There are plenty of ways that don't have to feel awkward or forced. One simple idea is organizing casual after-work hangouts. Nothing too intense—it could be grabbing drinks, hitting up a trivia night, or going out for a low-key meal after a long day. These relaxed settings allow for conversation that goes beyond work deadlines, and that's where the real bonds start to form.

And if the bar scene isn't your thing, no worries—there are plenty of other options! How about a group hike, a workout class, or even starting a little book club? The activity itself doesn't matter—it's just about stepping out of "work mode" and into a more laid-back space where you can enjoy each other's company. It's less about what you do, and more about doing it together and creating those shared experiences outside the usual grind.

Let's not forget the digital side of things, either. In today's world, social connections don't always have to happen in person. A shared Slack channel or WhatsApp group for non-work banter can work wonders. Whether you're swapping memes, sharing weekend plans, or debating the latest TV show, these informal online spaces help keep connections alive even when you can't hang out in person. Plus, a little humor and lightheartedness during the workday can make things more enjoyable (and yes, sharing the perfect meme *is* an art form).

That said, it's important to maintain a healthy balance between those social connections and the professional dynamic at work. Just because you're grabbing drinks with coworkers on Thursday night doesn't mean you can toss professionalism out the window come Friday morning. Work is still work, and respecting each other's roles and responsibilities is crucial, no matter how tight-knit your after-hours crew becomes. It's all about balance—enjoy the fun outside of work, but keep things professional during office hours.

Here's the kicker: social connections at work benefit your organization in ways you might not expect. For one, they're great for reducing stress. When you've got good relationships with your coworkers, tough days don't feel quite as tough. It's like having your personal support crew right there, making everything a little more manageable. Plus, strong social bonds boost teamwork. When you trust and know your colleagues beyond their job titles, collaboration comes naturally, feedback is easier to give and receive, and even disagreements are handled with more grace and understanding.

And communication? That's another big win. Sometimes, those casual chats outside of work give you a better sense of how someone communicates, making workday conversations way smoother. Open, honest communication becomes much easier when you've built a solid connection outside the office walls.

So, how do you get those social connections started? There are plenty of ways, depending on your team's vibe. In-person meetups—whether casual dinners, group activities, or company-organized outings—are a great way to build deeper bonds. But if your team is remote or can't always meet up in person, virtual hangouts work just as well. A dedicated Slack channel for non-work chatter, a group text, or even a virtual happy hour can keep those connections alive when physical meetups aren't possible.

One super easy way to get the ball rolling? Just invite someone for coffee or a walk during a lunch break. It's a low-pressure, low-commitment icebreaker that gets the conversation flowing beyond just work-related stuff. From there, you can start organizing bigger group hangouts. And remember, the goal isn't to make this feel like another meeting or obligation—it should be organic and fun. The more relaxed the setting, the easier it is for people to let their guard down and enjoy themselves.

In the end, building social connections at work doesn't just make the workday more pleasant—it has real, tangible benefits for both individuals and the organization. So, go ahead, grab that coffee or set up that trivia night. You might be surprised at how a little social time can transform your workplace dynamic for the better. And hey, if nothing else, you'll finally get to know the person from accounting's *real* name!

* * *

Resilience Through Unity

Let's face it: tough times are inevitable. Whether it's a massive project hitting a brick wall, a team that's completely burned out, or interpersonal drama that has everyone walking on eggshells, challenges are part of the package. But here's the real test: it's not about how your team performs when everything is running smoothly—it's about how they rally together when the pressure's on. That's where *resilience through unity* comes in, and as a leader, your mission is to keep the team from unraveling when things get rocky.

So, how do you hold it all together when the going gets tough? First and foremost, acknowledge the situation. Ignoring the chaos and pretending everything's fine only frustrates people more. In my experience, addressing the elephant in the room head-on shows the team that you're in the trenches with them. Maybe the deadline is looming, and everyone's feeling the crunch, or maybe there's some tension brewing between colleagues. Whatever it is, call it out. Let your team know you see the problem and that you're ready to tackle it *together*. Trust me—a little transparency goes a long way.

Next, it's crucial to remind everyone of the bigger picture. When things start to fall apart, people tend to focus on the immediate frustration and what's going wrong. That's when I step in and ask, *"How does this situation fit into our overall goal?"* It shifts the conversation from dwelling on the problem to remembering the purpose. You're all on the same team, working toward the same goal, and sometimes that shared focus is all it takes to reignite the team's energy.

Now, let's talk about the classic case of teammates not getting along—it happens. We're all human, and not everyone is going to click perfectly all the time. I've seen my fair share of situations where two team members just couldn't find common ground. They'd bicker, undermine each other, or simply avoid working together. It's draining for everyone, and the worst part? The wasted potential. As a leader, you've got to step in, address the conflict, and help bridge the gap. Whether through mediation, redirecting their energy toward shared goals, or reminding them that they're both essential to the team, it's up to you to steer them back toward unity. Because once the dust settles, a team that's been through the trenches together is nearly unstoppable.

When things get tense, honest conversations are your best friend. I usually start by talking to each person separately to understand their side of the story, then bring them together for a calm, structured discussion. This isn't about playing referee or forcing a "hug it out" moment—it's about giving them space to air their grievances and, hopefully, find some common ground. Sometimes, it's a quick fix, like clearing up a misunderstanding. Other times, it takes more effort. The goal is always the same: help them see each other's perspective, even if they don't agree 100%. Mutual respect is key.

But what if you've had the tough conversations, done all the listening, and even thrown in a pizza party or two, and things still aren't clicking? At that point, it's time to shift the focus from trying to create best friends to finding ways for the team to work together productively—even if they aren't sending each other holiday cards. In these cases, I find it helpful to clearly define roles and responsibilities. Sometimes the conflict isn't personal—it's just that people are stepping on each other's toes without realizing it. By setting clear boundaries and expectations, you can reduce tension and create a space where everyone can focus on their work without getting in each other's way.

Another secret weapon for keeping the team motivated during tough times? Celebrate small wins. When the road ahead feels endless, those little victories can keep spirits up. I've seen this during massive projects where it felt like we'd never reach the finish line. By breaking the work down into smaller chunks and celebrating every accomplishment—no matter how small—you keep the momentum going. It's a reminder that, yes, progress is happening, and yes, we're all in this together.

And don't forget about fostering unity. When things get rough, it's easy for people to retreat into their own corners and stop collaborating. That's the last thing you want. As a leader, it's your job to pull the team back together, whether through team-building activities, regular check-ins, or just some casual bonding time. I've found that even something as simple as getting the team together for a meal or a relaxed conversation can go a long way in rebuilding those connections. When people feel like they're part of a team, rather than just a group of coworkers, they're more likely to stick together through tough times.

But here's the thing: sometimes, no matter how hard you try, things won't magically fall into place. People may still have their differences, and the stress might not disappear overnight. That's when you've got to be flexible and realistic as a leader. You can't force everyone to be best friends, and that's okay. What you *can* do is create an environment where people feel safe to speak up, supported in their work, and respected as part of the team. That's the real foundation of resilience—knowing that even when the going gets tough, your team has each other's backs and can push through together.

Building resilience through unity isn't about crafting a picture-perfect team where everyone's holding hands and singing campfire songs. It's about understanding that tough times are part of the journey, and with the right mindset and some solid effort, you can keep your team moving forward—even when things get messy. As a leader, your role is to guide them through the rough patches, remind them of the bigger picture, and show them that together, they're stronger than any challenge that comes their way.

10

Setting New Standards

Setting new workplace standards is like taking your team to the next level after you've built a strong foundation. Once your team trusts you and fully embraces the company culture, it's time to raise the bar. At this stage, they're not just following instructions—they're ready to push themselves, and as a leader, it's your job to help them see what more they're capable of.

Why set higher standards? Because your team is ready for it. They've bought into the culture, they trust the leadership, and now they're eager for a challenge. It's not about demanding more work or putting pressure on them—it's about giving them space to grow, encouraging them to think outside the box, and allowing them to take more ownership of their roles. When the groundwork is solid, setting new goals becomes a shared vision. The team wants to hit those higher targets because they know their contributions matter, and they feel your trust in their abilities.

In my experience, raising expectations creates a sense of momentum. When your team sees you're setting new goals, they understand that the company is committed to constant growth and improvement. Stagnation? No thanks. By always striving for more, you send a clear message that progress is key and that personal and professional development is an ongoing journey.

The beauty of raising the bar is that it strengthens the idea that excellence is baked into your company's DNA. It's not just about doing what's required; it's about always reaching for that next level. That mindset can be incredibly motivating for a team that's already bought into the vision—and it's how you take a good team and make it great!

A great example of a company that grew its business by setting new standards is Netflix. In the early 2000s, Netflix was a DVD rental service, competing with the likes of Blockbuster. However, as the industry began shifting toward digital streaming, Netflix saw the opportunity not only to embrace change but to raise the bar for the entire entertainment industry. This shift wasn't just about embracing new technology—it was about redefining their business model and workplace culture and pushing boundaries in how they approached customer experience and employee performance.

The turning point for Netflix came when they recognized the limitations of their DVD rental business and boldly decided to pivot toward streaming. This was a massive risk at the time, as streaming was still a relatively untested technology. But instead of playing it safe, Netflix set a new standard for how content could be delivered. They pushed boundaries by developing a streaming platform that was user-friendly, reliable, and scalable on a global level. This move redefined success for the company, shifting its focus from physical media to digital content delivery and, eventually, content creation.

Internally, Netflix set equally high standards for their team. Reed Hastings, Netflix's CEO, famously promoted a culture of "freedom and responsibility." The company eliminated traditional corporate hierarchies and rigid rules, giving employees more autonomy in their roles while holding them accountable for delivering high performance. Netflix introduced unlimited vacation time, encouraged flexibility, and placed a strong emphasis on hiring top talent who could operate independently while meeting the company's elevated standards.

At the same time, Netflix redefined how performance was measured. Success wasn't just about doing your job—it was about doing it exceptionally well and contributing to the overall mission of innovation and customer satisfaction. Teams were free to experiment and take calculated risks, but the expectation was that those risks would drive results. Leadership communicated clearly that while failure was acceptable in pursuing innovation, mediocrity was not. Employees who couldn't keep pace with the company's high standards were encouraged to seek opportunities elsewhere. It was a tough-love approach, but it worked.

Netflix also pushed boundaries by investing in content production. Rather than relying on third-party studios for licensing content, Netflix started creating its original programming. Shows like *House of Cards* and *Orange Is the New Black* set a new standard for streaming content, challenging the traditional television and film industries. Netflix raised the bar on quality, storytelling, and production value, redefining what success looked like in the entertainment industry.

So, how did Netflix hold their team to these high standards? First, they emphasized transparency and communication. Employees knew exactly what was expected of them, and they were given the resources to succeed. The company embraced a feedback-driven culture, where employees were encouraged to speak openly about what was working and what wasn't, and leaders provided frequent, constructive feedback. Performance reviews weren't annual—they were ongoing, fostering an environment of continuous improvement.

The outcome of Netflix's new standards was revolutionary. By embracing streaming early and raising expectations for content quality, customer experience, and internal performance, Netflix grew from a DVD rental service into a global entertainment powerhouse. Today, Netflix has over 230 million subscribers worldwide, and its influence on the entertainment industry is undeniable. The company not only transformed how we consume content but set the bar for what a high-performance, innovative company could achieve.

Netflix's success came from its willingness to push boundaries, set new standards internally and externally, and redefine success in its industry and workplace. By holding its team to a higher performance bar and fostering a culture that thrives on innovation and accountability, Netflix built a business model that continues to shape the future of entertainment.

Raising the Bar on Workplace Standards

Raising the bar in the workplace isn't just about pushing for higher performance—it's about creating a culture of excellence that energizes and transforms the way things get done. As a leader, it's not enough to simply tell your team to "do more." It's about fostering an environment where high performance feels natural, where people are not only challenged but also supported, and where success means consistently exceeding expectations, not just meeting them.

From my experience, the first step in raising the bar is figuring out where you are. You've got to take a good, hard look at your workplace culture and current expectations. Are people just coasting along, or are they pushing themselves? Are they generating fresh ideas, or are they stuck in the same old routine? Getting a clear picture of your starting point helps you understand what needs improvement and where the potential for growth lies.

Once you've identified where things stand, the next move is communicating your vision for the future. Simply saying, "We need to step it up," won't cut it. You need to paint a clear picture of what these higher standards look like. Maybe it's about improving the quality of work, sparking more creativity, or streamlining processes. Whatever it is, your team needs to understand why these raised expectations matter—not just for the company, but for them as individuals. Show them how these new standards will help them grow in their careers, not just add to their workload.

Now, raising the bar doesn't mean you raise expectations and then walk away. You've got to make sure your team has the tools, training, and support they need to meet these new goals. Maybe that's offering additional training, upgrading technology, or mentoring individuals through the transition. Raising the bar without giving people the resources they need is a recipe for frustration and burnout. As a leader, your role is to ensure your team feels prepared and empowered to thrive under these higher standards. After all,

SETTING NEW STANDARDS

the goal is for them to succeed, not just survive.

Accountability is also crucial in this process, but it doesn't have to be the bad guy. Clear expectations should be set from the start, with defined success metrics. Everyone on the team needs to know exactly what's expected of them and how their performance will be measured. Accountability should feel like a support system, not a punishment. It's not about catching people when they fall; it's about helping them stay on course and pushing them to achieve more. When paired with support, accountability becomes a growth tool, not a stick to wave around.

One of the most effective ways to raise the bar? *Lead by example.* If you want your team to push boundaries, take risks, and aim for excellence, guess what? You've got to be doing the same. Leaders who "walk the walk" inspire their teams far more than those who just give orders. Whether it's being fully prepared for meetings, staying up-to-date on industry trends, or rolling up your sleeves and tackling tough challenges head-on, your actions set the tone for the entire team.

And here's a secret to keeping the momentum going—*celebrate progress.* Don't wait until the end of a project to acknowledge hard work. Recognize and reward those who rise to the challenge throughout the process. Celebrating those small wins not only boosts morale but also reinforces the behavior you want to see. When people feel appreciated, they're more likely to stay motivated and keep pushing themselves. Plus, it shows that high performance doesn't go unnoticed—it's valued.

But what happens when someone doesn't meet the new, higher standards? That's where empathy and curiosity come in. Instead of jumping to conclusions, take the time to understand why someone might be struggling. Is it a skills gap? Are there external factors at play? As a leader, you must offer guidance and support to help them get back on track. Sometimes raising the bar means delivering some tough love, but it should always come from a place of wanting to help your team grow, not just pointing out failures.

Now, let's be real—raising the bar can ruffle a few feathers. Not everyone will jump on board immediately, and that's okay. Change can be uncomfortable, and it's natural for some people to feel uneasy when expectations rise. As a leader, you've got to stay patient and persistent. Have conversations with those who are resistant, listen to their concerns, and work through them. Over time, as the team starts to see the benefits—better results, more personal growth—resistance usually fades away.

And remember, raising the bar isn't a one-and-done deal. It's an ongoing process. The standards you set today might need to evolve as your company grows or the industry shifts. Regularly assess how your team is performing against those standards, and be ready to adjust when needed. This keeps your organization dynamic, innovative, and always striving for improvement.

In my experience, raising the bar can truly transform a team. It takes clear communication, the right resources, accountability, and a lot of support, but the results are worth it. When done right, you create a culture of excellence where people aren't just meeting expectations—they're exceeding them. And that's where the magic happens. When your team starts pushing beyond what they thought was possible, your organization reaches new heights.

***

Breaking the Mold: Crafting New Success

Redefining success within a team is one of the most transformative moves a leader can make. It's like giving your team a new lens through which they can see beyond the typical "hit the deadline, meet the goal" mindset. Sure, traditional success metrics like revenue targets and project completions are important, but when you redefine success, you challenge your team to think differently, break the mold, and tap into potential they didn't even know they had. And let me tell you, that's where the magic happens.

So, what does it mean to redefine success? It's about shifting the focus from just counting how many tasks get done to looking at the quality of the work, the innovation behind it, and the collaboration that brought it to life.

Think of it like making a sandwich: anyone can slap together some bread and cheese, but it's the perfectly toasted bread, the secret sauce, and maybe that surprise addition of bacon that turns it into a masterpiece. In team terms, it's about how creatively, thoughtfully, and collaboratively projects are completed, not just checking off boxes.

Take a real-world example: instead of measuring success purely by projects finished on time (yawn), focus on how much innovation went into those projects, how the team grew from the experience, and how well they supported each other along the way. It's not just about finishing the task—it's about evolving as a team, creating something fresh, and maybe even having some fun while doing it.

As a leader, the first job is to explain this new way of thinking to the team. Let them know that while traditional goals still matter, success now includes growth, creativity, and continuous improvement. This isn't just about crossing the finish line; it's about how you run the race. You're setting the expectation that trying new things, learning from mistakes, and collaborating like a well-oiled machine are just as important as hitting the numbers.

Next, help your team set goals that align with this broader view of success. Encourage them to think beyond just getting tasks done—ask how they can innovate, how they can grow, and how they can collaborate more effectively. By doing this, you're giving them the freedom to think creatively and push themselves, not just meet quotas. It's about fostering a mindset that says, "How can we do this better, smarter, and more collaboratively?"

Now, here's where it gets fun: redefining success means embracing risk. Yep, you heard that right—encouraging your team to take risks and accept that failure is part of the process. If you want your team to break the mold, they need to know it's okay to take a leap, even if they occasionally miss. And as a leader, you've got to lead by example. Share your own stories of risk-taking and flops (we've all had them), and show them that failure isn't the end of the road, but another step toward success. When your team sees that you're not obsessed with perfection, they'll feel more comfortable thinking outside the box.

One of the best parts of redefining success is watching the transformation unfold. When your team realizes success isn't just about meeting a deadline, they start aiming higher. They take more ownership of their roles, push for better results, and work together in ways that can take the team from good to great. And trust me, the energy and motivation that comes from working toward something meaningful is contagious.

So, let's toss the old success playbook out the window. It's time to redefine what winning looks like, encourage some bold moves, and celebrate growth in all its forms. After all, success isn't just about reaching the top—it's about the journey that gets you there. And if that journey includes a few detours, risks, and bacon-worthy wins along the way, even better!

Of course, not everyone will jump on board right away, and that's where the real leadership work comes in. Resistance is common when change is involved. Some team members might prefer sticking to the old ways, clinging to their comfort zones like a cozy blanket. It's human nature to resist change, especially when it involves taking risks or trying something new.

As a leader, it's important to handle this resistance with empathy and patience. Start by having one-on-one conversations with those who seem hesitant. More often than not, their resistance comes from fear—fear of failing, fear of the unknown, or fear of losing control over what they've mastered. By getting to the root of their concerns, you can address them head-on. Sometimes, all they need is reassurance that they'll be supported through the change.

It's also essential to equip your team with the tools and resources they need to succeed. A lot of resistance comes from feeling underprepared or uncertain about what's being asked of them. Offering training, mentorship, and opportunities for growth can help ease that anxiety and show them that they have what it takes to succeed in this new environment. In my experience, once people feel equipped and confident, they're much more likely to embrace change.

That said, there will always be a few who resist, no matter what you do. At that point, you may need to evaluate whether they're a good fit for the team moving forward. To maintain a culture of growth and innovation, everyone has to be committed to the journey. Sometimes, the hardest decision is helping someone find a new opportunity where they'll feel more comfortable. After all, not everyone wants to come along for the ride, and that's okay.

In the end, redefining success is about more than just shaking things up—it's about giving your team the opportunity to grow, innovate, and truly excel. When you break the mold and encourage bold thinking, you create a culture where the team isn't just aiming for the finish line—they're redefining the entire race.

* * *

Turning a Good Team Into a Great Team

Taking a team from good to great is like upgrading from regular coffee to a double shot of espresso—it's a game-changer! A team that consistently meets expectations is fine, but a great team goes above and beyond. They don't just complete tasks—they innovate, collaborate, and push boundaries. But making that leap from good to great? It requires setting high-performance norms where your team stretches beyond what they know and feels empowered to take on bigger challenges. It's all about finding that sweet spot between raising expectations and keeping your team motivated (without needing that extra espresso shot every day).

Step one in this journey to greatness is defining what "great" looks like. Every team has basic expectations—meet deadlines, check tasks off the list, and maintain quality. But "basic" won't get you to the next level. To raise the bar, you need to communicate exactly what high performance means. Maybe it's delivering a "wow" factor to clients, sparking more collaboration, or improving the quality of the work itself. Be clear about the new standards and—just as importantly—explain why they matter. No one gets excited about running faster if they don't know where the finish line is.

Once everyone's on board with the vision of greatness, it's time to set some stretch goals. These are the kinds of targets that make people pause and think, "Wait, can we pull this off?" Spoiler alert: yes, they can! But you've got to find the balance between challenging and achievable. Push too hard, and you risk your team burning out. Think of it like a workout—you don't start by lifting the heaviest weights. You build up to it. Your team should feel stretched but not overwhelmed, and they'll need the right resources and support to succeed. No one reaches those goals alone.

I'll share a story from my consulting days with a retail company that was doing well, but they wanted to do more than just meet their quarterly targets. They wanted to become the top player in their market, but their team was stuck in a cycle of "good enough." I worked with them to redefine what success looked like—moving away from simply hitting sales numbers to fostering a culture of innovation and customer service that would set them apart. We set stretch goals that challenged every department to push beyond what they thought they were capable of. And guess what? Not only did they meet their new goals, but the team also felt more energized and engaged than ever before. The shift in mindset was the real win.

Now, keeping the team energized on this journey to greatness requires regular check-ins and celebrating wins—big and small. Every milestone is a reason to pause and say, "Look at what we've accomplished!" Celebrating progress keeps the momentum alive and shows the team that the hard work is paying off. Plus, it reinforces that high standards are not only achievable but also rewarding. And let's face it, who doesn't love a good celebration—even if it's just a well-deserved donut break?

Accountability is another key ingredient in turning a good team into a great one. High-performing teams don't just work hard; they work smart. Everyone takes ownership, not just of their tasks but of the team's overall success. In a great team, people don't just show up to do their jobs; they solve problems, take initiative, and invest in the whole squad's victory. Accountability doesn't have to be about pointing fingers—it's about creating a supportive environment where feedback is a regular part of life, not just an annual "you could do better" chat.

As a leader, you need to be in the mix, offering feedback and encouraging the team to do the same with each other. Think of it like a basketball team—everyone's calling plays, giving pointers, and cheering each other on. When feedback flows in all directions, the team isn't just working—they're improving. And that's how you build a culture where greatness becomes the everyday norm.

One of the most powerful aspects of a great team is collaboration. Individual talent is important, but it's the synergy between team members that kicks things into high gear. When diverse perspectives come together, creativity skyrockets, and solutions improve. As a leader, fostering collaboration means tearing down silos, encouraging communication, and creating opportunities for cross-functional teamwork. The more your team works together, the more they'll inspire each other to push higher.

Now, let's be real: aiming for greatness doesn't mean smooth sailing all the time. In fact, teams aiming for greatness often hit more bumps in the road because they're pushing boundaries. But here's the thing—what sets a great team apart is their resilience. They don't crumble when they hit a roadblock; they learn from it and keep moving forward. As a leader, you can model this resilience by showing your team that failure isn't the end—it's just a plot twist in the journey to success.

But how do you push a team to greatness without pushing them too far? That's the million-dollar question. The secret is balance. Know your team, understand their limits, and watch for signs of burnout. If you see enthusiasm fading or performance slipping, it's time to pause, recalibrate, and give the team space to recharge. This doesn't mean lowering the bar, but adjusting the pace so the team can maintain their energy and focus.

In the end, turning a good team into a great one isn't a one-and-done process—it's a continuous effort. You've got to set high-performance norms, encourage accountability, and foster collaboration. But the best part? The result isn't just better outcomes. When a team goes from good to great, it becomes more than a group of individuals—it becomes a powerhouse, a team driven by a shared commitment to excellence.

Ultimately, a great team is defined not just by what they achieve, but by how they work together. They're adaptable, innovative, and driven by a passion for constant improvement. As their leader, your job is to guide them on that journey, raising the bar and showing them that greatness isn't just a dream—it's the new normal.

* * *

Creating a Team of Excellence: The New Normal

Creating a new normal at work, especially one built on a culture of excellence is a game changer. It's more than just introducing new rules or raising expectations—it's about getting the entire team to shift their mindset. Excellence isn't a finish line to cross; it's a standard you live by daily. Reflecting on how I helped transform a receptionist team that once felt like a revolving door shows just how powerful this kind of shift can be.

When I first stepped in to lead the receptionist team, the problem was clear: turnover was high, and stability was non-existent. People were coming and going so fast that it felt like there was a new face at the front desk every week. This wasn't just creating chaos within the team—it was sending the wrong message to clients. Receptionists are often the first point of contact for anyone walking through the door, and we all know that first impressions matter—a lot. To elevate the company's image, the front-line team had to reflect the professionalism and excellence we were striving for. It was time to shake things up and create a new normal.

The first big change I made was setting a clear, non-negotiable standard: 100% customer service, 100% of the time. No exceptions. The receptionists weren't just there to answer phones and point people in the right direction—they were the face of the company. They set the tone for how clients, customers, and visitors perceived us. Let's be honest—it wasn't the CEO or VP making that first impression; it was the receptionist team. That one interaction could shape the entire relationship going forward.

But this wasn't just about delivering top-notch customer service. It was about changing how the receptionists saw themselves and their role in the company. They weren't just filling a seat; they were ambassadors of the brand, and their work mattered. This shift in perspective created a sense of ownership and pride that completely transformed the team dynamic. They went from just showing up to showing up—with confidence, purpose, and a commitment to making every first impression count.

Of course, not everyone was thrilled about this new standard. Whenever you aim for excellence, there's bound to be some pushback. A few team members were comfortable coasting at the bare minimum and didn't quite see the point of striving for more. They questioned why we needed such high standards for what they saw as a "simple" or "routine" role. But as a leader, I knew anything less than 100% was a no-go. The team needed to be all in, or we risked undermining the culture we were working so hard to build.

When it came time to confront the naysayers, I approached it with a mix of empathy and firmness. Balance is key, right? I had honest conversations with those resistant to the change, explaining why this new level of excellence wasn't just important but crucial to the company's success—and their personal growth. I made it clear: their role wasn't just about answering phones or greeting guests. It mattered. For many, this was an eye-opener. I framed it as an opportunity to step up, not a critique of their past work, and a chance to grow into a position with more responsibility and impact.

But for those who still resisted? That's where the tough love came in. As leaders, we have to recognize when someone isn't on board with the vision and be ready to make hard decisions. Despite mentoring, coaching, and pep talks, some individuals weren't willing to embrace the new standard. That's when I had to make the tough call to part ways. It wasn't easy, but holding onto team members who weren't aligned with the new culture would've dragged everyone down—and that wasn't the direction we were heading.

The real magic happened when the rest of the team began to take ownership. They started holding each other accountable, taking pride in being the first point of contact for everyone who walked through the door. We began regular feedback sessions where receptionists could share their thoughts and ideas on how we could raise the bar even further. This fostered a culture of collaboration and constant improvement—two key ingredients in any recipe for excellence.

The result? Total transformation. The receptionist team became one of the most rock-solid, high-performing groups in the company. Client feedback skyrocketed, with many praising the professionalism and warmth of the front office staff. Even better? That revolving door stopped spinning. The team became stable, engaged, and proud of their role in shaping the company's image. The shift didn't just stop with them—it sent ripples throughout the organization, raising the bar for how all teams approached their work.

What I learned from this experience is that creating a new normal at work isn't a one-time deal—it's an ongoing journey of setting and upholding high standards. It takes clear communication, strong leadership, and, yes, some tough decisions when necessary. You have to be ready to face those who resist and approach them with empathy and a willingness to coach. Sometimes, people just need a little guidance. But when that doesn't work, you've got to make the call to let them go for the sake of the team's success.

Building a culture of excellence is about more than just setting expectations. It's about creating an environment where every team member feels valued, challenged, and inspired to bring their best every day. When you nail that, excellence becomes the new normal. It turns good teams into great ones and pushes the entire organization to new heights.

***

Challenging the Status Quo

Challenging the status quo at work is one of the most exciting ways to ignite growth, innovation, and improvement. As a leader, I've come to understand that pushing boundaries isn't just about achieving bigger goals—it's about rethinking how we define success. Encouraging teams to push beyond what they once thought possible opens up a new world of problem-solving and creativity. But let's be honest—there's a fine line between productively pushing boundaries and pushing them too far.

I still remember my first retail job as a sales associate, where our Regional Vice President would always ask, "How high is high?" Back then, I thought it was just a catchy corporate pep talk meant to hype us up to sell more. But as I've grown in my career, I've realized it was far deeper than that. She wasn't just pushing us to sell more—she was challenging us to question our limits. Her message was clear: don't settle for what you think is possible. Push further. But there was an art to pushing boundaries, and she balanced it with her other mantra, "under-commit and over-deliver."

"Under-commit and over-deliver" stuck with me ever since. It's simple: set realistic goals, but aim to exceed them. It's about quietly working behind the scenes to surprise and delight, creating a kind of magic where you set expectations but then blow them out of the water. When you can lead a team to do that, you're not just meeting expectations—you're surpassing them. It's like promising someone a regular cup of coffee and surprising them with a perfectly made cappuccino with fancy foam art.

But here's the million-dollar question: how do you know when it's time to challenge the status quo, and how do you avoid pushing too hard?

One clue is when things start feeling too comfortable. If your team is hitting goals easily, going through the motions, and everything feels routine, it's time to shake things up. Consistency is great, but it can also lead to complacency. As a leader, it's your job to spot when the status quo has become a cozy blanket everyone's snuggled under. If there's no challenge, no new ideas, and no innovation, it's time to stretch the boundaries and see how high "high" really is.

Now, let's not get carried away—challenging the status quo doesn't mean taking wild risks or setting impossible targets. It's about creating an environment where trying new things is the norm, where a little discomfort is embraced because that's where growth happens. This is when your team has the opportunity to shine. Involving them in the process of challenging the norm is crucial. If they're not on board with the vision or don't understand why it's important, pushing boundaries will feel like unnecessary stress. But if they see the value—not just for the company, but for their own development—they'll be ready to rise to the occasion.

As leaders, we must loop the team into the conversation from the start. Ask for their input, get them involved in the planning—it's not just about making them feel included, it's about giving them ownership of the challenge. When people feel they've had a hand in shaping the game plan, they're more invested in the outcome and more open to thinking outside the box. Plus, involving the team ensures you're not tossing them into the deep end without a floaty. They're helping build the boat, and that creates accountability and excitement.

That said, pushing boundaries can backfire if it's done recklessly. If you push too hard, too fast, without clear objectives or the right support, your team can quickly feel overwhelmed. That's when the boundary-pushing goes from "Heck yeah, we got this!" to "Wait, what are we doing again?" As leaders, we need to be attuned to our team's capacity—not just in terms of workload, but in terms of their mental and emotional stamina. If you start seeing burnout, frustration, or disengagement, that's your cue to hit pause and reassess.

The key is setting stretch goals that are challenging but achievable. Think of it like a rubber band—you want to create enough tension to stretch, but not so much that it snaps. When stretch goals feel impossible, they can backfire, making the team feel destined to fail no matter what they do. A good stretch goal should make people a little uncomfortable but in a "let's stretch our skills and see what we can do" kind of way, not an "oh no, we're doomed" way. It's about pushing them enough that they're growing, but not so far that they want to throw in the towel.

And communication is key when you're challenging the status quo. It's not enough to just say, "Let's crush it!" You need to explain why the current way of doing things isn't cutting it and what you hope to achieve by going beyond it. Clear communication acts as a roadmap—it shows the team where they're headed and how they'll be supported along the way. It helps ease nerves and gives everyone a clear sense of direction.

For team members who resist change or find challenging the status quo unsettling, it's all about empathy and curiosity. Some people thrive on boundary-pushing, while others prefer the stability of what they know. The key is understanding the root of their resistance. Is it fear of failure? Lack of confidence? Plain old discomfort with change? Once you know what's holding them back, you can help them overcome it through reassurance, extra support, or just giving them time to adjust.

Transforming a good team into a great one is all about continuously challenging the norm in ways that build people up, not break them down. It's about setting higher standards, encouraging innovation, and keeping an eye on your team's well-being. It's a delicate balance—pushing boundaries without pushing people too far.

And honestly, "How high is high?" is a question with no final answer. It's a mindset—a way of always striving for more, always reaching further, and never settling for "just good enough." When leaders and teams embrace that mindset, that's when the real magic happens.

**

Follow the Leader: Learning to Lead by Example

Leading by example is one of those timeless leadership principles that never goes out of style. It's the bedrock of effective leadership, especially when it comes to shaping company culture. In any organization, the tone and behavior set by leadership trickle down to everyone else. When leaders live and breathe the values they want to see in their teams, the organization naturally follows. But when that leadership is missing or inconsistent, things can quickly spiral into chaos. As a business consultant, I've seen both sides of this—companies where leadership takes a "do as I say, not as I do" approach (spoiler alert: it doesn't work) and others where leaders walk the talk, completely transforming the company's culture.

I remember working with a mid-sized company that was, frankly, a mess. The workplace vibe was more "wild west" than professional. Employees came and went whenever they pleased, dressed however they felt (let's just say the dress code was more of a suggestion), and professionalism. Nonexistent. Unprofessional language was the norm, and respect for the workplace was an afterthought. But it wasn't just the employees—the leadership team wasn't setting a better example. Senior executives strolled in late, dressed like they were headed to a beach day, setting the tone for the entire office. Accountability was nonexistent, and the company had no clear standard of excellence.

It didn't take long to realize that if things were going to change, it had to start at the top. I sat down with the senior leadership team and laid it out: the company's culture mirrors its leadership. If they wanted employees to be professional, respectful, and punctual, they had to model those behaviors themselves. It's simple—you can't expect your team to show up on time if the leadership is rolling in late. You can't preach about professionalism while wearing flip-flops and jeans. If the leaders wanted a culture shift, they had to lead that change.

The first step was setting clear expectations. We established a solid code of conduct that emphasized professionalism, punctuality, and respectful communication. But this wasn't just about creating new rules. The leadership had to walk the walk. They needed to dress the part, show up on time, and use every interaction—whether with clients or staff—as an opportunity to model the excellence they wanted to see. It was all about showing, not just telling.

As the leadership team started making these changes, it was like watching a slow but steady transformation unfold. There was no need for a company-wide memo or strict enforcement of rules. The shift happened organically. Employees began to notice that their leaders were taking things seriously—arriving on time, dressing professionally, and treating others with respect. And guess what? The rest of the team followed suit. It's human nature—when leaders set a high standard, people tend to rise to it. Suddenly, "casual Friday" became just that—a day reserved for dressing down, rather than a daily occurrence. Language in the office became more respectful, and people started showing up on time. The company's culture was transforming, and professionalism became the new normal.

But leading by example didn't just set a professional tone—it fundamentally rewired the workplace culture. Employees weren't simply following rules; they took pride in their work because they realized they were part of something bigger. Excellence, respect, and integrity became the baseline. And that's where the real shift happened—when people took ownership of the culture change themselves.

Of course, not everyone jumped on board right away. Some employees were still stuck in their old habits—rolling in late, dressing like it was always the weekend, and ignoring the new standards. So, what do you do when your team isn't quite falling in line? You don't just throw up your hands and say, "Well, I tried." You tackle it head-on.

For those who were slow to adapt, we had some direct conversations. The leadership team was encouraged to meet with these employees one-on-one, not to reprimand them but to have an honest discussion about the company's values and why these changes mattered. It wasn't about punishment—it was about aligning everyone with the new expectations and helping them succeed in the new culture. The message was clear: "We want you to be part of this change, and here's how we can help."

Now, let's be real—not everyone made the shift. Some employees just weren't interested in adjusting to the new culture. And after several conversations, it became clear that they weren't going to change. As tough as it is, there comes a point where leaders need to make the call to part ways. You can't let a few holdouts derail the culture you're trying to build. Allowing one or two people to continue operating outside the new standards can drag everyone down. And protecting the team's culture? That's non-negotiable.

The biggest lesson I learned from this experience is that leading by example isn't a one-time thing—it's an ongoing commitment. Your team is always watching, and if you start slacking off, so will they. However, when leadership consistently models the values they expect from their teams, it creates a ripple effect that shapes the entire organization.

In the end, that mid-sized company did a complete turnaround. What was once a loose, unstructured workplace became a company where professionalism and respect were the new normal. And it wasn't just the leadership team that changed—this shift trickled down to every level of the company. Employees were more engaged, accountable, and motivated. They weren't just meeting expectations; they were exceeding them because they saw their leaders doing the same.

At the end of the day, leadership is about more than just setting policies—it's about living them. If we want our teams to be professional, punctual and committed to excellence, we need to embody those qualities ourselves. Lead by example, and you'll set the tone for an entire organization. And trust me, that's how you build a winning culture every time.

* * *

Accountability in Action: The Recipe to Success

Accountability is like the secret sauce that keeps a high-performing team running smoothly, and let's face it—every successful team needs a solid recipe. In my experience, when accountability is part of the workplace culture, it drives excellence, builds trust, and ensures everyone knows they're an essential part of the bigger picture. But let's be clear: holding people accountable isn't about hovering over them like a helicopter boss or dishing out punishment for every little misstep. It's about motivating the team to meet high standards and recognizing that what they do matters.

So, why is accountability so crucial? Well, without it, even the best-laid plans can unravel faster than a poorly made suit. You might start with a great game plan, an inspiring vision, and high hopes, but if there's no follow-through, those big goals can quickly fizzle out. Accountability ensures that the bar stays high, making excellence more than a one-off achievement—it becomes a habit. Plus, it creates a sense of ownership. When people feel

SETTING NEW STANDARDS

their work truly makes a difference, they're much more likely to put in their best effort.

And here's the thing: accountability is everyone's job, not just the boss's. Whether you're the CEO or the newest intern, everyone has a role in maintaining high standards. I've seen firsthand how one person's lack of accountability can create a ripple effect. If someone regularly misses deadlines or cuts corners, others might start thinking, "If they're slacking, maybe I can too." Before you know it, the whole team's standards begin to slide. But when everyone is on board, delivering their best because they know it counts, that's when the magic happens.

One of the biggest myths about accountability is that it's all about the manager riding herd on the team. Sure, leaders set the tone, but accountability is a team sport. It's not just about the manager stepping in with reminders or corrections—it's about teammates holding each other to those high standards, not because they have to, but because they want to. Think of it like a relay race: everyone's success depends on a smooth handoff. And when that happens? You're not just cooking with gas—you're running on rocket fuel.

Setting clear expectations is the first key ingredient in building accountability. If people don't know exactly what's expected of them, it's hard to hold them accountable, right? In my experience, ambiguity is the enemy of accountability. If someone doesn't have a crystal-clear understanding of what success looks like, how can they hit the mark? That's why communicating those standards is so critical. Whether it's through team meetings, one-on-ones, or written guidelines, making sure everyone knows what they're aiming for is the first step to making sure they hit it.

Now, let's talk about feedback—the secret ingredient that keeps accountability in check. Too often, leaders shy away from giving constructive feedback because they don't want to be seen as the "bad guy." But here's the truth: feedback isn't about pointing fingers; it's about helping people improve. Most people want to do their best, but they can't if they don't know where they're going off course.

When you give feedback, focus on actions and results, not personality.

We're not here to critique someone's whole character—just guide them toward better performance. Accountability isn't about criticism; it's about growth. When done right, constructive feedback shows you believe in someone's potential, and that's what makes people rise to the occasion.

But don't think accountability is only about calling out mistakes. It's equally important to recognize those who consistently crush it. Positive reinforcement is just as crucial as constructive feedback, and when people see their hard work being noticed, it lights a fire in the entire team. Recognition shows everyone that high standards aren't just expected—they're valued. So, take the time to celebrate wins, big and small, and watch how it boosts team morale.

Of course, sometimes, despite the feedback and support, someone still doesn't meet the expectations. That's when you have to face it head-on. I've seen what happens when issues are ignored—it drags the whole team down. If someone consistently underperforms without any consequence, the rest of the team starts to question whether accountability really matters. That's why those tough conversations are necessary. Sometimes, it means putting a performance improvement plan in place, and other times, it means making the difficult decision to part ways. Accountability means protecting the team's standards, even if it's uncomfortable.

The beauty of accountability is that it's not a negative—it's empowering. When people know they're being held accountable, they step up. It gives them a sense of ownership and pride in their work because they understand that what they do has an impact. It's a motivator, not a threat.

So, as leaders, our job is to build an environment where accountability is embraced, not feared. It's about creating a culture where high standards are the everyday norm, where everyone knows their role, and where excellence is the ultimate goal. When accountability is in full swing, the whole team thrives, and the organization achieves great things.

In the end, holding each other accountable for high standards isn't just nice to have—it's a must for success. It builds a culture where everyone's best is expected and appreciated. As a leader, it's your job to set those expectations, provide feedback, and make accountability something everyone buys into.

When you do that, your team won't just meet expectations—they'll blow them out of the water.

* * *

Innovation in Progress: Learning to be a Forward Thinker

Innovation is the lifeblood of any thriving organization. It's what separates companies that merely survive from those that truly excel. In my experience, fostering a forward-thinking culture is one of the most powerful ways to keep an organization moving ahead. It's not just about coming up with the next big idea or a flashy product; it's about creating an environment where new ideas are constantly being explored, where employees are encouraged to think beyond the status quo, and where risk-taking and creativity are truly valued.

Encouraging forward-thinking starts with leadership. As leaders, we set the tone. If you want your team to be innovative, you've got to show that innovation is a priority in your work. Forward-thinking doesn't happen by accident—it requires intentional actions, ongoing encouragement, and a willingness to challenge the norm. I've learned that when leaders embrace forward-thinking, it signals to the whole organization that innovation isn't just welcome—it's expected.

One of the first steps in fostering a forward-thinking mindset is to create space for exploration. Too often, teams are so focused on day-to-day operations and meeting immediate goals that they don't have time to think about the future. As a leader, it's your job to carve out time for your team to be creative. This could be regular brainstorming sessions, innovation workshops, or even just setting aside time each week for employees to work on projects outside their usual responsibilities. By giving your team the freedom to explore, you're encouraging them to think beyond their immediate tasks and consider how they can contribute to the organization's long-term success.

But space alone isn't enough—leaders must actively encourage experimentation. In a forward-thinking organization, risk-taking is a natural part of the innovation process. I've found that teams often hesitate to try new approaches because they're afraid of failure or believe they'll be penalized if their ideas don't succeed. That's where leadership comes in. You have to create an environment where failure is seen as a learning opportunity, not a career-ending disaster. This doesn't mean lowering standards, but recognizing that innovation often involves trial and error. When team members know they have leadership's support, they're more likely to take risks, try new things, and push boundaries.

Another key to fostering forward-thinking is challenging assumptions. It's easy for teams to get stuck in a rut, continuing to do things the same way because "that's how we've always done it." As a leader, your job is to challenge these assumptions. Ask why things are done a certain way, whether there's a better solution, or what could be improved. By encouraging critical thinking and pushing the team to question the status quo, you create space for innovation to flourish.

To guide this process, I developed a formula that helps leaders systematically foster innovation within their teams: the IDEA formula.

Forward-Thinking Formula: IDEA

- **I – Inspire curiosity:** Curiosity is the spark that drives innovation. As leaders, we must model this behavior. Ask questions, explore new ideas, and encourage your team to do the same. When you show genuine interest in innovation, your team will follow suit.

- **D – Dedicate time for innovation:** Innovation doesn't happen if it's always playing second fiddle to deadlines. You have to dedicate time for creative thinking. Whether through innovation days or cross-functional teams tasked with tackling challenges, make time for it.

- **E – Encourage experimentation:** Innovation requires experimentation, and experimentation involves risk. Make sure your team knows that failure is okay—what matters is the learning that comes from it. When you encourage risk-taking, you create an environment where creativity thrives.

- **A – Align innovation with strategy:** Innovation should align with the company's strategic goals. Make sure your team's ideas contribute to the broader vision, keeping the focus on driving real value for the business.

By following the IDEA formula, leaders can make forward-thinking an essential part of their organization's DNA—not just a nice-to-have, but a driving force behind every decision.

I once worked with a team that was, let's say, a bit allergic to change. They'd been doing the same things the same way for years, and while they weren't exactly struggling, there wasn't much excitement either. Everything was just... fine. But as I often say, no one gets fired up about "fine." So, I worked with leadership to introduce the IDEA formula, starting with simple things—like setting aside time for brainstorming sessions where all ideas were welcome, no matter how off-the-wall they seemed.

At first, the team was hesitant. Some eye rolls, and a few "we've always done it this way" comments, but once they saw that leadership was genuinely open to new ideas, something amazing happened. Suddenly, ideas were flying around—some winners, some, well... learning opportunities. But the shift was remarkable. They went from being a team stuck in their old ways to becoming the go-to group for innovative solutions.

And here's the kicker: this shift didn't just lead to better products or processes—it changed the company's entire culture. When leadership gives the green light for forward-thinking, people feel empowered. They start thinking about how their work impacts the company's future. That's where the real magic happens. Forward-thinking isn't just about the next big idea—it's about fostering an environment where creativity and innovation thrive every day.

In the end, fostering a culture of innovation is one of the most powerful things a leader can do. It's not just about dreaming up new ideas—it's about setting the stage for long-term success. By carving out time for curiosity, experimentation, and fresh thinking, leaders can transform their teams into creative powerhouses. And when you follow the IDEA formula, you're building for a future where your team is ready to tackle whatever challenges come their way.

11

Thriving in Transition

Let's talk about transition—you know, that thing that makes everyone feel a little uncomfortable, like wearing brand new shoes that haven't quite been broken in yet. Whether it's a new boss, a department shakeup, or a full-blown company overhaul, change in the workplace is inevitable. But here's the good news: it doesn't have to be something to dread! In fact, when approached the right way, transition can be the best thing that happens to you and your team. Thriving in transition isn't just about surviving the change—it's about embracing it, making the most of it, and coming out stronger on the other side. Think of it as your chance to level up!

So, what does it mean to truly thrive during a transition? It means looking at change as an opportunity, not a threat. It's about adapting, evolving, and keeping your sense of humor intact when the new system inevitably crashes for the third time that week (yes, I've been there too). Thriving means seeing the shifting landscape and saying, "Alright, let's roll with this!" rather than clinging to the comfort of how things used to be. It's like surfing—you can't stop the waves from coming, but you *can* learn to ride them.

Why is it so important to embrace transition? Because, whether we like it or not, change is a constant in life and business. The companies—and individuals—that thrive aren't the ones who resist change; they're the ones who adapt, innovate, and pivot when needed. Embracing transition helps you stay relevant, opens doors to new opportunities, and gives you a chance to grow in ways you might not have considered before. Plus, being the person who stays calm, collected, and even positive during a shakeup? That's a leadership skill right there!

Let's focus on LEGO—the little bricks scattered across living room floors and painfully stepped on by parents for decades. While LEGO is now a global powerhouse of creativity, fun, and (occasionally) foot pain, there was a time when this beloved company was on the brink of collapse. They went from thriving to struggling—and then, like a true comeback story, they learned how to thrive in transition.

Back in the early 2000s, LEGO was facing some serious challenges. After years of success, they hit a rough patch. Sales were down, and kids preferred video games over building blocks. LEGO was at a crossroads: either stay stuck in the past or embrace change. Spoiler alert—they embraced change and turned it into one of the greatest corporate turnarounds ever.

LEGO realized that if they wanted to survive, they had to step up their game. Enter the world of digital transformation. Instead of fearing the rise of technology, they figured out how to integrate it. They created video games like *LEGO Star Wars*, *LEGO Harry Potter*, and *LEGO Batman*—and boom, suddenly, LEGO wasn't just a toy company anymore. They were a multimedia empire.

But LEGO didn't stop there. They tapped into the magic of storytelling by launching *The LEGO Movie*, which was a smash hit. And just like that, the little brick company wasn't just surviving in a world dominated by digital entertainment—it was thriving.

What's even more impressive is how LEGO navigated multiple transitions at once. They embraced technology with video games, expanded into Hollywood with movies, and even leaned into the rise of online communities. They built platforms where fans could share their LEGO creations, vote on new sets, and contribute to the brand's creative process.

The lesson here? LEGO didn't just stick to what worked in the past. They embraced change, even when it meant stepping out of their comfort zone of plastic bricks and diving into the digital world. By adapting and evolving, they proved that thriving in transition is about more than just keeping up with the times—it's about building (pun intended) a future where creativity and innovation lead the way.

* * *

Embracing Change

Let's talk about something everyone loves...just kidding! We all know change isn't exactly the warm, fuzzy topic most people want to embrace. But here's the thing: change isn't going anywhere. It's as much a part of work life as coffee breaks and performance reviews. Whether it's a new boss, a department restructuring, or the latest software that's supposed to make everything "easier" (cue the collective eye-roll), change is inevitable. So, instead of dreading it, why not learn to embrace it?

I get it—it's easier said than done. I used to be the person who would internally panic any time something at work shifted. "Why mess with a good thing?" I'd think. But over time, I realized something surprising: change can be a *good* thing. Shocking, I know! But once I shifted my mindset, I started seeing change not as a disruption but as an opportunity for growth.

Think of change like that awkward party you don't want to attend but end up having a blast at. You dread it, resist it, and then when you finally give in, you realize it's not so bad after all. Change works the same way. Sure, it can throw you off balance for a bit, but it also pushes you out of your comfort zone—and that's where the magic happens.

Let's take a minute and ask, "What's the worst that could happen?" Okay, now that you've imagined the absurd worst-case scenario (are aliens going to abduct your company?), let's focus on the other side: "What's the *best* that could happen?" New opportunities, skill development, personal growth, and maybe even discovering strengths you didn't know you had.

Ah, fear—everyone's unwelcome plus-one to change. It shows up every time something new is on the horizon. But here's the thing: fear is normal.

You don't have to let it run the show. Think of fear as a backseat driver—annoying, yes, but not the one steering the wheel. When fear creeps in, one of the best ways to deal with it is to break things down into manageable pieces. Instead of staring at the giant mountain of "new stuff" ahead, focus on one small step at a time. Got a new system to learn? Start by mastering the basics. Need to adjust to a new boss? Take it one conversation at a time. Small victories build confidence, and before you know it, that intimidating mountain looks more like a speed bump.

And hey, messing up along the way is totally fine. Failure is part of the process. I mean, did you ride a bike perfectly the first time? No, you wobbled, you fell, and eventually, you got it. Navigating change is no different. Give yourself permission to be imperfect, and treat every stumble as a step closer to mastering the new normal.

Once you've reframed change as an opportunity and are ready to face your fears, the next step is learning how to approach transitions with confidence—or at least fake it until you make it! Confidence isn't about having all the answers; it's about staying adaptable and open to learning as you go.

One of the best ways to stay confident during a transition is to take control where you can. Ask questions, gather information, and get involved in shaping the change rather than waiting for it to happen to you. Not sure how the new process works? Ask! Feeling uncertain about a new role? Seek out clarity from your manager. The more you engage with the change, the more empowered you'll feel.

And let's not forget the importance of leaning on your work buddies. Transitions are much less intimidating when you're not facing them alone. Your team, your colleagues, maybe even that friendly HR person with the candy at their desk—they're all in this with you. Support each other, share stories, and remember: today's "new normal" will just be "normal" before long.

At the end of the day, change is what you make of it. You can resist it, fear it, and stress over every little detail—or you can see it as a fresh opportunity to grow, learn, and maybe even have a little fun along the way. It's all about the mindset you bring to the table. You get to decide if change is the big, bad wolf or your next big adventure.

***

The Power of Adaptability

Adaptability is one of those superpowers we often don't realize we have—until we need it. Once you unlock it, though, it's like finding the key to making change your ally. I've learned over the years that being flexible—especially when things are shifting fast—is one of the most valuable skills in any career. Whether it's a change in leadership, a complete process overhaul, or even a new company direction, being able to roll with the punches is what separates those who thrive from those who flounder.

Now, I won't lie—adaptability isn't always easy. We're wired to seek stability and routines, so when change shows up, our first instinct can be to resist it. The trick is learning to recognize when change is inevitable and, instead of fighting it, finding a way to pivot and see the opportunity it brings.

Here's the thing: adaptability isn't about being wishy-washy or going along with every new trend that comes your way. It's about resilience and staying open to new possibilities, even when they aren't part of the original plan. Think of it like working with Legos—you might have a vision for what you're building, but sometimes the pieces don't fit the way you expected. Do you give up? No! You adapt, tweak your plan, and often end up with something better than you initially imagined. That's the beauty of adaptability.

The first step to being more adaptable is letting go of the idea that there's only one "right" way to do things. Some of the best solutions come when you're forced to abandon your usual approach and think outside the box. So when processes, leadership, or goals shift, instead of seeing it as a hassle, try viewing it as a chance to learn or improve. You'd be surprised how much opportunity is hidden in those moments of disruption.

Here's the secret sauce to adaptability: an open mind. When you're open to new ideas, new perspectives, and new ways of doing things, change stops feeling like a disruption and starts feeling like an opportunity. Now, staying open-minded takes practice, especially if you've been doing things a certain way for a while. But here's a little trick I use: whenever you're faced with a big change, ask yourself, "What's the opportunity here?"

When you approach change with curiosity rather than dread, your mindset shifts from resistance to possibility. For instance, if a new boss comes in and shakes things up, instead of thinking, "Oh great, now I have to learn a whole new way of working," flip that thought to, "What can I learn from this new leader? How could this change help me grow?" It's all about perspective.

Being adaptable also means being okay with not having all the answers. Change can feel overwhelming when you think you need to have it all figured out from the start. But the truth is, you don't. Flexibility is about being comfortable with uncertainty and trusting that you'll figure things out along the way.

So, how do you stay flexible when everything's shifting around you? Here are a few strategies that have helped me adapt with a little less stress and a lot more success.

- **Focus on what you can control:** When big changes happen, it's easy to feel like everything is spiraling out of control. But here's the thing—you don't have to control everything. Instead, focus on what's within your power. Maybe you can't control the new system being implemented, but you *can* control how you adapt, how you learn, and how you contribute to making it a success.

- **Embrace a growth mindset:** You've probably heard this before, but having a growth mindset is crucial to staying adaptable. When you see challenges as opportunities for growth, it's easier to stay flexible. Instead of fearing failure, embrace it as a chance to learn. Ask yourself,

"What can I take away from this experience that will make me better?"

- **Stay curious:** Curiosity is your best friend during change. When things are in flux, ask questions and explore new ideas. The more curious you are, the more engaged you'll be, and the less daunting the changes will seem. Plus, curiosity often leads to innovation—you might stumble upon the next big idea simply by being open to different approaches.

- **Build a support system:** Change is easier when you've got people in your corner. Surround yourself with colleagues, mentors, or friends who can offer advice and support. Having people to bounce ideas off or just vent to can make a world of difference. After all, navigating change with a team is always better than going it alone.

- **Practice patience:** Change doesn't happen overnight, and neither does adaptability. Give yourself time to adjust. It's okay if you don't immediately feel comfortable with the new way of doing things. Be patient, and remember that flexibility is a muscle you can build over time.

At the end of the day, change is inevitable, whether we like it or not. The organizations that thrive—and the people who succeed—are the ones who can adapt and keep moving forward. It all comes down to mindset. If you view change as an opportunity rather than a threat, you'll be far better equipped to handle whatever comes your way.

So next time a big change hits your workplace, take a deep breath, channel your inner Lego master, and start building something new. And remember, as the great Dory once said, "Just keep swimming." Because, with the right attitude and a little adaptability, you can ride any wave of change that comes your way.

**

Leading Through Change

Leading a team through change is a lot like steering a ship through rough seas—steady hands, clear communication, and a whole lot of patience are required to keep things on course. It can feel unsettling for everyone, but with the right approach, you can guide your team not just through the turbulence, but toward new horizons with confidence. Let's dive into how you can navigate these waters and lead your team through transitions while keeping spirits high and focus sharp.

First things first, communication is your best tool. When things start to shift, the last thing your team needs is to be left in the dark. We all know that the unknown breeds anxiety and one of the best ways to ease that anxiety is by keeping everyone in the loop. Be transparent about what's happening, why it's happening, and how it's going to affect the team. No, you don't need to have all the answers (honestly, who does?), but being open and honest goes a long way in calming nerves and building trust.

And remember, communication isn't just you talking. It's a two-way street. Make sure you create space for your team to ask questions, share concerns, and voice their thoughts. Let them know they're being heard, even if you can't solve every problem right away. Sometimes, just knowing that their leader is listening can make all the difference. It's kind of like when you're on a road trip and someone asks, "Are we there yet?" You might not be there, but at least they know you're paying attention to the journey.

Now, let's talk about resilience. Change can knock the wind out of anyone's sails, especially when it feels like it's coming out of nowhere. Part of your job as a leader is to help your team bounce back and move forward, even when the seas are rough. That doesn't mean pretending everything's fine when it's not—it's about acknowledging the challenges and helping your team shift their mindset. Remind them that while change can be uncomfortable, it's often the catalyst for growth. Sure, the old way of doing things might have felt comfortable, but growth rarely happens in comfort zones.

Here's a trick I've learned: instead of framing change as something happening *to* the team, present it as something happening *for* them. It's an opportunity to learn new skills, take on new responsibilities, and maybe even shake up some old habits that weren't working in the first place. Think of it like this: if your favorite coffee shop suddenly starts offering oat milk instead of just regular milk, you might resist at first, but hey, you could end up discovering your new favorite drink!

Maintaining morale during transitions is where things can get tricky. Change often brings a mix of excitement and anxiety, and it's your job to make sure the anxiety doesn't overpower the excitement. One way to do this is by celebrating small wins along the way. Even when the big picture feels overwhelming, find reasons to celebrate progress. Did the team hit a milestone? Celebrate it. Did someone step up and go the extra mile? Give them a shout-out in the next team meeting. Positive reinforcement keeps the energy high and helps remind everyone that they're capable of handling whatever comes their way.

And don't underestimate the power of humor during times of change. A little lightheartedness can go a long way in breaking tension. Crack a joke, share a funny story, or just be the person who can laugh at the absurdity of the situation when appropriate. Humor can be a great way to remind the team that, yes, we'll get through this. It's like keeping a stash of chocolate in your desk—sometimes, a small bit of sweetness is all you need to keep going.

But while it's important to keep things positive, don't shy away from acknowledging the tough parts of change. Transitions can be tough, and pretending otherwise doesn't do anyone any favors. Let your team know that it's okay to feel frustrated, stressed, or uncertain. Building resilience isn't about ignoring emotions; it's about acknowledging them and moving forward anyway. As a leader, your empathy will go a long way in helping your team feel grounded and supported.

Finally, be the role model your team needs. If they see you embracing change with confidence, they're more likely to follow suit. Show them that you're not just surviving the transition—you're thriving in it. Be flexible, open to new ideas, and willing to adjust your approach when necessary.

When you lead by example, your team will see that change isn't something to fear—it's something to embrace.

In summary, leading through change is all about guiding your team with clear communication, resilience, and a healthy dose of humor. Keep the lines of communication open, help your team see the opportunities in the challenges, and celebrate every win—big or small—along the way. With the right approach, you won't just lead your team through change—you'll lead them to success, and maybe even have a little fun doing it.

* * *

Navigating Organizational Restructuring

Navigating organizational restructuring can feel like riding a rollercoaster you didn't exactly sign up for. One minute, everything seems steady, and the next, there's a sharp turn, and the company's in the middle of a massive shake-up. Mergers, layoffs, leadership changes—whatever the reason, restructuring can shake things up and leave everyone feeling a bit off balance. But here's the good news: while you can't always control the changes, you *can* control how you navigate them. In fact, staying focused and positive during these shifts is like having a secret recipe for success when everything around you feels uncertain.

Let's start with the practical side of things. When an organization restructures, there are usually more questions than answers. It's tempting to get caught up in rumors and worst-case scenarios, but trust me—nothing good comes from that. The best thing you can do is stay grounded and focus on the facts. What do you *actually* know? What's been communicated officially? If the details are still up in the air, resist the urge to fill in the blanks with anxiety-fueled speculation. Trust me, creating imaginary problems won't help anyone—especially not your blood pressure.

One practical tip: stay informed. Read those company emails (yes, the ones you usually skim), attend all-hands meetings, and don't be afraid to ask for clarity when you need it. If you're feeling out of the loop, check in with your manager to get the latest updates. The more you know about what's happening, the better prepared you'll be to navigate the changes. Plus, staying informed shows you're engaged and adaptable, which never hurts when the company is re-evaluating roles during a restructuring.

Now, let's address the big, scary word in the room: layoffs. If there's talk of downsizing, it's hard not to worry about job security. But here's where it's crucial to focus on what you *can* control. Keep showing up and doing your best work. Sounds simple, but it's easy to let anxiety take over. Even during restructuring, your work still matters. Keep adding value, stay engaged, and show that you're adaptable. In my experience, the people who maintain their focus and contribute positively are often the ones who find themselves in good positions once the dust settles.

If the worst happens and your role is impacted, take a deep breath. Yes, restructuring can lead to tough outcomes, but it's not the end of the road. Look at it as an opportunity to pivot, reevaluate your goals, and maybe even find a new path that suits you better. I've seen plenty of people come out of layoffs stronger and more focused than before. Sometimes, the shake-up pushes you toward opportunities you didn't even know you wanted. Silver linings, right?

And let's not forget about mergers. They bring their own unique set of challenges. Suddenly, you've got new teams, new leaders, and maybe even a completely new culture to navigate. It can feel like someone redecorated your house while you were away, and now you have to figure out where everything is. My advice? Embrace adaptability. The company is changing, and clinging to the way things were will only make the transition harder. Get to know the new faces, learn the new processes, and find your place in the new structure. Change is inevitable, but how you adapt to it sets you apart.

Here's a little mindset shift that might help: instead of seeing restructuring as something happening *to* you, try viewing it as something you're actively *part of*. This is your chance to demonstrate your flexibility and prove your value to the new organization. When you look at it this way, it's easier to stay positive and see the bigger picture. You're not just surviving the change—you're helping shape the future of the company.

Of course, restructuring isn't just a logistical or professional challenge—it can also be an emotional rollercoaster. It's normal to feel unsettled during transitions, especially when uncertainty is in the air. My advice? Talk about it. Whether with your colleagues, manager, or someone outside of work, having a sounding board can help you process your feelings. Don't bottle it up. Change is tough, and pretending everything's fine when it's not only adds to the stress.

And hey, don't underestimate the power of humor. I've found that in the middle of the most chaotic restructurings, a little laughter goes a long way. Sometimes, you just have to laugh at the absurdity of it all. New org charts that look like someone spilled spaghetti? A dozen meetings with no clear agenda? Sure, it's chaotic, but finding moments to laugh helps relieve the tension and reminds everyone that we're all human and figuring this out together.

Finally, remember that stability isn't about everything staying the same—it's about finding your balance, no matter what's going on around you. Whether you're taking on new responsibilities, adjusting to a new team, or learning a new system, your ability to stay flexible and proactive will help you thrive through change. Keep a positive mindset, stay engaged, and don't be afraid to lean into the shifts instead of resisting them.

In the end, organizational restructuring is just part of the business landscape. It's not always comfortable, but it doesn't have to be terrifying either. By staying informed, keeping your cool, and finding humor in the chaos, you can navigate these shifts with confidence. And who knows? You might even uncover new opportunities you hadn't considered before.

***

Reinventing Your Role

Reinventing your role at work can feel a bit like being handed a script for a play you didn't audition for. One day, you know exactly what your job looks like, and the next—bam!—your responsibilities shift, new expectations pop up, and suddenly your role feels like it's still being written. But here's the thing: when your job evolves, it's not the time to panic—it's the perfect opportunity to reinvent your role and show what you're really capable of.

I get it—change can be unsettling. We're all creatures of habit, and having your daily routine upended might throw you for a loop. But here's the fun part: when your role starts to shift, it's like the universe is handing you a golden opportunity to grow, develop new skills, and prove your worth in ways you never imagined. Think of it like a rollercoaster—you didn't ask for the sudden twists, but now that you're on the ride, you might as well throw your hands up and enjoy it!

One of the biggest game-changers when your job evolves is the mindset you bring to the table. Instead of viewing these changes as overwhelming or out of your control, try to see them as opportunities to reinvent your role and expand your expertise. Your job description might have once been a neat little box, but who says you can't turn it into a treasure chest of new opportunities? The key is taking ownership of your evolving responsibilities rather than simply reacting to them.

Let's talk strategy. When you notice your role shifting—whether it's new tasks, changing processes, or increasing responsibilities—don't just sit back and wait for someone to officially redefine your position. Be proactive! Ask yourself, "How can I add value in this new scenario?" Then, identify the skills you already have that align with these new responsibilities—and don't be shy about highlighting those to your boss. You're showing that you're not just rolling with the punches, but ready to throw a few of your own (in a professional way, of course).

Next, embrace the learning curve. Yes, evolving roles often come with uncertainty. You might find yourself taking on tasks you've never done, learning new software, or leading projects you didn't even know existed.

Instead of seeing this as extra stress, look at it as free education. It's your chance to build new skills and broaden your experience. And trust me, there's nothing more satisfying than mastering a skill you once thought was out of reach. It's like suddenly realizing you've been playing chess while everyone else was stuck in checkers.

And remember, reinventing your role isn't just about you—it's about adding value to the entire organization. When you show that you're adaptable and eager to take on new challenges, you send a clear message to leadership: you're not just surviving change, you're thriving through it. You're not just keeping up—you're leading the way, and that growth-oriented mindset is what sets you apart.

Now, here's the secret: nobody expects you to have all the answers when your job starts evolving. It's perfectly fine to ask for help. Whether it's tackling a new task or navigating unfamiliar processes, don't hesitate to ask questions, seek advice, or collaborate with colleagues. Reinventing your role doesn't mean going it alone. You're building something new, and it's okay to lean on your team for support. Besides, chances are, others are in the same boat, and together you can create solutions that move the entire team forward.

Reinvention is a long game—it doesn't happen overnight, and that's okay. The goal is to take small, steady steps toward owning this new version of your job. Focus on mastering one new skill or responsibility at a time. Celebrate the wins, no matter how small, and use them to fuel your momentum. Reinvention is as much about the journey as it is about the destination, so pace yourself.

One last piece of advice: have fun with it! Yes, job evolution can be stressful, but it's also a great opportunity to shake things up and try new approaches. When you see these changes as personal growth and development opportunities, they become a lot less intimidating. And honestly, who doesn't want to add a few new superpowers to their resume?

In the end, thriving when your job evolves is all about mindset, ownership, and embracing the unknown. It's about stepping up, learning new skills, and finding ways to bring even more value to the table. So, the next time your role shifts, don't let it freak you out. See it for what it is: your chance to reinvent, level up, and thrive in ways you never thought possible.

* * *

Building Resilience

Let's be real—navigating organizational uncertainty can feel like trying to juggle flaming torches while riding a unicycle. It's stressful and unpredictable, and there's always a chance you might get singed along the way. Whether it's a company restructuring, a leadership shake-up, or a big project that has everyone on edge, staying strong and resilient during these times isn't just crucial—it's completely doable. You just need the right mindset and tools to keep moving forward without losing your balance.

Resilience is like the secret sauce that helps individuals and teams manage the rocky waters of uncertainty. It allows us to bounce back, stay productive, and maintain a positive outlook, even when everything around us feels like it's up in the air. Let's face it, in today's fast-paced work environment, uncertainty is a given. But instead of letting it knock us off course, we can use it as an opportunity to grow stronger, more adaptable, and—dare I say—better equipped to handle the next curveball life throws our way.

Let's start with personal resilience. This is all about how you handle stress and bounce back when things get tough. We've all had those days when it feels like everything changes for the worse. But the key is learning how to manage that stress and keep moving forward. One of the best ways to build personal resilience is to reframe uncertainty as an opportunity for growth. I know it sounds like a cliché, but stick with me. Think of challenges as little nudges pushing you out of your comfort zone—and we all know, that's where the magic happens. It's like going to the gym for your brain—every time you navigate uncertainty, you're building mental muscles.

Another great tool for staying strong is focusing on what you can control. In times of uncertainty, it's easy to get overwhelmed by everything that's out of your hands. But here's the thing: worrying about what you can't control is like trying to steer a ship by blowing on the sails—not very effective. Instead, put your energy into what you *can* control—your attitude, your work ethic, and how you support your teammates. When you focus on those areas, you'll feel more grounded and less overwhelmed by the chaos around you.

Now, let's talk about team resilience. Building resilience as a team is just as important as building it individually. Resilient teams can handle setbacks, adapt to changes, and still find ways to collaborate and move forward. One of the best ways to build team resilience is through open communication. When things are uncertain, keeping everyone in the loop is like giving the team a flashlight in a dark room—it makes everyone feel a little more secure and confident. Regular check-ins, transparent updates from leadership, and honest conversations go a long way in keeping the team focused and strong.

And let's not underestimate the power of humor. When the pressure's on, a good laugh can be a game-changer. I'm not suggesting you turn into the office comedian (though I've seen it happen), but lightening the mood during stressful times can work wonders. Whether it's sharing a funny meme in the team chat or cracking a joke in a tense meeting, humor helps break the tension and reminds everyone that, yes, we're human, and yes, we'll get through this. It's like hitting the "refresh" button on the group's collective stress level.

Flexibility is another key to handling stress and uncertainty. Think of it like being a tree in a windstorm—the more you can bend, the less likely you are to break. Teams that stay flexible and open to new ideas are the ones that thrive in uncertain environments. This might mean adjusting timelines, shifting responsibilities, or rethinking how to approach a project. When everyone on the team is willing to pivot, it keeps the momentum going, even when the road ahead looks unclear.

And while we're on the subject of staying strong, let's talk about self-care. Resilience during organizational uncertainty isn't just about powering through—it's about taking care of yourself too. I'm not just talking about bubble baths and meditation (though those are great). I mean making sure you're getting enough sleep, eating well, and finding time to disconnect from work when you need to. When you're physically and mentally in a good place, it's much easier to stay resilient and handle whatever the workday throws at you.

Lastly, one of the most important aspects of resilience is keeping your eyes on the bigger picture. When things get tough, it's easy to get bogged down in day-to-day stresses, but resilient people (and teams) keep their focus on the long-term goal. Ask yourself: What's the ultimate goal? Why are we doing this? By keeping the bigger vision in mind, it's easier to navigate the bumps in the road without losing sight of what really matters.

So, if you're dealing with organizational uncertainty (and let's be honest, who isn't?), remember that resilience is your secret weapon. Focus on what you can control, keep the team laughing, stay flexible, and always keep your eye on the prize. When the dust settles, you'll not only have survived the chaos—you'll have thrived through it. And hey, who knows, you might even discover some new juggling skills along the way.

***

Communicating in Times of Change

Communicating during times of change is like steering a ship through a storm—if everyone's not in sync, you'll end up off course, and someone's bound to feel seasick. When an organization faces transitions—whether it's a restructuring, new leadership, or even a shiny new process—clear, open communication is the anchor that keeps the team grounded and moving forward. The goal isn't just to survive the storm but to come out stronger on the other side.

One of the biggest roadblocks to effective communication, especially in times of change, is the infamous *silo effect*. Picture each department as its own little island, only sending the occasional message in a bottle to other departments. Sure, everything might seem fine on each island, but when the seas get rough and you're all rowing toward the same goal, those islands need to start talking—or you'll end up paddling in circles. Breaking down silos isn't just a "nice-to-have" during a company transition; it's essential. Cross-department communication helps ensure everyone is aligned, resources are shared, and surprises are minimized.

Let's paint a quick picture. Imagine marketing thinks they're launching a big campaign on Tuesday, but sales isn't ready until Thursday. That's a classic case of miscommunication. By opening up the lines of communication, leaders can make sure everyone's on the same page, aiming for the same goals. It's like making sure the whole orchestra is playing in tune—otherwise, it's just a bunch of noise (and nobody wants to listen to that kind of chaos).

So how do you keep the team informed during transitions? Here's where leadership really needs to step up. When change happens, the rumor mill can start working overtime, and if leaders aren't actively communicating, misinformation will spread faster than you can say, "Wait, what?" Suddenly, a minor change sounds like the company's about to go under. The best way to combat this? Get ahead of it. Be transparent, be proactive, and, most importantly, communicate often. The more information you share, the less room there is for rumors to take root.

Here's a tip: when it comes to communication during change, clarity is your best friend. Sending out long-winded emails full of corporate jargon won't help anyone. Instead, keep it simple, keep it clear, and make sure everyone understands what's happening and why. And, yes, you'll need to repeat yourself. I know it sounds redundant, but in times of stress or uncertainty, people don't always catch everything the first time around. Don't be afraid to reiterate key points and provide updates regularly—it'll help keep everyone grounded.

But let's not put all the responsibility on leadership. Employees, listen up—you've got a role to play too. If you're feeling out of the loop, don't just wait for someone to fill you in. Be proactive. Ask questions, attend those meetings (yes, even the long ones), and make sure you understand what's going on. The best way to stay informed is to take ownership of your understanding. And please, don't rely on the office grapevine for your news—go straight to the source. If something's unclear, raise your hand and ask for clarification.

And while we're on the subject, cross-department communication isn't just a leadership task—it's everyone's responsibility. If your team is working on something that affects another department, reach out and loop them in. A simple "Hey, just wanted to update you on this project" can prevent a last-minute fire drill. It's not just about keeping your team informed—it's about keeping the whole ship sailing smoothly.

Now, let's talk alignment. It's one thing to communicate; it's another to make sure everyone is on the same page. Regular check-ins and updates can make a world of difference here. I'm not suggesting hour-long meetings every day (no one has time for that), but quick, focused conversations can ensure that everyone knows the priorities and any updates to the plan. These touchpoints are essential for catching misalignments before they become bigger problems.

Leaders can also foster alignment by being transparent about the "why" behind the changes. When people understand the reasoning behind a shift, they're much more likely to buy into it. It's like going on a road trip: if you know where you're headed and why, the journey makes more sense. But if your driver keeps taking random turns without explaining, everyone in the car is going to get frustrated. During transitions, explain not just *what* is happening but *why* it's happening. That will keep your team focused on the bigger picture rather than getting stuck in the weeds.

And don't underestimate the power of humor. In times of change, a little lightheartedness can go a long way in easing tension. You don't have to turn into a stand-up comedian, but cracking a joke or sharing a funny story in a tense moment can help remind everyone that, yes, things are shifting, but we're all human, and we'll get through this together. As they say, laughter is the best medicine—and during times of uncertainty, it might just be the best communication tool too.

In the end, communicating during times of change is about keeping the ship steady. Whether you're leading the charge or navigating from within the team, clear, transparent communication is the key to ensuring everyone stays on course. Break down those silos, stay proactive, and keep the conversation going. And when in doubt, remember: a little humor can make the ride a whole lot smoother.

***

Creating a Culture of Continuous Improvement

Creating a culture of continuous improvement is one of the most effective ways to ensure that a workplace doesn't just survive but thrives in today's fast-paced, ever-changing world. And let's be honest, getting to that point where change becomes part of the daily routine isn't about forcing it on people—it's about getting them genuinely excited for it. After all, who wouldn't want to feel like they're constantly growing, learning, and becoming better at what they do? It's like turning your workplace into a gym for your brain and your skills—always stretching, always improving. And the best part? Once you build momentum, everyone starts to enjoy the process.

The key to fostering a culture of continuous improvement is to make it about small, consistent tweaks rather than overwhelming, big changes. Do you know how a great cup of coffee can set the tone for your whole morning? It's the little things that can add up to huge improvements over time. As leaders, we need to help everyone understand that "better" is something we're always chasing—there's no finish line in sight, and that's actually a good thing! We're always evolving, adapting, and finding new ways to be more efficient, creative, and productive.

In my experience, the best way to get started is by normalizing feedback—a lot of it. And I don't mean the kind of feedback that makes people feel like they're in trouble. I'm talking about constructive, forward-thinking feedback that's all about growth. It's like saying, "Hey, that was great, but have you thought about trying this next time?" or "I loved how you handled that; now let's see if we can streamline it even more." Feedback should be part of everyday conversations, where people get used to talking about how they can improve. No one should dread feedback; they should look forward to it because it's how they get better!

Another powerful way to foster continuous improvement is by encouraging curiosity. When employees are curious, they naturally start looking for ways to do things better. They ask questions, dig into processes, and think critically about how things work (or don't work) and how they can be improved. In my opinion, curiosity is the fuel for innovation. So, as a leader, you've got to make space for people to explore and experiment. If someone comes to you with an out-of-the-box idea, don't shoot it down—encourage them to run with it. Some of the best improvements come from those wild, creative moments that push the boundaries.

Of course, to build this kind of culture, you need to eliminate the fear of failure. This one's tricky because, let's face it, no one likes to fail. But here's the reality: failure is a natural part of improvement. If you're not failing at least a little, you're probably not pushing yourself enough. I like to say, "Fail fast, learn faster." If something doesn't work, that's fine—what did we learn from it? How can we use that failure to get better next time? It's all part of the process.

Here's the fun part: if you want to thrive in a constantly evolving workplace, you need to get everyone on board with the idea that change isn't something to fear—it's something to get excited about. Change isn't just something we *have* to deal with; it's something we *get* to embrace. The organizations that adapt the fastest are the ones that succeed in the long run. And that all starts with the right mindset.

You've probably heard about having a "growth mindset," but let me tell you, it's the real secret sauce. People with a growth mindset don't see challenges as roadblocks—they see them as opportunities to learn. When the company rolls out a new process or a system update, instead of resisting it, they say, "Okay, how can we make this even better?" They're not afraid to learn new things, and they certainly don't get stuck in the "that's how we've always done it" mentality. As leaders, it's our job to encourage this mindset across the board.

One strategy I love is rewarding small improvements. It doesn't always have to be about the big wins. If someone can streamline a process by five minutes or make a customer interaction smoother, celebrate it! Recognition goes a long way in motivating people to keep looking for ways to improve. When employees see their efforts are noticed and appreciated, they're more likely to keep at it. Before you know it, continuous improvement becomes contagious, and soon the whole team is in on it. That's when the real magic happens.

And speaking of magic, flexibility is essential. Change isn't always going to be tidy; sometimes, it'll throw people off their game for a bit. The key is to stay adaptable. When goals shift, leadership changes or processes evolve, remind your team (and yourself) that flexibility is part of the journey. Embrace the messiness because that's often where the best opportunities for improvement arise. It's like rearranging furniture—you might make a mess first, but the room looks fantastic once it's done.

Lastly, the best way to build a culture of continuous improvement is by leading by example. If you want your team to always look for ways to improve, you've got to do the same. Show them that you're constantly learning, adapting, and striving to be better. Whether you're picking up a new skill, trying out a new approach, or being open to feedback, when your team sees you embracing change and improvement, they'll be much more likely to follow suit.

In the end, thriving in a constantly evolving workplace isn't about dodging change—it's about leaning into it with enthusiasm and curiosity. It's about creating a culture where improvement is part of the everyday, where change is embraced, and where everyone is always looking for ways to grow. When you get that right, the company thrives, and so does every individual within it. And remember, as the wise saying goes, "Strive for continuous improvement, not perfection."

* * *

Managing Emotional Reactions to Change

Let's talk about something we all *love*—change. Just kidding! Most people don't love change; it can stir up a whirlwind of emotions—and not the fun kind. But whether we like it or not, change is inevitable, and how we manage our emotional reactions can make all the difference between sinking and swimming through times of transition.

Now, I get it—when change hits, especially at work, it's easy to feel overwhelmed. You might experience everything from anxiety and frustration to excitement and hope, sometimes all at once! It's like riding an emotional roller coaster, and not everyone enjoys those loops and dips. But here's the secret: those emotional reactions are completely normal. Yes, even the messy ones. The key is learning to navigate them without letting them take the wheel and drive you into a ditch.

First off, let's address the fact that when change shows up, our brains tend to react like we're facing a saber-toothed tiger. It triggers that fight-or-flight response because of change = unknown = potential danger. Of course, in today's workplace, most changes aren't life-threatening (though it might *feel* like it when you get that email about restructuring). But our emotional responses are still valid, and the first step is recognizing that it's okay to feel a little freaked out.

One of the best things we can do is permit ourselves to feel those emotions. You don't have to pretend everything's fine when you're secretly wondering, "What's happening to my job?!" Whether it's anxiety, confusion, or even excitement, acknowledging your emotions helps you process them. Suppressing feelings only leads to that inevitable emotional outburst in the break room, and nobody wants that.

Once we've allowed ourselves to feel all the feelings, it's time to work on managing them. A strategy that's helped me (and plenty of others) is focusing on what we can control. Change often feels overwhelming because it highlights how much is out of our hands. But here's a little secret: worrying about what you can't control is like trying to steer a ship by blowing on the sails. Not very effective. Instead, focus on the areas where you *do* have influence—your attitude, how you approach new tasks, or how you communicate during the transition. Shifting focus from the big, scary unknown to the small things you can control reduces stress and gives you a sense of empowerment.

Speaking of communication, it's a lifeline when dealing with emotional reactions to change. If something about the transition is unclear or you feel lost, ask questions! Whether it's a colleague, your boss, or even HR, seeking clarity can help soothe some anxiety-inducing "what ifs." And if you're the leader, communication is *everything*. One of the worst things you can do as a leader during times of change is to leave your team in the dark. Even if you don't have all the answers yet, being transparent and open about what you know goes a long way in easing uncertainty.

As a leader, it's important to understand that your team will have a range of emotional responses, and they won't all be in sync. Some people might jump into change with a "bring it on!" attitude, while others will be on the verge of panic. Your job is to meet them where they are. That means listening, acknowledging their feelings, and offering support. It could be as simple as a conversation to hear someone's concerns or offering resources like stress management workshops. Showing you genuinely care about their emotional well-being makes all the difference.

One thing that's helped me lead teams through emotionally charged transitions is creating space for people to process their emotions together. Whether it's a team meeting where everyone can voice how they're feeling or informal check-ins, it's important to make room for people to talk it out. Sometimes, just knowing they're not the only ones feeling frazzled can ease the emotional load.

Let's not forget the power of humor. When emotions are running high, a little lightheartedness can work wonders. I'm not suggesting laughing off someone's genuine concerns, but a well-timed joke can break the tension and remind everyone that we're all human and in this together. I've found that a shared laugh about "yet another system update" can help everyone feel a bit more relaxed and connected.

Another key piece of the puzzle is building resilience. Helping yourself and your team develop emotional resilience is critical during times of change. Resilience doesn't mean not feeling emotions; it means bouncing back from setbacks. Encourage your team (and yourself) to focus on past successes and remind them they've navigated tough changes before and emerged stronger. They have the skills and experience to handle what's coming.

And let's not forget about self-care. Change is exhausting, and if you're not taking care of yourself, burnout is just around the corner. Make sure you're getting enough sleep, eating well, and taking breaks when needed. Leaders especially need to model this for their teams. If your team sees you running yourself ragged, they'll think they need to do the same. Show them it's okay to take a breather and recharge, even during stressful transitions.

In the end, managing emotional reactions to change is all about balance. It's about recognizing the emotions, processing them, and then taking proactive steps to move forward. Change is inevitable, but emotional meltdowns don't have to be! With a little patience, a lot of communication, and maybe even a few laughs, you and your team can navigate the emotional roller coaster and come out stronger than ever. So buckle up, stay flexible, and remember: change isn't the enemy—how we react to it is.

***

Leveraging Technology During Transitions

Let's face it—technology has officially taken over, and there's no escaping it. Whether it's the latest app promising to streamline your day or that sleek gadget on your desk, the future isn't just a far-off sci-fi concept—it's happening right now. And in the workplace? It's one of the biggest arenas for these innovations. The good news? If we learn to embrace these tools and tech, we can stay ahead of the game, especially during times of transition.

I'll admit, there was a time when I felt a bit intimidated by new technology at work. That moment of, "Wait, what does this button do?" hits us all. But whether we like it or not, technology is key to staying agile in today's workplace. The trick is learning how to leverage it, especially when everything else is in flux. And let's be honest—there's a certain satisfaction in mastering that new software before anyone else does.

When transitions hit—whether it's a company restructuring, a leadership shuffle, or a strategic shift—technology is your best ally. Why? Because technology isn't just about making things faster or flashier; it's about creating opportunities to adapt, innovate, and ultimately thrive during times of change. Plus, it doesn't hurt that when you're the first one to figure out how to use that new tool, you look like a total rockstar.

One of the biggest advantages of technology during transitions is its ability to streamline communication. Remember when you had to wait for email replies or, worse, schedule endless meetings just to get everyone on the same page? Thanks to tools like Slack, Microsoft Teams, and Zoom, that's a distant memory. These platforms have become lifelines, especially when change is happening. When teams are scattered across departments, locations, or even time zones, these tools keep everyone connected, aligned, and—let's be real—probably a little too reachable. The key is using them wisely: keeping communication flowing without drowning in endless notifications.

Here's the fun part: technology doesn't just keep you in the loop—it simplifies transitions. Automation tools, for example, take those repetitive tasks off your plate so you can focus on the more strategic, creative work. Whether it's automating customer follow-ups, scheduling, or tracking project progress, tech can make transitions smoother by handling the nitty-gritty, freeing you to tackle the bigger picture. And let's be honest—who wouldn't want robots taking care of the boring stuff?

But the real game-changer? Data. Yes, data has become the secret sauce for navigating workplace transitions. With the right tech, you can gather insights, track performance, and make informed decisions faster. If your company is going through a major shift, technology provides real-time data to adapt strategies, measure success, and identify areas for improvement.

And when you're the one armed with all the facts, it's a whole lot easier to stay calm and focused during uncertain times.

Now, not everyone jumps for joy at the thought of learning a new software program or adapting to the latest tech trend. But here's the secret to staying ahead: embrace it, don't fight it. Every time you pick up a new tool or master an innovative process, you're future-proofing your career. The workplace is evolving at lightning speed, and those who embrace technology won't just survive—they'll thrive.

So, how do you ensure you're not left behind in the tech race? First, adopt a mindset of curiosity. Instead of groaning when the IT department rolls out a new tool, see it as an opportunity to sharpen your skills and add something new to your toolbox. Play around with it, ask questions, and find ways it can make your job easier. The more you experiment, the quicker you'll adapt. And who knows? You might become the office tech guru (which comes with the bonus of impressing your boss).

Another key strategy? Stay ahead of the curve by keeping an eye on emerging trends. Don't wait for your company to implement the next big thing—do a little research yourself. Whether it's AI, machine learning, or augmented reality, there are always new tools and innovations making waves in the workplace. By staying informed, you can position yourself as a forward-thinker who's not afraid of a little disruption. And let's be honest—nothing boosts your street cred like casually dropping phrases like "blockchain technology" or "machine learning" in the break room.

But perhaps the most important thing to remember is that technology is here to support us, not replace us. It's easy to feel like tech is just another thing we have to learn on top of everything else, but the truth is, it's designed to make our lives easier—if we let it. By leaning into new tools during transitions, we give ourselves the flexibility and freedom to focus on the bigger goals. Instead of getting bogged down by the details, technology empowers us to keep moving forward, even when everything around us is shifting.

So, whether you're a tech whiz or someone who still isn't quite sure what "the cloud" is, the future is here, and it's time to embrace it. Take ownership of the tools at your disposal, stay curious about innovations, and use technology to navigate transitions confidently and creatively. The next time change comes your way, you won't just survive—you'll thrive. And who knows? You might even have a little fun along the way.

* * *

Thriving in Remote or Hybrid Transitions

When the COVID-19 pandemic hit, it was like the world collectively slammed the "remote work" button. Overnight, Zoom replaced the conference room, pajamas became office attire, and "You're on mute" became the most repeated phrase in history. Companies scrambled to figure out virtual operations, and employees had to quickly adapt to working from home. Fast forward a few years, and while some people have returned to the office, many companies continue to embrace remote or hybrid work models. In fact, these models have become the new normal.

Now, I'll admit, I used to be a little skeptical about remote work. The appeal of skipping the commute and grabbing snacks from your kitchen between emails is undeniable. But when your office becomes your living room, it can feel like your work life and personal life start blending in odd ways. That said, whether you're full-on remote, splitting your time between home and the office, or still showing up to the office every day while others dial in from their couches, staying productive and engaged in any setting is the key to thriving.

For those of us transitioning to remote or hybrid work environments, the first thing to embrace is structure. In an office, there's a natural rhythm to the workday—scheduled meetings, lunch breaks, and the occasional chat by the water cooler. When working from home, you've got to create that rhythm for yourself. The couch might look inviting, but having a designated workspace helps keep your mind in "work mode." Trust me, separating where you work from where you binge Netflix will save you a lot of trouble.

And no, your bed doesn't count as an office.

One thing I've learned is that creating a routine while embracing flexibility is crucial. Sound like a contradiction? Here's what I mean: It's good to have a daily schedule—start your day at a set time, take regular breaks, and try to wrap up work around the same time each evening. But, one of the perks of remote work is that you don't have to stick to the traditional 9-to-5 if it doesn't work for you. If you're more productive in the evening or need a mid-day walk to clear your head, go for it. Flexibility is your friend, as long as you're meeting deadlines and keeping communication open with your team.

Speaking of communication, it's essential to stay connected when you're not physically in the office. Without those natural interactions, like bumping into someone at the coffee machine, it's easy to feel isolated. Make a point to engage with your colleagues beyond the required meetings. Whether it's through Slack, Microsoft Teams, or a good old-fashioned phone call, keep the conversations flowing. And hey, it's not all about work—sometimes sending a funny meme or checking in on someone's weekend is just as valuable as a meeting. Don't underestimate the power of these small moments to keep the team spirit alive.

Now, let's talk about one of the trickier parts of remote work—distractions. When you're at home, you're surrounded by things that can easily pull you away from your work: laundry, pets, kids, or even the endless allure of social media. Finding a balance is key. Whether you need productivity apps like the Pomodoro technique or just putting your phone out of reach during focus time, figure out what keeps you on track. And remember, it's okay to have off moments. The beauty of remote work is that you can find your own flow. Just try not to let a quick Instagram check turn into a two-hour scroll session (we've all been there).

For those working in a hybrid model, switching between home and office can be its own challenge. The pace and structure of office life are often much different than the more relaxed atmosphere of working from home. The trick here is consistency. Try to maintain the same habits whether you're at home or in the office. When you're in the office, maximize that time for face-to-face collaboration, brainstorming, or tackling projects that benefit from being in person. At home, find a routine that helps you stay productive without feeling disconnected.

At the end of the day, whether you're remote, hybrid, or holding down the fort at the office while the world works from home, adaptability is the name of the game. Embrace change rather than resist it. These new work models offer flexibility, autonomy, and a chance to rethink how we approach productivity. Sure, it might feel odd giving a presentation in sweatpants or attending a team meeting from your kitchen table, but if the last few years have taught us anything, it's that we can get the job done from just about anywhere.

So, whether you're working from your desk, your couch, or even a hammock in your backyard, the key is to stay flexible, stay connected, and embrace the shift. Who knows? Maybe your best ideas will come to you during that mid-day walk instead of in a conference room. The future of work is here, and the only thing left to do is thrive in it.

* * *

Setting New Goals During Periods of Change

When change hits, it can feel like someone's flipped the board game, sending all the pieces flying. You thought you were close to winning, but now the rules have changed, and you're not even sure where the board is anymore. Welcome to transition! Whether it's a company restructuring, a shift in leadership, or a new business direction, these periods can throw your goals into a tailspin. But here's the good news: when everything is in flux, it's the perfect opportunity to redefine success and set new goals. Think of it as being handed a fresh set of puzzle pieces—you might not know exactly how they fit together yet, but there's potential to build something completely new.

I've been part of teams that resist change, clinging to old goals that no longer make sense. Trust me, trying to achieve outdated milestones during a transition is like running a marathon in flip-flops—it's awkward, frustrating, and bound to give you blisters. Instead, the smart move is to take a step back, breathe, and acknowledge that what was important before may no longer be relevant. And that's okay! It's an opportunity to rethink what success looks like for your team and for yourself.

So how do you redefine success during a period of change? First, you need to assess the new landscape. What's changed? What's stayed the same? Maybe your team was focused on hitting certain revenue targets, but now the company is shifting to prioritize customer satisfaction. Or perhaps your role has transitioned from project management to more of a leadership position. Whatever the case, getting clarity on what has shifted and why is crucial. Talk to your team, leaders, and anyone with insight into the new direction. Clarity is key, especially when things feel uncertain.

Once you understand the changes, it's time to set new goals that align with the new direction while still giving your team a sense of purpose. Here's the fun part: redefining success isn't about abandoning what you've built—it's about leveraging your strengths in a fresh context. Ask yourself and your team, "What can we achieve now to help us grow in this new environment?" Your goals might shift from hitting specific numbers to building stronger client relationships, or from launching products to improving internal processes. It's all about staying flexible and adjusting your milestones to fit the new reality.

During times of transition, it's crucial to break down those big, overwhelming goals into smaller, achievable milestones. Change is already challenging, so don't add to the stress by setting goals that feel out of reach. Instead, focus on small wins that you can celebrate along the way. These mini-milestones will keep your team motivated and give everyone a sense of progress, even when the finish line seems to keep moving. Besides, who doesn't love an excuse to celebrate a win, no matter how small?

Clear communication is essential when setting new goals. Your team needs to understand not just what the new objectives are but also why they matter. This is where storytelling comes into play. Share a vision of what success looks like now and why it's exciting. Show your team how these new goals align with their strengths and contributions, and get them excited about the journey ahead. The more you connect the dots between the transition and their roles, the more motivated they'll be to move forward confidently.

It's also important to stay realistic. Transitions are rarely smooth, and there will be bumps along the way. Your team might not hit every new milestone right out of the gate, and that's perfectly fine. The goal is progress, not perfection. Redefining success during times of change isn't about nailing every target—it's about setting goals that push you in the right direction, even if you have to take a few detours along the way. Remind your team (and yourself) that growth takes time, especially when adjusting to a new normal. Patience and resilience will be your best allies.

Speaking of flexibility, don't be afraid to revisit and revise your goals as things evolve. Just because you've set new targets doesn't mean they're set in stone. One of the benefits of transition is that it's a fluid process, and as new challenges and opportunities arise, your goals might need to shift again. Stay open to this possibility and encourage your team to do the same. Adapting and pivoting when necessary is one of the most valuable skills you can develop during periods of change.

And don't forget to celebrate the wins—both big and small. It's easy to get bogged down by uncertainty and overlook the progress you're making. Whether you've hit a major milestone or just survived a particularly tough week, take the time to recognize your team's efforts. These moments of celebration will keep morale high and remind everyone that, despite the changes, you're still moving forward.

At the end of the day, setting new goals during periods of change is about embracing the unknown and using it as a platform for growth. It's not always easy, but with the right mindset and a willingness to adapt, you and your team can emerge from the transition stronger, more focused, and more aligned with the future. So let's ditch those flip-flops, lace up our running shoes, and start running this marathon with confidence, clarity, and maybe a little bit of fun along the way.

Pivoting and Thriving in a New Role or Industry

So, you've decided to make a career transition—a bold move! Whether it's switching roles within your current field or jumping headfirst into a completely new industry, the process can feel a little like walking into a party where you don't know anyone. You're excited but also wondering if you're wearing the right thing and hoping someone offers you chips and dip. Trust me, I've been there. Career transitions can be intimidating, but they're also packed with opportunity if you approach them with the right mindset.

Let's start with something that might ease your nerves—transferable skills. You might not realize it yet, but you're already carrying a toolkit that can help you succeed in just about any role or industry. Think of these as your superpowers—the skills you've built over the years that apply no matter where you end up. Communication, problem-solving, leadership, adaptability—these are the gems that can smooth out your transition. Whether you're moving from marketing to sales, finance to tech, or corporate life to a freelance hustle, these core skills will serve you well.

I remember when I made a major career pivot myself, and at first, it felt like I was starting from scratch. It was overwhelming. But then I took a step back and really thought about the skills I'd built in my previous roles. I had experience managing teams, solving complex problems, and—let's not forget—navigating tricky office politics (every workplace has its own unique flavor of that). Once I realized these skills were just as valuable in my new role, I felt more confident. It wasn't about throwing away everything I knew—it was about repackaging it for a new context. Suddenly, I wasn't starting from scratch; I was building on a strong foundation.

Next up: continuous learning. You can't just waltz into your new role, throw down your laptop (or briefcase if you're feeling retro), and declare yourself an expert. Embrace the fact that you're going to be a learner again. This is your chance to absorb new knowledge, master new tools, and maybe even reinvent your work. It's an exciting process when you lean into it, not to mention a great way to prove to yourself (and others) that you're adaptable and ready for anything.

And here's a pro tip: Stay curious. When you're new to a role or industry, you have the perfect excuse to ask all the questions. Take advantage of that honeymoon phase! Ask why things are done the way they are, how processes could be improved, or what the key challenges are in your new field. People are usually happy to share their insights, especially when you approach with genuine curiosity and a willingness to learn. And hey, they might even give you a few pointers that will save you from those classic rookie mistakes.

Now, let's address the elephant in the room: imposter syndrome. If you haven't felt it yet during your career transition, don't worry, it's probably just waiting for the right moment to make its grand entrance. That little voice that says, "What are you doing here? You don't belong in this role!" Yeah, we've all been there. Here's the thing: it's normal. The fact that you're feeling out of your depth means you're stretching yourself—and that's a good thing! Every expert was once a beginner. Own your learning curve, make a few mistakes, and keep pushing forward. Remember, growth happens outside your comfort zone.

Speaking of mistakes, let's reframe how we think about them. During a career pivot, you're bound to have a few missteps. Maybe you'll take the wrong approach in your new job, or maybe you'll have that awkward moment where you forget a basic industry term (yep, been there too). Instead of beating yourself up, treat those moments as learning experiences. Every stumble is a stepping stone to mastery, and the faster you embrace that, the more resilient you'll be.

Another key to thriving in a new role or industry? Build your network. Don't isolate yourself, thinking you need to figure everything out on your own. Find mentors, connect with colleagues, and get involved in industry groups or online forums. Not only will you gain valuable insights, but

THRIVING IN TRANSITION

you'll also build relationships that can support you as you grow in your new career. Plus, having a solid network makes the whole process much more enjoyable. After all, who doesn't want a few allies in the trenches when things get tough?

And don't be afraid to reinvent your personal brand. If you've spent years as the "numbers guy" but are now transitioning into a more creative field, it's time to showcase a different side of yourself. Update your resume, LinkedIn profile, and how you talk about your experience to reflect where you're headed, not just where you've been. It's about shifting your narrative to highlight the skills and experiences that are relevant to your new direction. Reinvention is exciting—it's like getting a fresh start without losing all the work you've already put in.

Lastly, celebrate the small wins. Career transitions can be a long process, and it's easy to feel like progress is slow. But every new skill you learn, every relationship you build, and every challenge you overcome is a victory. Keep track of those wins, no matter how small they seem. They'll help you stay motivated and remind you that you're making progress, even if you're still finding your footing.

So, whether you're pivoting into a new role, diving into a new industry, or completely reinventing yourself, remember this: you've got the tools to succeed. Lean into your transferable skills, stay curious, and embrace the learning process. Don't let imposter syndrome hold you back. Reinvent your brand, build your network, and keep celebrating those small victories along the way. Career transitions aren't always easy, but they're an opportunity for growth and reinvention. And if you can navigate this pivot, you can navigate anything! Just remember to keep a sense of humor—you'll need it for the ride.

* * *

How Disruption Sparks New Ideas

Change often feels like that unwelcome guest who arrives at the worst possible time—uninvited, unexpected, and disruptive. But here's the thing: that disruptive guest? It's actually a catalyst in disguise, nudging us out of our comfort zones and into innovation. When the usual ways of doing things are upended, it creates the perfect conditions for fresh thinking, creative solutions, and bold new ideas that may never have been considered otherwise. In fact, some of the most groundbreaking innovations have emerged from moments of major disruption.

Take Airbnb, for example. In 2008, founders Brian Chesky and Joe Gebbia weren't exactly dreaming of revolutionizing the hospitality industry—they were just trying to pay their rent in San Francisco. A design conference was coming to town, hotels were booked, and they needed a solution. So, they offered up their living room air mattress to attendees, along with breakfast, and advertised it on a simple website: Air Bed & Breakfast. They got three takers. That's when the lightbulb moment hit.

Initially, Airbnb faced skepticism from investors, and the idea of staying in a stranger's home seemed a little weird to most people. But instead of backing down, Chesky and Gebbia leaned into the discomfort. They saw the hotel industry as ripe for disruption and decided to challenge the status quo. The 2008 financial crisis, which left many homeowners looking for new ways to make money, actually fueled their growth. As people became more open to alternative income streams, Airbnb's model took off. What started as a way to make rent became a multi-billion-dollar company that completely redefined the way we think about travel.

What's the lesson here? Disruption forces us to rethink how we operate. It pushes us to get creative, challenge norms, and see things differently. When everything is running smoothly, we tend to stick with what we know works. But when the usual methods break down, we're given a unique opportunity to innovate and explore new possibilities. It's often in these moments of uncertainty that the best ideas emerge.

I've seen this happen firsthand. I once consulted for a retail company facing a sharp decline in foot traffic—no surprise in the age of e-commerce. The easy option would have been to continue as usual and hope for the best. But instead, the company took the disruption as a sign to rethink the entire shopping experience. We brainstormed what could make their physical stores not just relevant, but irresistible in a world of online shopping. The result? They transformed their stores into interactive experiences, complete with digital fitting rooms and personalized services that couldn't be replicated online. By embracing the disruption, they didn't just survive—they thrived.

What makes this approach so powerful? It's all about mindset. Rather than seeing disruption as a roadblock, successful innovators view it as a catalyst for creativity and growth. When the status quo is shattered, we have the chance to build something better. Disruption forces us to ask, "How can we do this differently?" It opens the door to experimentation, which can lead to solutions that are not only creative but often far superior to what existed before.

This mindset applies just as much to individuals as it does to companies. When personal or professional disruption hits—a job loss, a major industry shift, or even a global pandemic—it's easy to focus on what's been lost. But if you step back and look at the bigger picture, there's almost always an opportunity hidden in the chaos. Instead of asking, "Why is this happening to me?" ask, "What can I create from this?"

It's easy to resist change. Let's face it, we like our routines. But when disruption shakes things up, it's a chance to pivot, adapt, and explore new paths that might not have been obvious before. It's the perfect time to leverage what you already know and reimagine how it can be applied in a new, innovative way.

The key to thriving during disruption is adaptability. You don't need to have all the answers, but you do need to be willing to experiment, fail, learn, and keep moving forward. I often tell teams I work with, "Don't fear the mess—embrace it." The messiness of change is where the magic happens. It's where new ideas get sparked, where creativity takes over, and where the most exciting breakthroughs occur.

And let's not forget that humor can go a long way when everything feels upside down. Sometimes, in the middle of a chaotic transition, the ability to laugh at the absurdity of the situation can provide the clarity and levity needed to spark fresh ideas. After all, if you can't laugh at the unpredictability of it all, you're missing out on the best part of the ride!

Ultimately, disruption is an opportunity in disguise. It may not feel comfortable—change rarely does—but it's a powerful driver of innovation. The next time you find yourself facing a significant shift, whether in your business, your industry, or your life, remember this: disruption sparks new ideas. The more you lean into it, the more you'll uncover the potential to create, innovate, and thrive. So, when life flips the board game, don't panic—just start playing with the new pieces. Who knows what you might build?

* * *

From Surviving to Thriving

Moving from simply surviving to thriving during workplace changes is a bit like crawling through mud and then breaking into a joyful dance in the rain. Change can feel messy, unpredictable, and uncomfortable, but it's also the space where real growth and innovation happen. It's where your team gets the chance to turn challenges into opportunities and show that they're not just reacting to change but embracing it and thriving because of it. To thrive in times of transition, you don't need to have all the answers or avoid the occasional tough spot—it's all about resilience, adaptability, and staying forward-thinking. This is how challenges turn into opportunities, and disruption becomes a stepping stone to success.

Let's start with resilience, the secret weapon of any thriving team. Think of resilience like a muscle—the more you use it, the stronger it becomes. Being resilient doesn't mean avoiding setbacks; it means bouncing back from them, sometimes with a smile or even a laugh. As a leader, you can help set the tone by normalizing setbacks and framing them as opportunities to learn. When your team knows it's okay to stumble, they're more willing to take risks, recover from failures, and keep pushing forward. And, hey, cracking a joke after a setback can lighten the mood and remind everyone that it's okay to stumble as long as you get back up.

Building a culture of resilience starts with encouraging a growth mindset. When challenges arise, instead of the collective groan of "Oh no, not this again," inspire your team to think, "What can we learn from this?" This shift in mindset transforms obstacles into opportunities. A team that adopts this approach starts to see every challenge as a hurdle they can either leap over or at least stumble through with a little bit of grace. And remember, if you can laugh at the twists and turns, you're already halfway to success.

Next up is adaptability, the cornerstone of thriving during change. Adaptability is all about staying flexible when the ground beneath you keeps shifting, like playing a never-ending game of job-description Twister. You might be asked to touch red with your left foot while balancing new tasks with your right hand, all while keeping your cool. The key to thriving through all this is keeping an open mind and staying nimble.

One of the best ways to foster adaptability is by creating a culture of experimentation. Let your team know it's okay to try new approaches, even if they don't always work out. Think of it as a "fail forward" mindset—each misstep is another step toward figuring things out. Leaders can create low-risk opportunities for testing new ideas, like piloting a small change with a few team members before rolling it out more broadly. This not only reduces the fear of failure but also empowers your team to think creatively and take ownership of navigating the transition.

Forward-thinking is the final piece of the thriving puzzle, and it's all about staying ahead of the game—even when the present feels like a high-stakes round of Whack-a-Mole. Teams that thrive don't just react to change—they anticipate it. They stay curious, look for trends, and ask themselves, "How can we get ahead of this?" As a leader, you can encourage forward thinking by making continuous learning part of your team's culture. Whether through professional development, workshops, or simply keeping up with industry trends, the more informed and proactive your team is, the better they'll handle whatever changes come their way.

Setting new, relevant goals during a transition is also key. When things are up in the air, it's easy for your team to feel lost or aimless. That's why it's important to redefine what success looks like in the new context. Maybe the focus shifts from speed to quality or from individual performance to collaboration. Whatever the case, make sure your team understands the new priorities and feels a sense of ownership over them. And remember, not every goal has to be huge—sometimes, keeping the team engaged and moving forward is the win.

Now, let's talk communication. Open, clear communication is a must during any transition. It's not enough to send out a company-wide email and call it a day. Leaders need to actively seek input from their teams, ask questions, and listen to what's being said. Regular check-ins—not just about tasks, but about how people are feeling—are essential. It's not about coddling; it's about understanding where the team is emotionally and making necessary adjustments. Sometimes, just having a space to talk it out can defuse tension and bring some much-needed perspective. And, yes, humor can work wonders here, too. A little light-hearted banter can go a long way in easing stress and keeping spirits high during the chaos.

Lastly, don't underestimate the power of celebrating small wins. It's easy to focus solely on the big picture during a major transition, but recognizing the little victories along the way is crucial. Whether it's hitting a tight deadline, coming up with a creative solution, or just getting through a tough week, those small moments of success deserve acknowledgment. Celebrating them boosts morale and reinforces the positive behaviors that help teams thrive.

In the end, thriving during change isn't about having it all figured out. It's about fostering resilience, staying adaptable, and always keeping an eye on the future. The next time change comes knocking, don't brace for impact—invite it in and see where it takes you. Together, with the right mindset and a sense of humor, your team won't just survive the transition—they'll come out stronger, more innovative, and better connected than ever before.

THRIVING IN TRANSITION

After all, thriving in change isn't about perfection; it's about embracing the journey, one twist and turn at a time.

12

Firing With Compassion

Let's face it: firing someone is one of the toughest parts of leadership. It's not fun, and it's certainly not something anyone looks forward to, but sometimes it's necessary. Whether due to performance issues, a cultural mismatch, or a shift in company direction, not everyone is the right fit forever. And while the word "firing" carries a harsh ring, it doesn't have to be a cold, impersonal event. In fact, when done with compassion, it can be a respectful, even humane experience for both sides.

We've all heard horror stories—people getting let go by email or finding out when their keycard stops working. It's like breaking up with someone via text: impersonal and cruel. But firing someone doesn't have to feel like an execution. If handled with empathy and care, it can open the door to new opportunities for the person, while creating space for your team to thrive.

Here's the truth: keeping someone in a role where they're struggling doesn't help anyone. It's like forcing yourself into shoes that don't fit—they'll only give you blisters in the long run. Sometimes, the kindest thing you can do is help someone find a better fit elsewhere. It's not about kicking them to the curb; it's about supporting their next move, and who knows—they might even thank you later for the nudge.

Firing with compassion is all about your approach. You don't just drop the news and disappear into HR oblivion. You handle it with grace and respect—maybe even with a little humor to lighten the moment. After all, it doesn't have to feel like a courtroom drama. Be clear, kind, and constructive. Think of it as sending someone off on their next adventure, with honesty and appreciation for their contributions. Sure, maybe throw in a joke like, "It's not you, it's us—well, okay, maybe it's a little you," but make sure the person knows they're valued, even if the role wasn't the right fit.

Timing matters, too. No one should be blindsided by being let go, so ongoing feedback is key. By the time you have that final conversation, it shouldn't come as a shock. Address issues early, give people a chance to improve, and if it's still not working, at least they'll understand why.

Finally, offer support during the transition. Severance, job placement assistance, and extending benefits are ways to show you care beyond their time with the company. It's about parting ways with dignity and keeping the door open for positive future connections.

At the end of the day, letting someone go should be handled with the same respect and care you'd hope for yourself. It's tough, but it's not about being the villain—it's about making the best decision for everyone involved. After all, what feels like an ending today could be the start of something better for them—and for you. And let's be honest, we've all dodged a bad pair of shoes at some point!

Let's take a closer look at Airbnb, a company that faced one of its most challenging moments in 2020 and transformed how it handled layoffs. We all know Airbnb as the leader in home-sharing, connecting millions of travelers with unique stays around the globe. But when the COVID-19 pandemic hit, and travel ground to a halt, Airbnb found itself in crisis. Almost overnight, one of the fastest-growing companies in the world was forced to make the difficult decision to let go of a significant portion of its workforce to survive.

Layoffs are never easy, but Airbnb decided to handle this situation with as much compassion and respect as possible. CEO Brian Chesky and his leadership team made it clear from the start: if they had to let people go, they would do it in a way that honored the humanity of each employee. There would be no impersonal emails, no sudden pink slips, and certainly no cold, corporate handling like you see in some companies.

Airbnb began by being completely transparent. Chesky sent a heartfelt letter to the entire company, explaining the financial impact of the pandemic and the necessity of the layoffs. He didn't sugarcoat the situation, but he also didn't hide behind corporate jargon. He took full responsibility for the difficult decision and showed genuine empathy, expressing how hard this was for him and the leadership team.

The process itself was handled with an "employee-first" approach. Airbnb offered generous severance packages, extended healthcare benefits, and job placement support. They even created a talent directory—an online platform showcasing the profiles of laid-off employees to help them connect with other companies. On top of that, Airbnb allowed employees to keep their laptops, recognizing the practical need to job hunt with proper tools.

One of the most thoughtful gestures was how they communicated the layoffs. Instead of sending mass emails, managers reached out personally to each affected employee. These conversations were respectful and genuine, acknowledging each person's contributions to the company. It was clear that their time at Airbnb was valued, and the company made sure to handle the situation with dignity.

So, why did Airbnb choose such a compassionate approach? Because they understood the long-term impact of their actions. Companies that handle layoffs without care risk creating a culture of fear and mistrust. Employees who remain often feel demoralized, constantly wondering if they'll be next, which can stifle innovation and collaboration. By treating employees with kindness, even in tough times, Airbnb strengthened the morale and trust of those who stayed.

The response was remarkable. Instead of bitterness, many laid-off employees took to social media to express their gratitude, thanking Airbnb for how they were treated. This is almost unheard of in the corporate world. By handling the layoffs with empathy, Airbnb managed to preserve its reputation as a caring employer and turned a painful transition into a case study in compassionate leadership.

Firing with compassion does more than soften the blow for those who leave—it sends a powerful message to those who stay: "We value you, even when times are tough." It builds loyalty, preserves dignity, and fosters trust. While it may be easier to take a cold, procedural approach to layoffs, doing so can leave lasting damage to a company's culture.

Airbnb's story proves that handling layoffs with empathy and respect isn't just good for public relations—it's smart business. By showing that people matter, even in the hardest moments, Airbnb built a foundation of trust that will help them weather future challenges. In a world where circumstances can change overnight, that's the kind of company anyone would want to be part of.

***

The Ethics of Letting Go

Let's talk about one of the toughest parts of leadership: letting someone go. Yes, we're talking about the corporate equivalent of the "F" word—firing. It's awkward, and uncomfortable, and no one ever looks forward to it. But here's the reality: sometimes, it's necessary. Whether it's due to budget cuts, poor performance, or simply a bad fit, not every employee is going to be the right match forever. And while firing someone is never fun, it can be done with compassion, dignity, and respect.

First things first: firing with compassion isn't just about being nice; it's about doing what's right for both the individual and the company. As leaders, we have an ethical obligation to handle terminations in a way that honors the person, not just the position. People aren't just cogs in the corporate machine—they have lives, families, and futures to consider. Handling a termination carelessly can have lasting effects, not just on the person being let go but also on the morale of the entire team.

Let's rewind for a second and think about why terminations happen. Whether it's restructuring, financial cuts, or performance issues, the outcome is the same—someone's job is ending. It's a big deal, and if we handle it with cold efficiency, we miss the opportunity to do it right. Firing someone isn't just about clearing a desk; it's about managing the human element with empathy.

Now, I'm not saying you need to turn every termination into a heart-to-heart therapy session, but there's a huge difference between firing someone with grace and blindsiding them with a cold, impersonal email. I once knew a manager who actually fired people via text message—talk about setting a new low. Not only did that destroy trust, but it also tanked team morale. People remember how they're treated in tough moments, and bad exits leave lasting scars.

So, what does it mean to fire with compassion? First, it starts with honesty and transparency. If someone is underperforming or there's a chance they might be let go, they shouldn't be blindsided by the decision. Consistent feedback and open communication can help ease the shock. Think of it like ending a relationship—you don't just ignore the problems and then drop the breakup bomb one day. The same goes for letting someone go at work—give them the chance to improve and be clear about what's not working.

Next, offer support. Whether it's severance, extended benefits, or helping them transition to a new role, showing you care beyond their employment with your company is a key part of ethical leadership. And if you're thinking, "That's not my problem anymore," think again. Offering support isn't just ethical—it's smart business. It shows your team that you value people, even when things don't work out, and it maintains a level of trust and morale for those who stay.

Compassionate terminations also involve giving the individual a voice. No, this doesn't mean turning the decision into a debate, but simply acknowledging their perspective can go a long way. Sometimes, all it takes is a simple, "I understand this is tough, and I'm here to listen." It shows you respect them as a person, not just as a former employee.

And timing? It matters. Firing someone at 5 p.m. on a Friday isn't just inconsiderate; it leaves them without any support until the following week. Choose a time when you can be available for follow-up questions, and make sure they're not left feeling isolated or blindsided.

At the end of the day, firing with compassion is about more than just doing the right thing in the moment—it's about building a culture of trust and respect. Your team is watching how you handle tough decisions, and when they see you treat people with dignity, it reinforces that you care about them as individuals, not just as employees.

Firing someone is never easy, but it's an essential part of leadership. By approaching it with transparency, support, and respect, you maintain your integrity and uphold a company culture where people feel valued—even in difficult moments. Because no one wants to be remembered as the leader who fired someone like they were canceling a subscription. We can, and should, do better.

***

Preparing for a Difficult Conversation: The Steps to Take Before Terminating

Preparing for a difficult conversation, especially when it involves terminating an employee, is one of the toughest tasks a leader faces. It's never something to be done lightly or impulsively. Termination isn't just about ending someone's job; it's about impacting their livelihood, their self-esteem, and possibly their career trajectory. That's why preparation is absolutely key. Before initiating that conversation, you need to be sure the decision is fair, well-documented, and the best choice for everyone involved.

Let's break down the steps to take before you sit down for that tough conversation. Proper preparation not only makes the process smoother but also ensures you're acting ethically and responsibly.

- **Assess performance objectively:** The first step is to objectively assess the employee's performance. This isn't the time for vague impressions or gut feelings. You need hard facts—clear patterns of missed deadlines, underperformance, or behavioral issues. Look back at documented feedback, performance evaluations, and any discussions you've had about their work. Consistent underperformance over time is what you're looking for, not just a bad day here and there. Concrete evidence is key. This ensures the decision isn't based on emotion or a recent misstep, but on documented history. After all, firing someone shouldn't be the workplace equivalent of "Oops, wrong button."

- **Document issues and provide feedback:** One of the biggest mistakes leaders make is not documenting performance issues adequately. If an employee hasn't been told there's a problem, how can they be expected to fix it? Documentation is not just a way to cover your bases—it's about being transparent and giving employees a fair chance to improve. Whenever you've had feedback sessions—whether formal reviews or informal conversations—make sure they're well-documented. The employee needs to know what's going wrong, and there should be a clear record of that. If deadlines were missed or behavior was unacceptable, document what was discussed and the agreed-upon steps to improve. This helps ensure the employee isn't blindsided when you reach the point of considering termination.

- **Provide opportunities for improvement:** Before reaching the point of termination, make sure you've provided the employee with ample opportunity to improve. Whether through additional training, adjusted responsibilities, or a performance improvement plan (PIP), the goal is to genuinely help the employee succeed. A PIP isn't just a formality—it's your last-ditch effort to support the employee and set them on a better path. If you've offered every tool and resource, and still see no improvement, then you can move forward knowing you've done your due diligence as a leader.

- **Consult with HR and legal advisors:** Before making any final decisions, it's wise to consult with your HR team and, if necessary, legal advisors. This step ensures the termination is not only legally sound but also fair and in line with company policies. HR can help review documentation and make sure the process is consistent with past situations. The goal is to avoid any legal pitfalls and ensure you're treating the employee fairly, not just checking boxes.

- **Prepare for the conversation:** Once the groundwork is laid, it's time to prepare for the conversation itself. This is where things can get tricky—knowing what to say and how to say it. You want to be clear, concise, and to the point. Avoid long explanations or ambiguous language. State the decision, back it up with documented evidence, and outline the next steps. It's also important to practice your delivery. I know it sounds a bit silly, but saying the words out loud beforehand can make a huge difference. You'll feel more comfortable and composed, and the conversation will flow more naturally.

- **Anticipate reactions and prepare responses:** No two terminations are alike, and employees will react in different ways—some may be upset, others relieved. Try to anticipate how the employee might respond and be ready to address those emotions calmly and professionally. If they have questions, be prepared to reiterate the reasoning behind the decision without getting defensive. This is a difficult conversation for them, but it's also a moment where you can show empathy and maintain respect.

- **Plan the logistics:** Finally, plan the logistics. Where will the conversation take place? Who will be present? How will the employee transition out of their role, and what support will they receive? These details matter. Choose a private, respectful setting for the conversation and make sure any necessary paperwork—like severance agreements or benefits information—is ready. The smoother you can make this process, the more dignity the employee will feel during an incredibly tough moment.

Terminating an employee is never easy, but with proper preparation, you can ensure the decision is made fairly, documented thoroughly, and handled with the respect it deserves. At the end of the day, it's not just about making a difficult call—it's about doing it the right way, for everyone involved. And remember, this is a part of leadership that tests your character. Handle it well, and you'll maintain both your integrity and your team's trust.

* * *

Handling the Termination Meeting with Care

Walking into a termination meeting is like stepping into a high-stakes, heart-pounding moment—like walking a tightrope without a safety net. You know it's got to happen, and you've done all the prep work, but now it's time to deliver the news. And let's be honest: no matter how justified or well-documented the decision is, breaking the news to someone that they're losing their job will never be a pleasant experience. But here's the thing—how you handle this conversation says a lot about you as a leader and sets the tone for the individual's exit (and maybe even your whole company's culture).

The goal isn't just to get through it but to do it with empathy, respect, and as much care as possible. So, let's tackle handling the termination meeting like a leader who genuinely cares, even when the situation is tough.

The setting of the termination meeting is crucial. No one wants to hear they're being let go in the middle of a noisy office or a busy conference room with glass walls. Choose a private, quiet location where you won't be interrupted. It's not just about privacy; it's about creating a space where the person feels like they have a moment to process the news without the added anxiety of having others watch.

Think about the seating arrangement, too. Sitting across a big desk might feel too formal and cold, almost like you're placing a barrier between you and them. Instead, opt for a more conversational setup—two chairs next to each other, or at least sitting on the same side of the table, if possible. This setup communicates that you're on the same side, even in this difficult moment.

Before you say a single word, your body language is already speaking volumes. Walk in with confidence but not arrogance—no one needs to see you strutting in like you're about to win an award. Sit calmly, maintain an open posture, and make eye contact without staring them down. Crossed arms or leaning back with your hands behind your head? Hard pass. Those gestures can make you seem defensive or disconnected.

Your tone should be firm but compassionate. Consider the tone you'd use to break disappointing but important news to a friend. You're not there to sugarcoat the situation, but you're also not there to drop the hammer with a gleeful grin. Start with a calm, steady voice. Slow your speech a bit—rushing through will make you seem anxious or like you're trying to escape the conversation.

Here's the golden rule: keep it direct but kind. You're there to communicate a decision, not to justify it with a play-by-play of every mistake the person ever made. They likely already know why this is happening, especially if you've done your job leading up to this point with feedback and performance discussions.

Start with a straightforward statement, "I appreciate you meeting with me today. Unfortunately, I have to let you know that we've made the difficult decision to end your employment with us, effective immediately." Notice the key elements: it's clear and direct, and it doesn't leave room for confusion, but it also doesn't come off as harsh.

After delivering the news, pause. Give them a moment to process. This pause might feel like the longest ten seconds of your life, but it's necessary. Resist the urge to fill the silence with awkward explanations. Just let them absorb what you've said.

Now, this part is crucial: listen. After delivering the news, the individual might react with shock, sadness, anger, or indifference. Everyone processes news differently, and your job is to be there immediately without getting defensive or shutting down. Show empathy, not pity. Phrases like, "I know this is difficult" or "I understand this is not what you wanted to hear" go a long way in showing that you're aware of the emotional weight of the situation.

If they have questions or comments, let them speak. Don't interrupt or cut them off, even if what they say isn't easy to hear. Your role here is to be present and acknowledge their feelings without turning the conversation into a debate. Keep your responses short and focused: "I understand how you feel" or "I hear what you're saying." This isn't the time to get into the nitty-gritty details of every decision point; the termination meeting is about the present moment.

One of the worst things you can do in a termination meeting is to play the blame game. Saying things like, "You didn't meet your targets" or "You failed to improve" can feel like pouring salt in the wound. The decision has been made, and rehashing every misstep won't make it easier for anyone. Focus on the fact that this decision, while difficult, is the best course of action for both parties moving forward.

Instead, frame it in terms of fit or alignment: "We've reached a point where this role is no longer the right fit," or "We need to move in a different direction." This approach maintains the dignity of the individual without glossing over the truth.

Once the initial news is delivered, the next step is to outline what happens next. Whether it's discussing severance, how to handle their final paycheck, benefits, or the process for turning in company property, clarity is key. Be prepared with all the necessary information and any paperwork they'll need. If you have an HR representative present, let them handle the nitty-gritty details, but make sure the employee knows who to contact if they have follow-up questions.

If appropriate, offer resources or support, like career counseling or job placement services. Even if they don't take you up on it, the gesture shows that you care about their transition, not just that you're eager to show them the door.

As the meeting wraps up, be respectful and thank them for their contributions, even if their time with the company didn't end as planned. A simple "I appreciate the work you've done here" or "I wish you all the best in your next steps" can help soften the end of the conversation.

Avoid clichés like, "This hurts me more than it hurts you"—because honestly, no one wants to hear that. Instead, focus on acknowledging the situation for what it is: "I know this is hard, and I appreciate your professionalism during this conversation."

Remember: it's about humanity, not just business.

At the end of the day, a termination meeting isn't just a business transaction—it's a deeply human experience. Your goal is to deliver the news clearly and fairly but also with compassion and respect. The way you handle these moments reflects not only on you as a leader but also on the values of your organization.

When done right, even the toughest conversations can be conducted with dignity, leaving the individual feeling respected, if not entirely happy. And who knows? Handling these moments with care might just be the difference between someone leaving bitter or feeling like they've been treated with fairness and respect, even in tough circumstances.

Remember, it's not about making the news easy—it's about making it humane. And that, my friend, is how you lead with heart, even when the going gets tough.

***

The Role of HR During a Termination

Navigating the process of terminating an employee is one of the most challenging tasks any organization faces, and it requires a careful balance of empathy, fairness, and adherence to legal standards. In these moments, HR professionals play a crucial role, serving as the bridge between the company's need to maintain its standards and policies and the human element that underpins every termination. It's a delicate dance: we must uphold the law and company policy while ensuring that the process respects the dignity of the individual involved. As someone who's been involved in many of these situations, I've seen firsthand how critical HR's role is in making sure that compassionate termination isn't just a buzzword but a real practice.

HR's involvement in termination is not just about ensuring compliance with laws and company policies; it's about humanizing what is inherently a difficult and often painful process. HR professionals are often perceived as the enforcers of rules, but the best HR teams understand that their job is also to advocate for the well-being of employees. Balancing these two roles requires a deep understanding of both the legal landscape and the human impact of termination.

The first step HR takes in any termination process is ensuring the decision is justified and well-documented. This isn't just about protecting the company from legal repercussions; it's about fairness. Every employee deserves to be treated fairly, which means making sure the termination decision is based on solid grounds, whether it's performance issues, misconduct, or a necessary business restructuring. The role of HR is to meticulously review the situation, ensuring that all relevant policies have been followed, that any disciplinary actions were appropriately documented, and that the employee was given a fair chance to improve or rectify the situation where possible.

In my experience, this process often involves close collaboration between HR and management. It's our job in HR to ask the tough questions: Was the employee given clear expectations? Were they provided with feedback and support to address their performance issues? Did we exhaust all reasonable avenues for improvement before deciding to terminate? This diligence not only protects the company but also ensures that the employee has been treated fairly up to the point of termination.

Once it's clear that termination is the right course of action, HR's role shifts to balancing policy with compassion. We have to ensure that all legal requirements are met—things like final paychecks, severance agreements, COBRA notifications, and other compliance issues must be handled with precision. But the legal boxes to check don't have to overshadow the human element of the process.

One of the key ways HR can bring compassion into the termination process is by guiding managers on how to conduct the termination meeting itself. Many managers aren't comfortable with these conversations—who can blame them? Terminating someone's employment is never easy. HR's role is to coach and prepare the manager, providing them with guidance on what to say, how to say it, and most importantly, how to handle the conversation with empathy. We equip managers with phrases that convey respect and understanding, and we encourage them to listen actively, acknowledging the employee's emotions without getting defensive or dismissive.

HR professionals often participate directly in the termination meeting, not just as witnesses to protect the company but also as supporters of the employee. Our presence ensures that the conversation stays on track, remains respectful, and communicates all necessary information. We also answer questions the employee might have about their final pay, benefits, or next steps. In essence, HR's role is to ensure that the termination is handled with as much dignity and clarity as possible.

Compassionate termination goes beyond the initial meeting. HR's involvement continues as we help guide the employee through the transition. This can include offering resources such as career counseling, job placement assistance, or access to mental health services. Providing these supports isn't just about easing the employee's transition—it's also about maintaining a positive relationship even as the employment relationship ends. Employees who feel supported, even in termination, are less likely to harbor resentment and more likely to speak positively about the company in the future.

HR is also responsible for communicating with the remaining team members after a termination. The message must be handled delicately, respecting the privacy of the individual who was let go while maintaining transparency about the decision in a way that reinforces the company's commitment to fairness and high standards. The goal is to prevent rumors, reassure the team, and maintain morale during a destabilizing time.

While compassion is at the heart of a humane termination process, legal compliance cannot be overlooked. HR's role in managing terminations is as much about protecting the company as it is about supporting the employee. We have to ensure that all actions taken are in line with federal, state, and local employment laws, from anti-discrimination statutes to wage and hour requirements. This includes ensuring that any severance agreements are lawful, that any statements made during the termination are truthful and non-defamatory, and that the company has not inadvertently created a legal risk by failing to follow proper procedures.

HR also plays a critical role in handling any post-termination disputes that may arise. If an employee feels that their termination was unjust, HR often mediates the discussion, seeks to resolve the issue, or works with legal counsel to address any claims. By handling the initial termination with care and compassion, HR can often mitigate these disputes before they escalate, preserving the company's reputation and reducing legal exposure.

Compassionate termination isn't just about doing the right thing in a single meeting—it's about building a culture where empathy, respect, and fairness are woven into the organization's fabric. HR is instrumental in driving this culture. By training managers, setting clear policies, and modeling compassionate behavior in every interaction, HR sets the standard for handling the most difficult moments.

Ultimately, firing with compassion protects not just the individual but the entire company. It preserves the employee's dignity, reduces potential conflict, and helps maintain a positive work environment for those who remain. It shows that the company values people, even when tough decisions have to be made. As HR professionals, we are uniquely positioned to ensure that every termination is handled with the utmost care, balancing the needs of the company with the humanity of the employee. It's not just a job—it's a responsibility to uphold the organization's values, one difficult conversation at a time.

***

Choosing the Right Moment

Let's talk about something no one ever wants to say about delivering bad news, especially when it involves terminating someone's employment. If you've ever been on the delivering end of this news, you know it's not just about what you say but how, where, and when you say it. Timing, location, and setting play a massive role in how that conversation is received—and can make the difference between a respectful, compassionate exit and a complete and utter disaster. Trust me, the last thing you want is your conversation to become an episode of *Office Drama Gone Wild*.

Let's start with timing. You wouldn't break up with someone at their birthday party, right? (And if you would, well, we need to have a separate chat.) Delivering bad news at the wrong time can feel exactly like that—completely inappropriate and unnecessarily hurtful. Regarding terminations, picking the right moment isn't just polite; it's essential for maintaining the individual's dignity and keeping the process professional.

Timing is everything and a few things should be avoided at all costs:

1. **Avoid Mondays.** Nobody needs their week ruined right off the bat. If you terminate someone on a Monday, you set them up for a truly awful week. Not to mention, it makes the rest of the team start their week with a cloud of anxiety hanging over them. It's like throwing a gloomy rainstorm over everyone's sunny Monday morning coffee.

2. **Fridays aren't always a free pass.** While Fridays are often seen as "the day" for terminations because it gives people the weekend to process, it's not always the best choice. If the employee is going to feel isolated over the weekend without support or the opportunity to ask questions, this can lead to even more anxiety. It's all about balance—what works for one person might not work for another. It's key to consider the individual situation and the support structures available to them.

3. **Midweek is often ideal.** Tuesday, Wednesday, or even Thursday morning can be good options. It allows the person a few days to process the news during the workweek, reach out for support, and start planning their next steps. It also gives you, the leader, time to manage the transition without the rush of a Friday afternoon.

4. **Avoid right before holidays or big company events.** This one's a no-brainer, but you'd be surprised how often it's overlooked. Imagine getting let go right before the company holiday party—talk about a buzzkill. Timing matters for the morale of the entire team, so be mindful of what else is happening on the calendar.

Now, let's discuss where this conversation should take place. Spoiler alert: it's not at the employee's desk, in the breakroom, or, worse, in a public space where everyone can see or overhear. The setting for delivering bad news is just as important as the timing. It needs to be private, professional, and respectful. The goal is to maintain the employee's dignity and avoid turning the termination into a spectacle.

- **Rule #1: Privacy is paramount.** Choose a setting where the conversation can remain confidential. A private office or a quiet meeting room works best. Ensure the room is away from high-traffic areas, where people aren't likely to be passing by or overhearing bits of the conversation. I once heard about a termination that happened in a glass-walled conference room. It was like watching a fishbowl of despair—everyone in the office saw what was happening, and it was mortifying for everyone involved. Don't be that person.

- **Rule #2: Neutral territory helps.** Sometimes, your office might not be the best place if it feels too much like a power move. Choosing a neutral meeting room can help balance the power dynamic and make the conversation less confrontational. If you're sitting behind your big desk with all your plaques and accolades staring down at the person, it can feel a lot like judgment day.

- **Rule #3: Plan for comfort.** Consider simple things like seating arrangements. Sit at a table side-by-side rather than across a desk; it's less intimidating and makes the conversation feel more human. Have tissues on hand—trust me, it's better to be prepared than scrambling if emotions start to flow. Water bottles are a nice touch, too; a small gesture of care can go a long way in a tough moment.

One of the biggest mistakes leaders make is delivering bad news in a way that makes the situation even more uncomfortable and public than it needs to be. Think about the optics: walking an employee through the entire office to a meeting room can feel like the dreaded "walk of shame," with colleagues wondering what's happening. It's anxiety-inducing and can make a hard moment even harder.

To avoid this, consider how the employee is called into the meeting. A quiet, respectful email invitation or a quick private message is often best. You don't need to make a grand announcement or call them out in front of others. Discretion is key.

After the meeting, handle the exit with care. If the employee leaves the office immediately, give them the time and space to gather their things privately. Offer to help them pack up or arrange to send their belongings to them if that feels less awkward. The goal is to avoid making them feel like they're being paraded out of the office.

Delivering bad news, especially a termination, isn't just a logistical challenge—it's an emotional one. As much as we might want to get these conversations over, rushing the process or choosing the wrong moment can amplify negative emotions and make a tough situation even more painful.

As leaders, it's our responsibility to create the most humane and considerate environment possible for these conversations. Think about it: you're not just firing an employee; you're communicating a significant change in their life. Choosing the right time and setting shows that you respect them enough to make this difficult news as bearable as possible.

So next time you're faced with this tough task, remember: timing and setting aren't just minor details—they're crucial elements of handling the conversation carefully. And while there's no perfect way to deliver bad news, you can always strive to make it a little less terrible by being thoughtful, considerate, and downright human. Because at the end of the day, it's not just what you say, but how you say it—and where and when you say it, too.

***

Providing Resources and Guidance After Termination

Let's dive into an aspect of the termination process that can make a challenging situation a bit more manageable: offering support during and after the process. Now, you might be wondering, "Why invest in someone who's no longer part of the team?" But providing support to employees during and after termination isn't just a gesture of goodwill—it's a strategic move that benefits your business. Severance packages, career counseling, and outplacement services aren't just optional extras; they are key components of handling terminations with care and professionalism. Think of it as softening the impact—it's still a difficult situation, but at least you're helping ease the transition.

Let's be honest—no one is eager to allocate resources to someone leaving the company. The natural instinct is to cut ties quickly, save on costs, and move forward. However, offering support throughout and after termination isn't just about being considerate; it's about safeguarding your company's long-term reputation and fostering goodwill among current employees. By investing in support, you're not only protecting your brand but also sending a clear message to the remaining team that your organization values people, even when parting ways. Here's why that matters:

1. **Protect your reputation:** Newsflash—people talk. And in today's

world, where every experience can be blasted across social media in seconds, how you handle terminations will be part of your company's public narrative. By offering support, you're showing the world that you're a company that genuinely cares about its people, even when the going gets tough. Plus, no one wants to be the company known for tossing employees out on the street without a second thought. Trust me, that's a PR nightmare waiting to happen.

2. **Preserve team morale:** Your remaining employees are watching closely. How you handle a termination sends a clear message: "This could be you." By offering support, you're showing your current team that even if things go south, you'll still have their back. It reassures them they're working for a company with heart—a place that values people over profit margins.

3. **Reduce the risk of backlash:** Employees who feel wronged are far more likely to stir the pot after they're gone, whether through legal action, negative reviews, or even just badmouthing the company in professional circles. When you offer severance, career counseling, or outplacement services, you're giving them a smoother landing—and reducing the likelihood that they'll come back to haunt you like a ghost of terminations past.

4. **Boost your employer brand:** Think about it—what kind of company would you want to work for? One that leaves you high and dry the moment you're out the door, or one that helps you transition gracefully, even when the news isn't good? Offering support during and after termination enhances your employer brand, making you more attractive to top talent. You'll be seen as a company that does the right thing, even when it's hard.

Severance packages are like the corporate world's version of a "thank you for your time" gesture. They provide financial support while an employee searches for their next opportunity, offering some much-needed breathing room during what can be an incredibly stressful period. Yes, it's an expense, but it's also an investment in goodwill. Severance can range from a couple of weeks' pay to several months, depending on the employee's tenure and the company's policies.

Here's an interesting thought: many employees remember the severance package as the last positive interaction with their former company. It's the final gesture that says, "We understand this is tough, but we're still looking out for you." This classy exit leaves the door open for future opportunities because as we know, burning bridges isn't a great strategy in any industry.

Career counseling is another way to ease the transition. Imagine being let go and then expected to navigate the job market without any direction. It's a daunting prospect. Career counseling acts as a compass, helping employees refresh their resumes, improve their LinkedIn profiles, and fine-tune their interview skills. Essentially, it's providing them with the tools and guidance they need to find their next opportunity.

Offering career counseling is a powerful way to support employees as they take their next steps. Whether it's through mock interviews, personalized job search strategies, or resume reviews, this support can make all the difference in helping them bounce back quickly. Not only does it ease their transition, but it also reflects positively on the company, showing that you still care about their future success—even if it's outside your organization.

Outplacement services are like the ultimate care package for departing employees. These services go beyond offering basic job search advice and typically include coaching, networking opportunities, and direct access to job leads. It's a comprehensive approach to helping employees land on their feet faster and more effectively than they would on their own.

While outplacement services might seem like a significant gesture, the benefits far outweigh the costs. Employees who receive outplacement are more likely to find new positions quickly and leave with positive feelings toward the company. This can lead to fewer disgruntled ex-employees and more goodwill ambassadors for your organization—people who can still speak positively about their time with you long after they've moved on.

In the end, offering support during and after termination is about treating people as individuals, not just employees. It's easy to focus on the bottom line and forget the human side of these tough decisions. But providing severance, career counseling, and outplacement services shows that your company values its people—even during difficult transitions. It's about doing the right thing, even when it's not the easiest or most cost-effective option.

The way you handle terminations says a lot about your company's culture and values. It's a telling moment that shows how you treat your employees, both during the good times and the challenging ones. So, the next time you face a termination decision, consider going the extra mile. It's not just about closing a chapter—it's about helping someone start their next one with dignity and support.

In the end, we're all navigating the ups and downs of our careers, and when we lead with empathy—even in difficult moments—we create a more compassionate and respectful workplace. And that, in the long run, is worth every bit of effort.

* * *

Managing Your Emotions as a Leader

Firing someone is, without a doubt, one of the toughest responsibilities any leader faces. It's the leadership equivalent of a dreaded dentist appointment—necessary, but something no one looks forward to. And let's be honest, it's not just hard for the employee on the receiving end. As leaders, it can feel like a punch to the gut, causing sleepless nights and a mountain of stress. The guilt, the anxiety, and the immense weight of responsibility are real. If you've ever felt like you're carrying the hopes and dreams of an entire team on your shoulders, well, welcome to leadership.

Here's the reality: it's okay to feel all those emotions, but as a leader, you still have to navigate the situation professionally and compassionately.

There's no skipping out on the hard stuff just because it's emotionally draining. So, how do you handle your own emotions during a termination? How do you balance the weight of responsibility while ensuring you're doing right by everyone involved, including yourself? Let's dig into this emotional roller coaster and figure out how to keep it together when things feel overwhelming.

First, let's address the guilt. Ah, the guilt. That little voice in your head asking, "Could I have done more? Did I try hard enough to help them succeed? Am I wrecking their life?" It's completely normal to feel this way. If you don't feel at least a twinge of guilt, it might be time to check your empathy levels. However, guilt can also be a trap that keeps you from making the tough decisions that need to be made.

When the guilt starts creeping in, I remind myself that the decision to terminate an employee doesn't happen in isolation. It usually comes after multiple conversations, performance reviews, and efforts to help the person improve. As much as we'd love every coaching session to end with a breakthrough, that's not always how it goes. Sometimes, despite everyone's best efforts, it just isn't the right fit—and that's okay. Accepting that not every employee journey ends in promotions and celebrations will help you manage the emotional toll.

Now, let's talk about the stress. The pressure of knowing you're about to change someone's day (and possibly their career) can feel overwhelming. It's like holding a hot potato you don't want to drop, but you can't hold on to forever. My go-to strategy for managing this stress? Preparation. The more prepared you are, the more you can mitigate some of that anxiety. It's like studying for an exam you really don't want to take—if you've done your homework, you'll at least feel in control.

Before heading into a termination meeting, I make sure I've gathered all the necessary documentation, rehearsed what I'm going to say, and mentally prepared for the different reactions I might encounter. Preparation is like a safety net for your nerves—it won't make the task easy, but it will help you feel grounded. And remember, you're not alone. HR is there for a reason. Lean on them for support, guidance, and a reminder to follow the right procedures. They're not just there to tick boxes; they're there to ensure the process is handled legally and compassionately.

Then, there's the responsibility—the heaviest part of the equation. As a leader, the decision ultimately falls on you, and that can feel like a lot to carry. It's easy to feel like the bad guy, the one delivering the news no one wants to hear. But here's a mindset shift that's helped me: instead of seeing yourself as the villain, think of yourself as a guide. You're not there to ruin someone's day; you're helping them transition to something that's ultimately a better fit, even if that's outside your organization. It's about making the right decision for the individual, the team, and the business.

You're not doing this because you want to—you're doing it because it's necessary. And sometimes, letting someone go is the most compassionate thing you can do. Holding on to an employee who is struggling isn't doing them any favors; it's prolonging the inevitable. When that responsibility feels overwhelming, remember that making difficult decisions is part of leadership. It's okay to feel the weight of that, and it's okay to care. That's what makes you a good leader.

Another tip for managing your emotions? Lean on your support network. Whether it's a fellow leader, a mentor, or a friend who can listen without judgment, don't keep it all inside. Sharing your feelings can be a huge relief and help you process the situation. It's a reminder that you're not a heartless corporate robot—you're a human being navigating a difficult situation. Sometimes, that camaraderie is all you need to lighten the emotional load.

Finally, allow yourself to feel whatever you're feeling. Sad? Frustrated? Relieved? It's all valid. Once the meeting is over, take a moment to process it. Go for a walk, listen to music, or simply sit and breathe. The key is not to carry the emotional weight of every termination with you indefinitely. Do your best to handle it professionally, and then let it go.

Firing someone will never be easy, and it's never going to feel good. But by managing your own emotions—acknowledging the guilt, preparing for the stress, embracing the responsibility, and seeking support—you can navigate these tough moments with professionalism, compassion, and grace. At the end of the day, you're not just a leader; you're also a person, and it's okay to feel like one.

* * *

Communicating With Your Team After a Termination

Communicating with your team after termination is one of those leadership moments that can feel like walking a tightrope. You want to be transparent without oversharing, reassuring without sugarcoating, and, above all, maintain stability without creating panic. It's a delicate balance, but if handled correctly, you can preserve trust, keep morale steady, and guide your team with confidence through a period of transition.

The first thing to acknowledge is that you can't just pretend nothing happened. Your team is observant. They notice when a colleague's desk is suddenly empty or when they're no longer joining Zoom meetings. Silence in these situations can breed confusion and rumors. As a leader, it's your responsibility to provide clear communication that acknowledges the situation without diving into unnecessary detail.

When you start the conversation, be direct but concise. You don't need to turn this into a deep dive into why someone was let go. A simple acknowledgment like, "I wanted to inform you that [Employee] is no longer with the company," gets the message across and sets the stage for what's really important—the team's path forward.

Now, let's talk about what *not* to say. Avoid negative commentary or explanations that paint the former employee in a bad light. Phrases like "They weren't cutting it" or "They didn't meet expectations" do more harm than good. It's essential to keep the tone professional and respectful, using neutral language like, "This was a difficult decision made in the best interest of the team and company." This shows the team that the decision wasn't made lightly and protects the dignity of the departing employee.

After addressing the departure, the focus should shift to the team's future. Reassure them that this decision is not a reflection of their performance or the stability of the group. One of the most common reactions after a termination is fear—wondering if they're next. Calm those fears by clarifying that this was a specific decision and not the beginning of a series of terminations.

This is also the perfect time to rally the team. Highlight the goals ahead, and remind them of the progress they've made. Transitions like this are challenging, but they're also opportunities to refocus and strengthen the team's resolve. The message you want to send is, "Yes, we've hit a bump, but we're still on track, and we're moving forward together."

Transparency is key, but don't drag the team into unnecessary speculation or anxiety about the future. Acknowledge the emotional impact of the situation, but keep the conversation solution-oriented. You might say something like, "I understand it's tough when someone leaves, and it's natural to feel unsettled. But I'm here to answer any questions and make sure you have what you need to keep moving forward." This reassures the team that you're approachable while also emphasizing that the focus is on the future.

Maintaining morale is a crucial part of this conversation. Address any additional workload that may arise from the departure and offer solutions, whether that's temporary support or a plan to redistribute tasks. Show the team that you're mindful of their capacity and that you're committed to helping them navigate this transition.

One of the most effective ways to maintain morale is to remind the team of their strengths. Acknowledge their resilience and ability to rise to the occasion. Saying something like, "I've seen this team handle challenges before, and I have full confidence that we'll continue to do great work," can boost confidence and reinforce a sense of unity.

And yes, if the situation allows, injecting a little warmth can help ease the tension. A light-hearted comment, like, "I know change isn't everyone's favorite thing—if it were, we'd all be ordering pineapple on our pizza—but we'll get through this together," can bring some levity without undermining the seriousness of the conversation.

Finally, leave the door open for ongoing communication. This is not a one-time conversation. Check-in with your team over the coming days and weeks to see how they're doing, if they have any concerns, or if they need additional support. Letting people process in their own time is crucial, and regular follow-ups show that you're committed to their well-being.

Ultimately, how you communicate with your team after a termination sets the tone for how they will handle change moving forward. By being clear, compassionate, and forward-focused, you not only maintain stability but also strengthen your leadership and reinforce the trust within your team. It's never an easy task, but with the right approach, it's an opportunity to guide your team through adversity and come out stronger on the other side.

***

What Not to do When Letting Someone Go

Letting someone go is, without a doubt, one of the most challenging aspects of leadership. It's like walking through a minefield—you're trying to navigate a delicate situation without damaging relationships, team morale, or your own reputation. And even the most seasoned leaders can misstep if they're not careful. Let's go over some common mistakes leaders make when terminating employees and how to handle this process with more empathy and professionalism.

One of the biggest mistakes I've seen (and maybe even made in my early years) is giving unclear reasons for the termination. Imagine being told, "We're letting you go because... well, things just aren't working out." It's like breaking up with someone using, "It's not you, it's me." Vague explanations leave the employee confused and hurt, and worse, can lead to challenges down the road if they claim they never understood what they did wrong.

To avoid this, clarity is your best tool. Before you even walk into the room, ensure you have specific, concrete reasons backed by documented performance reviews and feedback. It's not about being robotic but about having a clear and honest conversation. Something like, "We're letting you go because your performance has not met the standards we discussed, despite our efforts to support you," is straightforward and respectful. No ambiguity, no guesswork.

Another classic mistake is being too harsh or impersonal. There's a fine line between being direct and being cold. Some leaders feel the need to put on a tough exterior to get through the discomfort, but delivering the news in a detached or robotic manner makes it feel as though the employee is nothing more than a name on a list.

The antidote is compassion. You don't have to go overboard, but showing humanity goes a long way. Start the conversation with empathy: "I know this isn't easy, and it's not a conversation I take lightly." Acknowledging the difficulty of the situation shows respect for the person's emotions and helps soften the blow.

Rushing through the conversation is another common misstep. Yes, it's uncomfortable, but speeding through it just to get it over with isn't fair to the employee. They deserve time to process what's happening, ask questions, and understand the next steps.

Instead, take a deep breath and slow down. Be fully present in the moment, allowing the employee to absorb the information and ask any questions they may have. Giving them that time makes the conversation feel less like a cold dismissal and more like a difficult but respectful dialogue.

Another avoidable mistake? Forgetting the human element entirely. In the rush to ensure paperwork is in order and legal protocols are followed, it's easy to overlook the fact that the person sitting across from you is dealing with a whirlwind of emotions. I've seen terminations where the manager, after delivering the news, handed the employee a box and said, "You've got 10 minutes to pack up." That's adding insult to injury.

Instead, think about how you would want to be treated. Give the person time to collect themselves and their belongings. Offer assistance—whether that's connecting them with HR for severance questions or providing a private space to process the news. Treat them with the dignity they deserve.

Then there's the mistake of losing your cool. Emotions can run high in termination meetings, especially if the employee reacts with anger or tears. But as the leader, it's your job to stay calm and professional. Getting defensive or letting your emotions dictate the conversation only escalates things.

If tensions rise, take a step back mentally and respond with calm, measured words. Something like, "I understand this is difficult, and I'm here to listen," can help de-escalate the situation and keep the conversation respectful, no matter how challenging it becomes.

Lastly, never bypass HR. This isn't just about legal protection—it's about making sure the termination is handled fairly and consistently with company policies. HR is there to guide you through the process, ensuring everything is done by the book and with the proper support. Skipping this step not only leaves you vulnerable to legal repercussions but also denies you valuable assistance that can make the process smoother and more compassionate for all involved.

In the end, while terminating an employee is never easy, avoiding these common mistakes can help you handle the process with grace, professionalism, and respect. By approaching the conversation with clarity, empathy, and preparation, you can ensure that the difficult decision is managed in a way that preserves both your dignity and theirs. And let's be honest—if you're the one letting someone go, at least you're not on the receiving end. That alone is reason enough to handle it with care.

***

Understanding the Impact of Firing

Firing someone is one of those leadership moments that no one truly prepares you for. You envision leadership as driving strategy, inspiring teams, and making tough decisions—but then you find yourself sitting across from an employee, facing the reality of having to let them go. It's in these moments that you realize leadership isn't just about the big wins and motivational speeches; it's also about navigating some of the toughest decisions that directly impact people's lives. And let's be honest: firing someone doesn't just affect them—it ripples out to everyone, including you.

For the person being let go, the experience can be a profound emotional shock. It's not just the loss of a paycheck; it's often the loss of identity, daily routine, and even social connections. I've seen a range of reactions—from tears and anger to silence or, occasionally, relief. No matter the response, it's clear that being fired is an intensely personal experience, even if the decision is "just business."

As leaders, we have to recognize the deeper impact of terminations. For many employees, a job is tied to their sense of self-worth, and losing it can lead to stress, anxiety, and uncertainty about the future. There's the practical side too—scrambling to update resumes, worrying about financial stability, and facing the job market again. When we understand this, we're better equipped to handle these moments with the empathy they require.

Handling a termination with empathy is key. It's not just about getting the paperwork right or ensuring their security access is revoked. It's about how you, as a leader, deliver the message. A simple acknowledgment like, "I know this is difficult, and I'm sorry we're in this situation," can set the right tone. It doesn't change the outcome, but it makes clear that you see the person, not just the employee.

The conversation shouldn't be rushed. It's essential to allow the individual space to process what's happening. Some may have questions, others might want to express frustration or disappointment, and some might just sit silently. The point is, you need to give them that room. Letting them speak—or not speak—shows you respect their response.

Offering support during the transition is another crucial step. No one wants to feel like they're being tossed aside. Severance packages, outplacement services, and even a letter of recommendation can make a big difference. These gestures say, "Your time here may be ending, but we want to help you succeed moving forward." It's not just the right thing to do—it sets a positive tone for your organization and shows the rest of your team how seriously you take these decisions.

Which brings me to your team. When someone is let go, the remaining employees feel the impact, too. They might worry about their job security or wonder if they could be next. It's important to address these concerns directly—without violating the privacy of the individual who was terminated. Reassuring the team with a clear, transparent message about why the decision was made helps keep morale steady and prevents speculation from spiraling out of control.

Lastly, let's talk about the emotional toll this takes on you as a leader. Terminating someone isn't easy, and it can leave you second-guessing your decisions or feeling the weight of responsibility for affecting someone's life. It's okay to feel that way—it means you care. But remember, while these decisions are difficult, they're also necessary for the health of the organization and the team. Understanding the impact of termination, and handling it with compassion, doesn't just help the person being let go—it also helps you maintain your integrity and strength as a leader.

In the end, firing someone with empathy isn't just a good practice—it's essential leadership. How we handle these difficult moments reflects who we are as leaders and how we approach the human side of business. And while terminations are never easy, doing it right can make the process a little less painful for everyone involved, turning a tough moment into an opportunity for growth—for both you and the individual you're letting go.

***

When Compassion is Tested

Terminating an employee is, without question, one of the most difficult tasks a leader faces. No matter how prepared you are or how justified the decision may be, there's always an unpredictable element—the emotional response of the person you're letting go. It's a moment that tests your compassion and professionalism in equal measure. As someone who's been through these conversations more times than I'd like to admit, I can tell you it never gets easier. But it is possible to navigate these moments with empathy and care, ensuring that even the hardest conversations are handled with dignity.

I've been in meetings where the employee's reaction took me by surprise—ranging from silence to shock, tears to anger. It's a whirlwind of emotions on their side, and while it's easy to focus on the logistics of the termination (paperwork, security access, etc.), the real challenge lies in managing the human emotions that come with the news. It's critical to remember that these reactions aren't about you—they're a response to the situation. Understanding that helps keep the conversation respectful and compassionate.

Staying calm and composed is essential. I've learned that my own emotional control sets the tone for the conversation. If I'm steady and focused, it's easier for the person across the table to process what's happening. That doesn't mean I shut off my own emotions—after all, we're human—but it does mean staying mindful of them. Empathy is key, but it's important not to let emotions dictate the conversation. I've found that acknowledging my own discomfort helps me stay grounded, and ultimately, it makes the conversation feel more respectful and productive.

One of the hardest reactions to manage is anger. It often stems from feeling blindsided or wronged, and it's easy for that anger to turn into blame. I've had employees question my decisions, accuse me of not valuing their work, or deny any wrongdoing. In those moments, the instinct might be to defend yourself or argue back—but trust me, that's not the way to go. Acknowledging their feelings without validating their anger is the best approach. Simple statements like, "I understand this is upsetting," or "I hear that you're frustrated," help diffuse the situation. It's not about winning an argument; it's about keeping the conversation professional and focused.

Then there's denial—a natural defense mechanism. Some employees, especially those who didn't see the termination coming, may insist there's been a mistake or that they didn't realize their performance was an issue. In these cases, patience is essential. I've found that giving the person a moment to process the news is often more effective than trying to fill the silence. A pause allows them to gather their thoughts and often leads to a calmer conversation. If the denial persists, I gently bring the focus back to the facts and remind them that the decision is final.

Sadness, especially tears, can be equally tough to handle. Watching someone cry in front of you is never easy, and it's a moment that stirs up emotions for everyone in the room. Offering a tissue or giving them a few minutes to collect themselves can go a long way in showing empathy. It's important to reassure them that their feelings are valid and that it's okay to be upset. If they need a break, I offer it. Sometimes, stepping outside or taking a few deep breaths can help them regain composure so we can continue the conversation in a calmer state.

Throughout these conversations, body language and tone play a crucial role. Staying open and approachable—maintaining eye contact, keeping a calm voice, and avoiding defensive postures like crossing arms—helps convey that you're fully present and respectful. Avoid rushing through the meeting or giving off cues that make the person feel unwelcome. Even though it's a tough conversation, creating an atmosphere of respect is essential.

It's important to accept that no matter how well you handle the conversation, the person may still leave feeling upset, hurt, or even angry. That's simply the nature of these situations. Your job isn't to fix their emotions—because you can't—but to manage the process with as much care and professionalism as possible. By staying calm and compassionate, you've done your part to make a difficult situation as humane as it can be.

As leaders, how we handle these challenging moments reflects our values. By approaching terminations with empathy, we maintain the dignity of the individual and uphold the integrity of our organization. Ultimately, it's not just about delivering difficult news; it's about helping someone transition with respect and grace, even when the road ahead looks tough.

* * *

Ensuring Compliance While Maintaining Compassion

Navigating the legal maze of terminating an employee can feel like tiptoeing through a minefield. One wrong step, and you're not just dealing with the emotional fallout—you're staring down potential legal headaches that could haunt you like a bad '80s hairstyle. As much as we'd like to believe that simply treating people with compassion and respect would cover all our bases, the reality is much more complicated. It's not just about doing the right thing; it's also about doing the legally sound thing. So, let's dive into the less glamorous but essential part of termination: keeping your termination practices on the right side of the law while still being human about it.

First, let's be clear: handling a termination with care doesn't mean throwing the rulebook out the window. It's the exact opposite. The most compassionate terminations are often the ones that are carefully planned, legally compliant, and impeccably documented. Why? Because when you follow the right procedures, you're not only protecting the company—you're also protecting the employee's dignity and minimizing the potential for misunderstandings, bad blood, or worse, lawsuits.

I remember working with a leader who was incredibly empathetic—almost to a fault. She was all about doing right by her people, which was great, but in her effort to be "nice," she sometimes skipped the paperwork and neglected key legal steps. One day, after letting someone go in what she thought was a friendly, mutual parting, she found herself on the receiving end of a wrongful termination claim. Talk about a wake-up call! As much as you want to lead with your heart, your head needs to be fully engaged in the process, too.

So, how do you balance the legal side of things with compassion? It starts with understanding your responsibilities and ensuring that every "i" is dotted and every "t" is crossed. Here are the top things HR managers and leaders need to keep front and center to avoid those dreaded legal missteps:

- **Know your employment laws inside and out:** Before you even think about having a termination conversation, make sure you're up to speed on federal, state, and local employment laws. These laws can vary significantly depending on where you operate, and they cover everything from wrongful termination protections to notice requirements and severance obligations. Ignorance of the law isn't an excuse that'll hold up in court, so take the time to familiarize yourself with the legal landscape—or better yet, partner with your HR team or legal counsel to ensure you're not missing anything crucial.

- **Document, document, document:** I can't stress this enough—documentation is your best friend in the termination process. From performance reviews to written warnings and any communication about issues leading up to the decision, having a clear paper trail is essential. This isn't just about covering your tail; it's about ensuring the termination decision is based on fair, documented reasons rather than knee-jerk reactions. Good documentation shows that you've given the employee every opportunity to improve and that the decision wasn't made lightly or without cause.

- **Review employment contracts and company policies:** Before pulling the trigger on termination, you need to review any employment contracts, union agreements, or company policies that apply. Are there specific procedures you're required to follow? Is there a stipulated notice period or severance package? The last thing you want is to get blindsided by a clause you overlooked in an employee's contract. Taking the time to review these documents can save you a lot of headaches (and legal fees) down the line.

- **Ensure compliance with anti-discrimination laws:** One of the biggest legal landmines in the termination process is running afoul of anti-discrimination laws. It's illegal to terminate an employee based on race, gender, age, disability, religion, or any other protected characteristic. Even if your intentions are pure, if the employee feels like they've been treated unfairly or discriminated against, you could be in hot water. To avoid this, make sure the termination decision is based solely on performance or conduct and not influenced by any personal biases, even unintentionally.

- **Provide proper notice and final pay:** Depending on where your business operates, there may be specific legal requirements around providing notice of termination and delivering final paychecks. In some states, you must provide the final paycheck immediately or within a certain time frame, including any unused vacation or PTO the employee is entitled to. Messing this up can result in fines, penalties, and one seriously disgruntled ex-employee. So, double-check those deadlines and make sure the financial side of the termination is handled smoothly and legally.

Now, with all the legal boxes checked, how do we maintain the human touch? The key is to blend these compliance steps with genuine empathy. You can stick to the rules while showing respect and kindness to the person on the other side of the desk. I've found that even the toughest conversations can be softened when you approach them with transparency and honesty. Tell the employee exactly why the decision was made, be upfront about their rights and next steps, and make sure they leave with their dignity intact.

It's also important to give them space to react—because, let's face it, nobody enjoys being told they're out of a job. Emotions are bound to run high, and as much as you might want to get through the meeting quickly, taking the time to let the employee process the news can make all the difference. It shows that while you're firm in your decision, you're also human and understand that this isn't just a business transaction—it's someone's life.

***

How Terminations Can Improve Leadership and Team Dynamics

Terminating an employee is one of those leadership tasks that no one looks forward to, but there's a lot we can learn from it. It's up there with getting a root canal or decluttering your entire house—not pleasant, but sometimes necessary. Yet, if you look beyond the discomfort, every termination holds valuable lessons that can improve your leadership and strengthen your team dynamics. So, let's dive in and see how firing someone—when done with thought and care—can make you a better leader and create a stronger, more resilient team.

First things first: nobody takes pleasure in firing someone. If you do, we might need a different conversation! But the reality is that, as leaders, we sometimes have to make tough decisions for the greater good. What's important is how we choose to approach those moments. Are we just checking a box, or are we using the experience to reflect and grow? Believe it or not, terminations can provide crucial insights into everything from your hiring practices to your leadership style. They're not just an unpleasant duty—they're an opportunity to learn.

Let's start with hiring. If you find yourself letting someone go because of poor fit or performance, chances are the red flags were there long before the termination meeting. Maybe during the interview, they threw out buzzwords like "perfectionist" (translation: "I'm going to drive you crazy with my micromanaging"), or perhaps you skipped a thorough reference check. When you reflect on a termination, it's an opportunity to scrutinize your hiring process. What did you miss? What could have been done differently? Tightening up your hiring strategy ensures that next time, you're bringing someone on board who's not just qualified but also a great cultural fit.

Performance management is another area where terminations can offer insights. In most cases, terminations don't happen overnight—they're the result of ongoing performance issues that weren't resolved. As leaders, we need to ask ourselves: Could this have been prevented? Was feedback clear, consistent, and actionable? Did I provide the right support, or did I avoid the tough conversations, hoping things would magically improve? Reflecting on these points helps you build a proactive performance management process, one that encourages growth and accountability before problems escalate to the point of no return.

And then there's the leadership growth that comes from navigating such tough conversations. We've all heard the saying, "What doesn't kill you makes you stronger." Well, firing someone won't kill you, but it sure will test your leadership muscles. Having that tough conversation, managing your own emotions, and handling the employee's reaction with empathy and professionalism can teach you more about leadership than any seminar or book. You'll sharpen your emotional intelligence, build resilience, and learn how to deliver difficult news with grace.

But it's not just about you. Terminations also impact the rest of your team, and if handled properly, they can strengthen team dynamics. After a termination, it's important to regroup with your team and have an honest discussion—not to gossip or point fingers, but to reflect on what can be improved going forward. Were there early signs the team saw but didn't address? Could the team have worked together better to avoid the situation? These conversations build a culture of transparency and mutual support, helping the team learn from the situation and grow stronger together.

Let's not forget the impact on your company culture. Each termination is an opportunity to reassess your values and whether you're truly upholding them. Are you living up to your cultural commitments, or have you let some things slide? A termination can be a wake-up call that prompts you to recommit to fostering a positive, supportive work environment where expectations are clear and people feel motivated to do their best work.

In the end, as uncomfortable as terminations are, they're valuable teachers. They challenge us to reflect on how we lead, how we hire, and how we manage our teams. When we embrace these lessons, we not only improve as leaders but also create a stronger, more resilient team. And who knows? With time, maybe we'll get so good at it that terminations become less about fixing mistakes and more about creating opportunities for growth—for ourselves, our teams, and our organizations. After all, leadership isn't just about making tough decisions; it's about learning from them too.

* * *

Preventing Future Terminations

Terminations are a bit like root canals—necessary at times, but no one looks forward to them. Wouldn't it be great if we could reduce the need for them altogether? The good news is that we can. By fostering a culture of development and feedback, we can address performance issues before they snowball into something unmanageable. It's like going for regular dental check-ups—consistent care can help avoid the dreaded drill.

As leaders, creating an environment where terminations are rare starts with adopting a proactive approach to feedback, development, and support. When employees feel valued, guided, and supported, they're far more likely to succeed. And when feedback becomes a natural, regular part of your team's day-to-day, it lays the foundation for success that prevents people from reaching a point where termination is the only option.

The first step? Embrace continuous feedback. I'm not talking about the once-a-year performance review marathon, where you try to summarize a year's worth of feedback in one conversation. Let's be real—that's about as helpful as trying to binge-watch an entire TV series in a weekend. Instead, think of feedback like seasoning—sprinkle it in regularly, not dumped all at once. Make feedback an ongoing conversation through one-on-one meetings, quick chats, or even shout-outs after team meetings. The goal is to make feedback a part of the daily routine, so it's not something to fear but something to grow from.

One piece of advice that stuck with me is, "Feedback should be more like GPS, not a post-game analysis." Instead of waiting until someone's already off course, give real-time guidance that helps them adjust before things go south. A quick "Let's work through that together" goes much further than a

"We need to talk about how you messed up." It's about keeping the focus on development, not just correction.

Providing the right tools and resources is another way to prevent future terminations. Imagine trying to win a cooking competition with a dull knife—it doesn't matter how good you are, you're going to struggle. The same applies to your team. If they don't have the right tools or training, it's only a matter of time before performance issues arise. Invest in professional development, mentorship, and skill-building opportunities. It's not just about sharpening technical skills either—focus on soft skills like communication, time management, and adaptability.

Creating a culture of self-reflection is another way to empower your team. Encourage them to regularly assess their performance and set personal goals for improvement. When employees take ownership of their growth, they become more engaged and proactive in fixing issues before they escalate. This isn't about setting people up for criticism; it's about giving them the tools to chart their path to success.

Recognition plays a crucial role in this, too. Often, feedback is all about what's going wrong, and we forget to celebrate what's going right. Take the time to catch people doing great work and acknowledge it. It doesn't need to be elaborate—a simple "You nailed that presentation!" can go a long way in reinforcing the behaviors you want to see more of.

At the heart of all this is trust. Employees need to know that feedback and support come from a place of care, not judgment. As leaders, we can build that trust by being approachable, transparent, and even vulnerable at times. Share your own challenges and growth areas—it helps to show that no one, not even the boss, is perfect.

Of course, there will be times when, despite your best efforts, an employee still struggles. In these situations, don't wait until it's too late. Have honest, compassionate conversations about where they're falling short, what they can do to improve, and how you're going to support them through it. If the issues persist despite all the feedback, support, and development, then yes, a tough decision may be necessary. But termination should always be the last resort, not the first.

Preventing future terminations isn't about lowering standards; it's about increasing support and commitment to your team's success. By embedding continuous feedback, development, and open communication into your leadership approach, you create a work environment where people aren't just surviving—they're thriving. So, let's trade those pink slips for feedback forms and help our teams grow, not go.

***

Leading With Compassion

Leading with compassion—it's like adding the secret sauce that takes leadership from "just okay" to truly exceptional. Let's be honest, no one wants to follow a leader who operates like a malfunctioning robot, spitting out commands without a shred of empathy. Especially when dealing with tough situations like terminations, compassion isn't just a "nice-to-have"—it's the glue that holds the whole process together. And believe me, when you lead with empathy and integrity, you're not only softening the blow, you're building trust that will carry your team through the toughest storms.

Throughout this journey, we've explored firing with compassion, managing emotions, and communicating with care. Now, let's tie it all together by digging into why leading with empathy isn't just about being a good human being (although that's a great reason). It's about fostering an environment where people feel valued, even when things aren't going perfectly. Compassionate leadership ensures that your team and organization maintain their integrity, no matter the difficulty of the situation.

Here's the bottom line: Leading with empathy doesn't mean avoiding tough decisions or sugarcoating reality. It means recognizing that behind every title is a person with hopes, concerns, and the occasional caffeine addiction. When you lead with empathy, you build trust, loyalty, and a team that feels supported—even when the news isn't good.

FIRING WITH COMPASSION

I once worked with a CEO who handled terminations like a cold, clinical task—no explanations, no empathy, just a quick "goodbye and good luck" on the way out the door. Sure, it was efficient, but it left a wake of low morale and a revolving door of talent spinning faster than anyone could keep up with. Contrast that with a leader who took the time to be transparent, compassionate, and supportive during a termination. She didn't rush through the process; she explained the decision, offered resources, and made sure the individual knew they were valued beyond this one tough moment. The result? The rest of the team felt respected, the trust in leadership remained intact, and morale stayed strong. The difference was night and day.

Compassionate leadership doesn't mean avoiding hard conversations. It's about approaching those conversations with empathy—prioritizing the person and their dignity while staying aligned with the organization's values. When you lead this way, you build integrity that reinforces your leadership. Your team knows you're not just making decisions to check boxes, but that you genuinely care about the impact on them.

Empathy also requires transparency. People aren't mushrooms—you can't keep them in the dark and expect them to thrive. When you're open and honest, especially during difficult times, it builds trust. Sure, your team may not love every decision, but they'll respect how you handled it. And that respect builds loyalty—something every leader dreams of.

And here's the kicker: When you lead with compassion, you set the tone for your entire organization. Your team sees how you handle pressure, navigate conflict, and treat others in their most vulnerable moments. This behavior trickles down and creates a culture where compassion isn't just a leadership trait—it becomes part of the company's DNA. The result? A workplace where people feel supported, valued, and willing to go the extra mile because they know their leader has their back.

At the end of the day, leaders who lead with empathy don't just gain respect—they gain loyalty. And loyalty is a rare gem in today's workplace. Teams that trust their leaders are more engaged, innovative, and dedicated. They know they're more than just a cog in the machine—they're part of a community that values them, even when times are tough.

So, here's the takeaway: Compassionate leadership isn't about being soft—it's about being strong enough to show empathy when it matters most. It's about making hard decisions while keeping humanity at the center. Because how you lead during the toughest moments defines your leadership—and your team will never forget that.

Here's to leading with heart, building trust, and embracing the power of empathy. When you lead with compassion, you're not just doing right by your team—you're setting the gold standard for leadership. And that's a legacy worth leaving.

13

From Theory to Practice

As we wrap up this rollercoaster ride through the ups and downs of business management and leadership, let me be the first to say—congratulations! You've made it through the gauntlet of team dynamics, navigating chaos (like a pro, I'm sure), investing in success, and creating visions that inspire more than just your daydreams about retirement. If you're still here, that means you survived my personal stories, questionable life choices, and what I like to call "hard-earned expertise" (AKA, all the times I messed up so you don't have to). Hopefully, you've picked up some golden nuggets of wisdom—and maybe even had a laugh or two along the way.

By now, you've probably realized that leadership isn't about the fancy title on your business card or the window office with the "executive view" (though I'm not knocking a good view—it can really help when you need to daydream your way out of a Monday morning meeting). It's about showing up, connecting, and, yes, occasionally hiding under your desk with a strong coffee—or something a bit stronger, no judgment here. It's about finding the courage to steer through the mess, setting new standards, and leading with compassion—even when everything around you feels like a circus and you're the reluctant ringmaster.

So, here's my parting advice as you step into your next chapter as a leader: First off, remember that leadership is more like a marathon than a sprint.

There will be days when you feel like the CEO of the universe, making decisions left and right like a seasoned pro. And then there will be days when you're just trying to figure out how your to-do list turned into a small novel. That's the game. Embrace the chaos. Every misstep is a learning opportunity—trust me, I've created more than my fair share of "learning moments," like the time I delivered a pitch with slides in the wrong order. (Pro tip: always double-check your PowerPoint game before going live.)

One major lesson I hope you've picked up: investing in other people's success is the true secret sauce to becoming a great leader. When you lift others, you're not just building a team—you're creating a squad that's got your back. And hey, if you need help changing that flickering lightbulb in your office, they'll be there for that, too. Don't hog the spotlight—share it, celebrate wins together, and create a culture where everyone feels like a rockstar.

Now, let's talk about change. I get it, change can be about as welcome as a surprise performance review, but it's where the magic happens. Embrace it, because a leader who sees opportunity in the unknown is one who gets things done. Be the person who not only adapts but inspires others to take that leap with confidence. After all, a great leader doesn't just survive change—they make it look like part of the plan.

Oh, and communication? Yeah, that's key. Whether you're shifting the company's strategy or just trying to get people to agree on lunch, clear communication will save you every time. Break down the silos, keep those conversations flowing, and encourage your team to ask the tough questions. And sometimes, the best thing you can do in a meeting is just listen. Trust me, that's when the real magic happens.

Finally, lead with empathy. You're going to have to make hard choices—it's part of the job. But if you approach every decision with compassion and a genuine commitment to doing right by your people, you'll build trust and respect that money can't buy. People may not remember every decision you make, but they will always remember how you made them feel.

So here we are at the end of our journey. I hope you've laughed, learned, and maybe even found a little inspiration to tuck away for later. You've

FROM THEORY TO PRACTICE

got everything you need to lead with confidence and make a real impact. And remember, when in doubt, just keep showing up, keep learning, and keep pretending you know what you're doing—because eventually, you will. Works every time.

Now, go out there and lead like the rockstar you are!

About the Author

Justin Calabrese, MSM, is an entrepreneur, author, and business consultant, born in Hartford, Connecticut. His entrepreneurial journey began at a young age, earning him national recognition when he was featured on National Public Radio (NPR) in 2008 for his early ventures in eCommerce. He went on to earn a Master's in Business Management from the University of Hartford, where he graduated as a top honor student. His outstanding academic achievements also led to his rare dual induction into a lifetime honors society, placing him among the top 3% of business students globally.

Justin's professional experience spans multiple disciplines, including eCommerce, web design, marketing, business strategy, and sales. As a business consultant, he has successfully guided over 150 small businesses, leveraging his expertise to drive growth and innovation. His insights have been shared widely through his contributions to both the Huffington Post and NewsBreak.

Outside of his professional life, Justin enjoys traveling, spending time with his family, and exploring his passion for cooking. He remains committed to helping businesses achieve their full potential through innovation and strategic growth.

Printed in the USA
CPSIA information can be obtained
at www.ICGtesting.com
CBHW011016241024
16331CB00026B/232/J